from the kitchen of:

_____

_____

MARTHA STEWART'S
BAKING HANDBOOK

The perfect madeleine or fruit pie can only be created with the perfect pan. Martha has amassed a collection of baking tins in every shape and size. Some of her favorite ones are pictured on the following pages.

MARTHA STEWART'S
BAKING HANDBOOK

CLARKSON POTTER/PUBLISHERS, NEW YORK

ACKNOWLEDGMENTS

THIS BOOK REQUIRED the hard work and dedication of many talented people. I'd like to thank all of them for working to ensure that it is everything we intended it to be—filled with delicious recipes, enticing photographs, and clear and concise instructions for the very best baked goods. A special thank you to Ellen Morrissey for shepherding the project the whole way through with the utmost care. Shelly Kaldunski spent the better part of two years developing outstanding, must-try recipes and leading our team of bakers. John Barricelli, longtime test kitchen manager at Martha Stewart Living television, created some of our favorites, most notably those in the Yeasted Baked Goods chapter. Our friend Susan Sugarman was instrumental in getting the project off the ground and organizing the chapters and recipes in their early stages. A very special thank you to the talented members of the Martha Stewart Living Omnimedia food departments who contributed excellent recipes and ideas, most notably Lucinda Scala Quinn, Jennifer Aaronson, Christine Albano, Tara Bench, Sarah Carey, Abigail Chipley, Sandra Rose Gluck, Susan Hanemann, Allison Lewis, Hayat Piñeiro, and Melissa Perry. Thank you, too, to our colleagues who keep our kitchens running smoothly, including Tylia Chevalier, Marie Cristino, Aida Ibarra, Lillian Kang, Gertrude Porter, and Darlene Schrack.

Photographer Jonathan Lovekin beautifully captured the essence of the baked goods, finding just the right style to highlight their appeal. Brooke Hellewell Reynolds created the gorgeous design under the direction of Mary Jane Callister and Eric A. Pike. Lisa Wagner helped shape the look and feel of the book through her careful eye and stylistic sensibilities. Duane Stapp did a wonderful job implementing the design, with the guidance of Denise Clappi. Meesha Diaz Haddad was invaluable in keeping the project on track; Elizabeth Alsop and Evelyn Battaglia kept watchful eyes on the accuracy of every recipe. Rory Evans and Bunny Wong wrote the text to introduce each chapter. Several readers helped ensure the book's quality, including Marc Bailes, Robert Bowe, Amy Conway, Natalie Ermann Russell, Kristen Croker Fiordalis, Kimberly Fusaro, Jennifer Jarett, Adam Kuban, Claire Lui, Kellee Miller, Andrea Peabbles, Debra Puchalla, Sarah Rutledge, Alex Van Buren, Miranda Van Gelder, and Penelope Wood.

Many thanks to Margaret Roach, Lauren Podlach Stanich, and Gael Towey for their guidance for the duration of the project, and to our friends at Crown and Clarkson Potter, Jenny Frost, Lauren Shakely, Pam Krauss, Jane Treuhaft, Elissa Altman, Mark McCauslin, Amy Boorstein, and Linnea Knollmueller. Finally, thanks to our readers and television viewers, who continue to inspire us with their feedback every day.

CONTENTS

chapter one
SIMPLE BAKED GOODS

chapter two
COOKIES

chapter three
CAKES

chapter four
PIES, TARTS, COBBLERS, AND CRISPS

chapter five
YEASTED BAKED GOODS

chapter six
PASTRIES

THE TASTES I BEST remember—the vast majority of them—are tastes that have to do with baking. For me there is something important about the flavor and texture of the best French baguette, the buttery flakiness of the perfect croissant, the subtle sweetness of the whitest cake, and the dense richness of the ultimate petit four.

I've long wanted to share the recipes for my favorite baked goods, which have not all been easily accessed or readily available to everyone. We, and I do mean *we* (a talented group of dedicated bakers) and not the royal we (I), have worked long and hard to assemble the best ones in a comprehensive, orderly, easy-to-use compendium for all of us.

Here, you will find the recipes and how-tos for the popovers you dream about, and for the simple crumb cake that you always want to whip up on Sunday morning, and for the double-chocolate brownie cookies that will make you a bigger hero with the after-school crowd, and for the citrus bars that you could only find on the eastern tip of Long Island in that little bakery that's no longer under the same management.

We, the team, got together and compiled our lists, gathered our desires, dug through our files, and collated everything into what we hope are sensible chapters, organized for easy use, with workable, clear recipes. Not everything you'll find on these pages is

Martha's pantry (opposite) in her home in Bedford, New York, has every type of pan, tin, and mold imaginable. Open wire shelving keeps the baker's tools readily available.

traditional, and some of the techniques are a bit unusual. But the best results are what we strive for in each one of our recipes, and because freshness of ingredients, exact measurements, accuracy of oven temperature, and careful preparation are tantamount to success, we focused on bringing a new understanding and artistry to the science of baking.

Speaking of techniques and baking essentials, I have always been fascinated with the baker's tools. Starting around the time I first visited Mr. and Mrs. Maus (extraordinary German-born bakers) next door on Elm Place in my hometown of Nutley, New Jersey, I have collected every possible kind of baking tray, sheet, mold, bowl, whisk, rolling pin, frosting tip, pastry bag, icing comb, and pie tin (you'll see many of my favorite, most beautiful ones photographed on these pages). The heavy edgeless steel pans I dragged home from Paris many years ago, from the legendary store Dehillerin, are still the very best for baking puff pastry for Napoleons and light-as-air cheese straws. And Mr. Maus's German tin-coated steel kugelhopf molds are the ones I like to use for babkas. And just when you think you have everything, you might discover the custardy excellence of cannelés and will want to invest in the copper molds shaped like tall little turbans that are for them and only them. These days I have silicone rubber molds, too, which bake perfect meringues. And I cannot live without my Silpats and rolls upon rolls of parchment paper that cut out so much scrubbing and scraping, leaving you more time to enjoy in the kitchen.

Baking, you will find, as you indulge in this home art, offers comfort and joy and something tangible to taste and savor. As much as any other culinary activity, it can bring countless smiles and much laughter into your home. We all hope that these recipes provide you with years of pleasure.

Martha Stewart

Read a recipe all the way through before you begin, and note the ingredients and equipment you will need. A read-through will also give you a sense of the techniques involved and the time required.

Prep ingredients before you proceed; you will work more efficiently. Measure out ingredients, and bring them to the right temperature, if necessary.

Your oven's internal temperature might not be accurately reflected by the dial or digital display. For a better reading, **set an oven thermometer** in the center of the oven. Preheat the oven, and check the temperature before you begin baking.

Preheat the oven 20 to 30 minutes before you plan to use it; the broiler, 10 minutes beforehand. Unless instructed otherwise, place baking pans and sheets on the oven's middle rack, in the center. Rotate pans and sheets halfway through the baking time, turning them front to back. If you're using the upper and lower racks at once, switch the positions of the sheets or pans (top to bottom and bottom to top) when you rotate them.

Baking times are important, but **pay attention to visual clues** as well. If a recipe calls for a baked good to achieve a certain color or texture, remove it from the oven when it arrives at that point, even if the baking time is not up.

Measure flour using the dip and sweep method (see page 18). Sift flour and other dry ingredients only when specified. Remember, too, that recipe wording is important. For example, "1 cup flour, sifted" means to measure first, then sift. If a recipe calls for "1 cup sifted flour," sift a generous amount onto parchment paper, then measure out 1 cup.

Similarly, when a recipe calling for chopped or ground nuts lists the volume amount first, **measure the nuts, then chop or grind them.** For example, "1 cup walnuts, coarsely chopped" means that the nuts are measured whole, then chopped.

Always use unsalted butter in baking recipes, rather than salted. This will allow you to control the amount of salt in the recipe.

Some recipes call for butter at room temperature; the **butter should be pliable,** but not runny or melted. Test its softness by pressing your forefinger into the top. Butter is ready when the indentation remains but the butter still holds its shape. To soften butter quickly, cut ¼-inch-thick slices, lay them flat on a work surface, and let stand for about 10 minutes.

When mixing, **scrape down the sides of the bowl** occasionally with a flexible spatula to make sure all of the ingredients are incorporated.

Use cold eggs when **separating whites from yolks;** the yolks will be less likely to break (and spill into the whites). You can refrigerate leftover whites and yolks in an airtight container for up to 3 days. Whites can be frozen for up to 2 months. Two tablespoons of whites is equal to one large egg white; 1 tablespoon of yolks is equal to one large yolk.

To bring eggs to room temperature quickly, soak them in warm water for 10 to 15 minutes.

Foods that contain raw eggs (or eggs that have not been heated to at least 160 degrees) should not be prepared for pregnant women, babies, young children, the elderly, or anyone whose health is compromised.

Invest in the best ingredients and equipment that you can afford. You will be more likely to achieve good results and be encouraged to bake more often.

1 Kitchen scale

When precise amounts are important, use a kitchen scale. In those instances, dry ingredients, such as flour, are often called for by weight. You can also use a scale to weigh nuts, dried and fresh fruits, and chocolate—and to measure out portions of dough. Digital models often have special functions, such as the ability to convert metric measurements.

2 Graduated dry measuring cups

Measure dry and semisolid ingredients (such as jam, sour cream, and peanut butter) in graduated dry measuring cups, preferably metal, which let you level ingredients with a straightedge.

3 Sieve

A fine-mesh sieve can be used to sift ingredients (such as flour) into a recipe, or to sprinkle ingredients (such as confectioners' sugar) over baked goods. Look for sturdy mesh that won't stretch or bend.

4 Mixing bowl

Keep a set of glass or ceramic bowls in graduated sizes on hand. Stainless-steel bowls, which are heatproof, are useful for recipes that require setting a bowl over hot water. Avoid plastic bowls; they retain flavors and traces of grease.

5 Liquid measuring cups

Measure liquids in clear liquid measuring cups (preferably heat-resistant glass), which allow you to read measurements at eye level and have a spout for pouring. This kitchen essential seems to always be in use, so it's helpful to have more than one.

6 Flexible heatproof spatula

Choose spatulas with silicone heads, which tend to be more resistant to heat and stains than rubber ones.

7 Whisk

Look for a stainless-steel whisk with fine wires and a bulbous shape—also called a balloon whisk.

8 Rasp grater

This stainless-steel grater has tiny, razor-sharp teeth that remove the flavorful zest from citrus fruits and leave the bitter white pith behind. This tool can also be used to finely grate chocolate, hard cheeses, whole nutmeg, and fresh ginger.

9 Graduated measuring spoons

Measure ingredients carefully. Pour liquids, such as vanilla extract, to the rim of the spoon; level dry ingredients, such as salt, with a straightedge.

10 Pastry blender

This utensil is indispensable for blending butter into flour, a crucial step in making simple doughs for biscuits and scones. It is also useful when making pie and tart doughs by hand.

11 Bowl scraper

This inexpensive plastic gadget collects dough or batter from a bowl, making it easy to transfer these goods to a work surface or a pan. It is especially helpful for manipulating large amounts of dough that a flexible spatula is too small to handle.

12 Citrus reamer

Pick out seeds from halved citrus fruits with the tip of this tool; twist the ridged body to express juice.

13 Cheesecloth

Use this cloth to bundle pie weights or to sift small amounts of confectioners' sugar over baked goods.

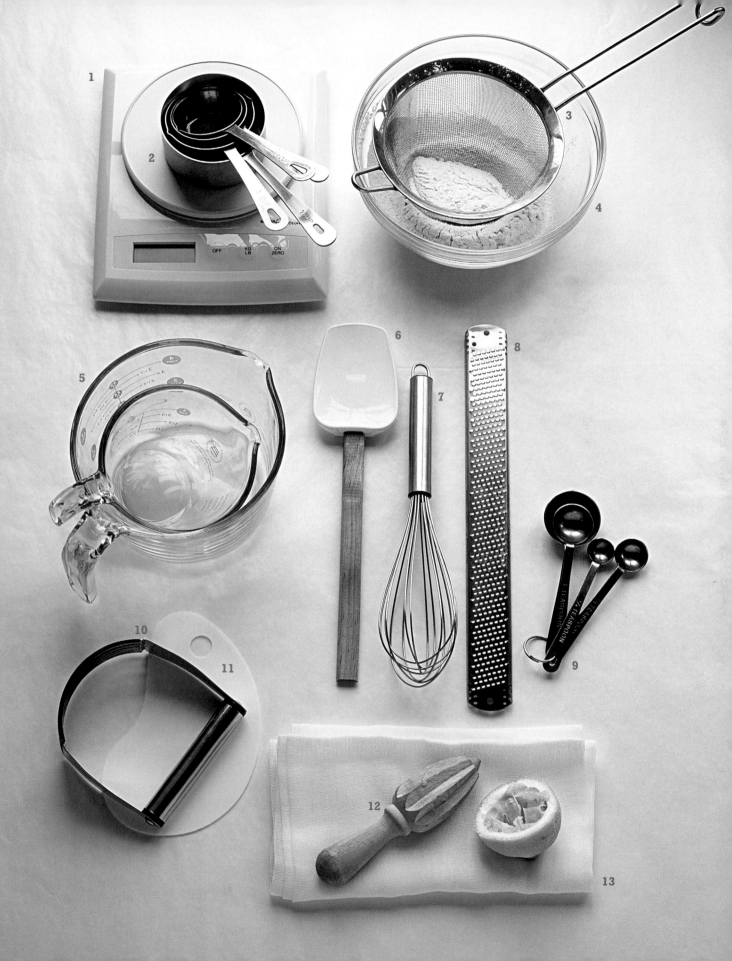

GENERAL BAKING EQUIPMENT

1 Rolling pin
Look for a wooden pin that is slightly heavy. The weight of it will help when rolling out laminated doughs, which have layers of butter and dough. A pin without handles will offer the most control.

2 Serrated knife
A long serrated knife is indispensable for leveling the tops of cake layers, slicing bread without compressing it, and chopping chocolate and nuts.

3 Ruler
Use a metal ruler to judge the spacing between cookies on baking sheets, to guide you in splitting cakes into equal layers, to measure cookware, to square corners and trim pastry dough, and more.

4 Bench scraper
A metal or plastic bench scraper is helpful for loosening dough from a work surface as you knead, scoring certain cookies, such as shortbread, cleanly dividing scone dough, and transferring chopped nuts or chocolate from a cutting board into a bowl.

5 Kitchen shears
Look for heavy blades and durable plastic handles. Label the shears "kitchen" so no one will mistake them for regular scissors. Use them to trim dough in a pie plate, cut out parchment rounds for cake pans, and cut dried fruit (such as apricots).

6 Pizza wheel
This cutter is used most frequently for slicing pizza and other flatbreads, of course. However, it also can stand in for a pastry cutter. Use it to cut lattice strips from pastry dough, trim rolled-out cookie dough, and divide pastry dough into neat shapes.

7 Pastry brushes
Look for pastry brushes with natural, tightly woven bristles that are securely attached to the handle. A large brush (1½ to 2½ inches wide) is ideal for brushing excess flour from work surfaces and pieces of rolled-out dough. A medium brush (1 inch) is good for buttering pans and applying egg washes to piecrusts. A small brush (½ to ¾ inch) is handy for dabbing egg wash on tiny pieces of dough. Reserve at least one brush for dry tasks and another for wet ones; mark each and store separately.

1 Parchment paper

This heat-resistant, nonstick, disposable paper can be used to line sheets and pans, making it easier to release baked goods. A sheet of parchment used to cover a work surface makes cleanup easier (try it when rolling out dough or frosting a cake). Doughs and baked items can be wrapped in parchment before being stored. Look for unbleached white or natural parchment. Waxed paper is not an acceptable substitute for most baking tasks.

2 Baking sheet (cookie sheet)

These sheets have small rims on the short sides for easy gripping; flat edges on the other sides let you slide off cookies without disturbing their forms. Choose sheets made from shiny, light-colored metals, such as heavy-duty aluminum, which encourage even baking and will not curl or warp. If using dark-metal sheets, such as nonstick, be aware that these tend to brown baked goods faster; you may need to lower the oven temperature (by 25 degrees) and reduce the baking time slightly.

3 Kitchen timer

Even if your oven comes with a built-in timer, it's a good idea to have a stand-alone model or even a multijob timer as well. Bakers often find themselves timing goods that are baking in the oven, cooling on a rack, or chilling in the freezer—all at once.

4 Nonstick baking mat

A heat-resistant silicone mat, such as a Silpat, can be used instead of parchment paper to line baking sheets; it's also washable and reusable. Wipe after each use with a damp sponge or, for more thorough cleaning, run it under warm water. Never scrub the mat with an abrasive sponge, which damages the surface. After it's dry, store the mat flat or rolled up. Don't fold it or store objects on top of it.

5 Metal spatula

A wide, thin-edged spatula can slide under just-baked cookies, rolls, and pastries and gently move them from hot sheets to wire cooling racks.

6 Large offset spatula

The thin metal blade makes this tool invaluable for frosting cakes, and the angled design allows it to double as a spatula, lifting cookies from baking sheets and brownies from pans. Steer clear of plastic ones; they are thick and might crush what you are picking up—and they are not as heat-resistant.

7 Small offset spatula

A small offset spatula, which can cover hard-to-reach spots and offer more control with tiny goods, is a must-have for cake and cookie decorating.

8 Rimmed baking sheet (jelly roll pan)

These sided sheets (really shallow baking pans) are used to make bar cookies, shortbread, sponge cakes, focaccia, and more. Position a sheet under a baking fruit pie, and it will catch juices, preventing them dripping onto the oven floor. Buy sheets made from heavy-duty, shiny aluminum.

9 Wire rack

These raised racks allow air to circulate around cooling baked goods. Look for a rack with stainless-steel mesh and feet on the bottom. Avoid plastic racks, and skip those with bars that go in only one direction (small items won't sit level on them).

10 Oven thermometer

Because oven temperature is critical to well-baked goods, an oven thermometer is one of the baker's most important gadgets.

1

2

3

4

5

6

7

8

9

10

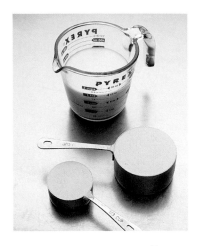

CHOOSING MEASURING CUPS Measure liquids in clear cups; place the cup on a work surface as you pour, and bend down so the markers are at eye level. Measure dry ingredients in graduated cups and level them off; use the right size cup (don't estimate portions).

PACKING BROWN SUGAR When a recipe calls for "packed" brown sugar, the sugar should look compact (above), not loose (top). Compress it with the back of a spoon so the sugar is level with the top of the measuring cup.

MEASURING FLOUR Employ the dip and sweep method: Dip a dry measuring cup directly into the flour, then use a straightedge—such as an offset spatula—to level the top. This will remove any hidden air bubbles and ensure an accurate measurement.

CHILLING INGREDIENTS Cold ingredients are crucial to the success of certain recipes. If chilling many ingredients, group them on a rimmed baking sheet so you can quickly move them in and out of the refrigerator or freezer.

MEASURING PANS The right size is important. If a baking pan is too small, batter may overflow; too large, and the end result will be thin and dry. Use a ruler to check: Measure the diameter (between inside edges) and the depth.

PREPARING PANS When a recipe calls for a parchment liner, first cut out parchment to fit the pan, then butter the pan and fit it with the liner. Next, butter the liner and dust it with flour. Rotate pan to distribute flour; tap out excess.

FOLDING IN BEATEN EGG WHITES
To combine egg whites with a heavy base, gently fold in about one-third at a time: Cut a spatula through the center of the mixture, sweep up the side of the bowl, and turn spatula over. Repeat, rotating bowl as you go, until just combined.

WHISKING TO COMBINE When a recipe calls for combining dry ingredients in a mixing bowl, whisk them just until the lumps are removed and the mixture has an even appearance.

WHIPPING CREAM To whip heavy cream, begin by briefly chilling the bowl and whisk attachment of an electric mixer. Start with the mixer on low speed, then gradually raise the speed and continue beating until peaks form.

CREAMING BUTTER AND SUGAR
Many recipes call for beating together butter and sugar, or "creaming" them. Beat the two until thoroughly blended and the mixture is pale and fluffy—that is, lightened in both color and texture.

ADDING LEMON TO CARAMEL When making caramel, you can eliminate the need to brush the sides of the pan with a wet pastry brush (to prevent crystals from forming) by first adding a drop of fresh lemon juice to the sugar water.

JUDGING CARAMEL The caramel samples above are (from top) light golden, light amber, amber, and deep amber. To test your batch, drop a spoonful onto parchment and compare the color to those shown here.

CHOPPING NUTS **1.** To coarsely chop nuts, use a serrated knife; the pieces should be about ¹/₃ inch. **2.** To finely chop nuts, use a serrated knife; the pieces should be about ¹/₈ inch. Before adding finely chopped nuts to doughs and batters, sift them in a fine sieve; the result will be a more professional-looking baked good. **3.** To finely grind nuts, or to make nut flour, use a nut grinder or pulse the nuts in a food processor. Watch that you don't overprocess the nuts, which will turn them into nut butter.

BEATING EGG WHITES **1.** Egg whites are beaten so that they attain volume and become stiffer. Start with room-temperature whites and a clean stainless-steel (or copper) bowl. As the whites are beaten they will begin to look foamy. **2.** With continued beating, the whites will form soft peaks, or peaks that gently droop when the whisk attachment is lifted. **3.** More beating yields glossy stiff peaks, or peaks that hold their shape even when the bowl is tilted; be careful not to beat past this point.

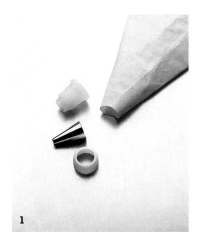

ASSEMBLING A PASTRY BAG **1.** To fit a pastry bag with a pastry tip, drop the larger piece of a plastic coupler into the bag so that its smaller opening is even with the opening of the bag. Place the pastry tip over the end of the plastic piece to fit snugly. **2.** Fit the ring piece of the coupler over the tip, and turn the ring until it locks. **3.** Fill the bag halfway with frosting; squeeze from the top of the bag down to release any air bubbles. Twist the end of the bag just above the filling; tightly seal with a rubber band.

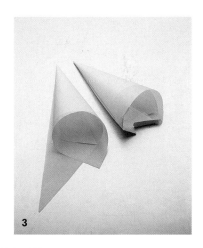

MAKING A PAPER CORNET FOR PIPING **1.** Cut a piece of parchment paper into an 8-by-12-by-14 1/2-inch triangle. **2.** Fold the lower right-hand point up toward the middle of the shortest side to form a cone shape; form the cone's point at the middle of the longest side. **3.** Wrap the slack around the cone shape, while pulling the inside flap of parchment taut to keep the point tight and completely closed. Tuck the top flaps inside the cone. To keep the cone closed, make a small (1/2-inch) tear in the folded side you have just created. Snip the tip of the cone after filling it.

SIMPLE
BAKED GOODS

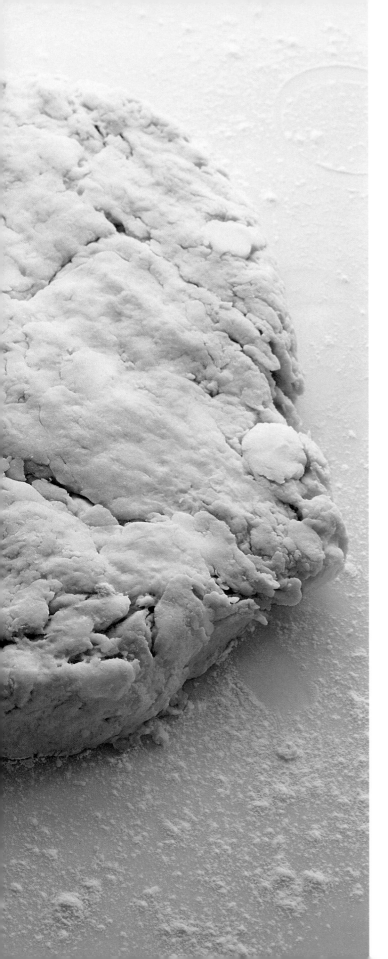

recipes

T

You don't need to wait for a special occasion to make biscuits, muffins, scones, and quick breads. These and other simple baked goods are meant for any Sunday breakfast or afternoon cup of tea—or for whenever you're in the mood to nibble on familiar favorites.

HE RECIPES in this chapter are simple and straightforward, calling for just a handful of ingredients to be combined in a few short steps. They are well suited to spur-of-the-moment urges to roll up your sleeves, tie on an apron, and create. In fact, it's likely that your pantry and refrigerator already hold the required components. Lots of the recipes call for little more than flour, sugar, baking powder and soda, eggs, butter, and milk or cream. You may already know the roles of these cornerstone ingredients—such as the way cold butter blends into flour to produce flaky biscuits, and how lightly beaten milk, eggs, and flour help give popovers their essential loft. You will find that such interactions recur throughout all baking: It is method, not magic, that turns out sublime Cornbread and sugar-crisped Chocolate Scones—and that enables you, with a little practice, to approach recipes for any baked good with confidence.

Look to the following recipes for direction not only on basic techniques, but also on the value of fresh ingredients and original combinations. The flavor of a just-baked Brown Sugar Pound Cake or Cranberry-Zucchini Muffin is unlike anything found in the grocery store. Even the local bakery doesn't compare: A coffee cake taken from a white cardboard box simply cannot compete with one straight from the oven. Just watch as your family congregates in the kitchen, clamoring for samples.

Don't overmix ingredients or overwork dough. A light touch will keep the finished product tender, not tough. When directed to do so, mix ingredients until just combined (or until the dough comes together). Then gently pat the dough into shape.

Bring milk, eggs, and butter to room temperature when making muffins. Take these ingredients out of the refrigerator before you start, and let them warm up as you measure the dry ingredients.

Cold butter is essential when making biscuits and scones. Cut the butter into small pieces, and then return it to the refrigerator to chill before adding it to the dry ingredients. If your kitchen is warm, chill the mixing bowl and pastry blender as well. If the butter becomes too soft while blending it into the flour, chill the bowl in the freezer for about 10 minutes before proceeding. Make sure you don't over-handle the dough; the warmth of your hands can affect the final product.

Gather together and reroll the scraps of dough when cutting out biscuits. Or you can try this easy alternative: Dip your finger into the cream or buttermilk left in the measuring cup, then use it to moisten the cut edges of the leftover dough; press the scraps together, gently pinching the surface to make it smooth before cutting out more rounds.

When working with biscuits, scones, and soda bread, **use only a small amount of flour** to dust your hands and the work surface. Too much flour will cause the dough to become dry and stiff.

Sanding sugar lends a sparkly finish to simple baked goods and doesn't melt when baked.

Experiment with variations. Any number of fruits and toasted nuts will add flavor and texture to muffins, scones, quick breads, and coffee cakes.

Most biscuits, scones, and other individual-size baked goods are **best eaten the same day they are baked.** If you are making a batch that can't be served all in one day, set aside a portion of unbaked pieces to bake at a later date. Chill the pieces in the freezer until firm, and then transfer them to resealable plastic bags. Return the pieces to the freezer, and store them for up to 3 weeks. To serve, bring the pieces to room temperature, and bake as directed.

When you do have **leftover biscuits and scones,** wrap them in plastic wrap and foil, and then freeze them for up to 3 weeks. To serve, bring the pieces to room temperature, and then warm them in a 300-degree oven for about 15 minutes.

1 Bundt pan

Created in the 1950s by an American company, this pan features fluted edges and a long tube in the center. The design encourages even baking and works nicely for Bundt cakes, of course, but also for pound and coffee cakes. Look for one in nonstick aluminum, a durable and easy-to-use option.

2 Muffin pans

This baking staple typically has 12 cups, each with a ½-cup capacity. Nonstick models in aluminum result in evenly browned muffins. Pans with smaller cups, which generally hold about 2 tablespoons of batter, come in handy when you want to make minimuffins. You can bake any muffin batter in these pans, but be mindful that the baking time will need to be greatly reduced. Batter poured into the little cups bakes quickly; use a light-colored metal pan, which will heat at a slower rate than a dark one.

3 Biscuit cutters

A clean cut is important for biscuits (it makes them rise higher), so a metal cutter with beveled edges is the best choice. Avoid plastic cutters, which are not sharp enough. Buying a boxed set provides a variety of diameters to work with. As for handles, with or without is a matter of personal preference. The former allows for a secure grip; the latter, for pushing down on the cutter evenly.

4 Popover pan

Traditionally this pan was made of cast iron, but newer ones are made with anodized aluminum, a much lighter material. Unlike a muffin pan, which has cups that are wider than they are deep, a popover pan has tall and narrow cups. This design encourages steam in the batter to rise quickly and puff up the tops of the popovers.

5 Loaf pans

There are two sizes given for standard loaf pans, 8½ by 4½ inches and 9 by 5 inches. The recipes in this book use both, but they are interchangeable as long as you pay attention to visual cues and adjust the baking time accordingly. For fewer issues with sticking and burning, choose metal loaf pans over glass ones. Lining the pans with parchment paper will let you quickly and cleanly lift out baked goods. A small version of the standard loaf pan is perfect for baking quick breads to give as gifts. Ours measures 6 by 3 inches and holds about 2 cups of batter.

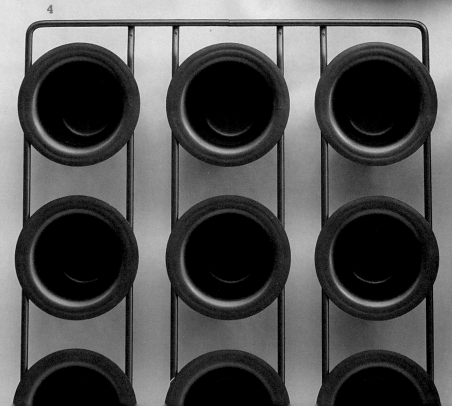

1

2

3

4

5

MAKING BISCUIT DOUGH 1. A pastry blender is used to blend small pieces of cold butter into the flour mixture; the tool is pressed down quickly and with as few strokes as possible. (If you don't have a pastry blender, two table knives make an acceptable—though less efficient—substitute.) **2.** The mixture has achieved the proper consistency when it resembles coarse crumbs with a few larger clumps remaining. **3.** The liquid is added and folded in just until the dough begins to come together; the dough will still be slightly sticky. The dough is then turned out onto a lightly floured work surface.

MAKING SCONE DOUGH 1. After the dry ingredients have been whisked together and the butter and dried fruits have been worked into the dough, liquid is added and mixed in just until the dough begins to come together. **2.** The dough should still be a little crumbly when it is turned out onto a lightly floured work surface; it is patted—with minimal handling—into a rectangle. **3.** After the dough has been patted to the proper size, it is cut into individual pieces (in this case, into triangles) with a bench scraper or a sharp knife. Before the pieces are baked, they are chilled in the freezer until firm.

CUTTING OUT BISCUITS A lightly floured cutter is used to cut rounds from the dough, which has been gently patted out to a 1-inch thickness. Scraps can be patted together and then cut into additional rounds.

MAKING DROP BISCUITS Wet biscuit dough, such as that of our Cornmeal Drop Biscuits, is scooped from the mixing bowl with a spoon; then, with the back of another spoon, the dough is eased onto a parchment-lined baking sheet.

SLASHING SODA BREAD A very sharp paring knife is used to cut a clean, deep cross (about ¾ inch) in the top of an unbaked round of Irish Soda Bread. A razor blade or bench scraper can be used in place of a knife.

PREPARING MUFFIN PANS A pastry brush—which can cover hard-to-reach spots—is used to thoroughly coat pans with softened butter. The surface between cups is brushed to prevent the muffin tops from sticking to the pan.

FILLING MUFFIN CUPS Prepared pans are filled using two spoons, one to scoop out the sticky batter, the other to push it into the muffin cups. The batter can also be scooped and dropped with an ice cream scoop.

COOLING MUFFINS Baked muffins are turned on their sides while they're still in the cups of the pan. This prevents them from steaming and cooking further—and makes them cool faster.

biscuits

BAKING POWDER BISCUITS

MAKES 1 DOZEN *These rich, flaky biscuits are best eaten warm from the oven. As with all biscuits, it's important not to overwork the dough while you are patting it out.*

- 4 cups all-purpose flour, plus more for dusting
- 2 tablespoons baking powder
- 2 teaspoons sugar
- 1 teaspoon salt

- 2 sticks (1 cup) unsalted butter, cold, cut into small pieces
- 2 cups heavy cream, plus more for brushing

Preheat the oven to 400°F. In a large bowl, whisk together the flour, baking powder, sugar, and salt. Using a pastry blender, cut in the butter until the mixture resembles coarse crumbs with a few larger clumps remaining.

Pour in the heavy cream; using a rubber spatula, fold cream into the dough, working in all directions and incorporating crumbs at the bottom of the bowl, until the dough just comes together. The dough will be slightly sticky.

Turn out the dough onto a lightly floured work surface. With floured fingers, gently pat the dough into a round about 1 inch thick, pressing in any loose bits. Do not overwork the dough. Use a floured 2¼-inch round biscuit cutter to cut out the biscuits as close together as possible. (Use one cut edge as the edge for the next biscuit.)

Place the biscuits on an unlined baking sheet about 1½ inches apart. Generously brush the tops of the biscuits with cream. Bake, rotating the sheet halfway through, until the biscuits are golden and flecked with brown spots, 20 to 25 minutes. Transfer the biscuits to a wire rack to cool.

HERB BISCUITS VARIATION Follow instructions for Baking Powder Biscuits, adding ¼ cup of finely chopped herbs, such as rosemary, oregano, thyme, or parsley, to the flour mixture after the butter has been cut in. Proceed with the recipe.

STRAWBERRY SHORTCAKE VARIATION Follow instructions for Baking Powder Biscuits, increasing sugar to ½ cup, and reducing butter to 1½ sticks (¾ cup). Pat dough to about 1¼ inches thick before cutting out rounds. Before baking, brush rounds with 1 lightly beaten large egg (do not brush with cream), and sprinkle generously with sanding sugar, if desired.

While biscuits bake, slice 3 pints hulled fresh strawberries in half (or in quarters, if large). In a medium bowl, toss to combine with 1 tablespoon freshly squeezed lemon juice and ⅓ cup granulated sugar. Let mixture macerate for 20 minutes.

After baking biscuits, cool them on a wire rack for 15 minutes, then split in half horizontally with a serrated knife. Place the bottom halves on serving plates, and top each with a dollop of Vanilla Whipped Cream (page 391). Spoon strawberries and juice over each, and cover with the biscuit tops. Serve immediately, with additional strawberries and whipped cream on the side, if desired.

Baking Powder Biscuits

Buttermilk Biscuits
(Cheddar Biscuits variation)

Cornmeal Drop Biscuits

Buttermilk Biscuits

BUTTERMILK BISCUITS

MAKES 1 DOZEN *These are delicious served warm or at room temperature with butter and jam. The cheddar variation makes a nice accompaniment to thinly sliced ham.*

- 4 cups all-purpose flour, plus more for dusting
- 1 tablespoon plus 1 teaspoon baking powder
- 1 teaspoon baking soda
- 1 teaspoon salt
- 1 teaspoon sugar
- 2 sticks (1 cup) unsalted butter, cold, cut into small pieces
- 1¾ cups buttermilk, plus more for brushing

Preheat the oven to 375°F. In a large bowl, whisk together the flour, baking powder, baking soda, salt, and sugar. Using a pastry blender, cut in the butter until the mixture resembles coarse crumbs with a few larger clumps remaining.

Pour in the buttermilk; using a rubber spatula, fold buttermilk into the dough, working in all directions and incorporating crumbs at the bottom of the bowl, until the dough just comes together. The dough will be slightly sticky; do not overmix.

Turn out the dough onto a lightly floured work surface. With floured fingers, gently pat the dough into a round about 1 inch thick, pressing in any loose bits. Do not overwork the dough. Use a floured 2¼-inch round biscuit cutter to cut out the biscuits as close together as possible. (Use one cut edge as the edge for the next biscuit.)

Place the biscuits about 1½ inches apart on an unlined baking sheet. Generously brush the tops of the biscuits with buttermilk. Bake, rotating the sheet halfway through, until the biscuits are golden and flecked with brown spots, 18 to 20 minutes. Transfer the biscuits to a wire rack to cool.

CHEDDAR BISCUITS VARIATION Follow instructions for Buttermilk Biscuits, adding 3 cups (9 ounces) grated sharp cheddar cheese to the flour mixture after the butter has been cut in. Proceed with the recipe.

CORNMEAL DROP BISCUITS

MAKES 10 *These biscuits are very quick and easy to prepare, since the dough is dropped onto the baking sheet without first having to roll it out or cut it.*

- 1½ cups all-purpose flour
- ¾ cup fine yellow cornmeal
- 2 teaspoons baking powder
- ½ teaspoon baking soda
- 1 teaspoon salt
- 2 tablespoons sugar
- 1 stick (½ cup) unsalted butter, cold, cut into small pieces
- 1 cup milk

Preheat the oven to 375°F. Line a baking sheet with parchment paper; set aside. In a large bowl, whisk together the flour, cornmeal, baking powder, baking soda, salt, and sugar. Using a pastry blender, cut in the butter until the mixture resembles coarse crumbs with a few larger clumps remaining.

Pour in the milk; using a rubber spatula, fold milk into the dough, working in all directions and incorporating crumbs at the bottom of the bowl, until the dough just comes together. The dough will be slightly sticky; do not overmix.

With two large spoons, drop mounds of dough (about ⅓ cup each) about 1½ inches apart on the prepared baking sheet.

Bake, rotating the sheet halfway through, until the biscuits are golden, 15 to 20 minutes. Slide the parchment and biscuits onto a wire rack to cool.

CREAM CHEESE AND CHIVE BISCUITS

MAKES 1 DOZEN *You can freeze the unbaked biscuits on a baking sheet, then store in a re-sealable plastic bag for up to three weeks. When ready to serve, bake them (without thawing) on a parchment-lined sheet (the baking time will be the same).*

2½ cups all-purpose flour, plus more for dusting	¼ cup finely chopped fresh chives
1½ teaspoons baking powder	1 stick (½ cup) unsalted butter, cold, cut into small pieces
¼ teaspoon baking soda	4 ounces cream cheese, cold, cut into pieces
1¼ teaspoons salt	1¼ cups buttermilk
1 tablespoon sugar	

Line a baking sheet with parchment paper; set aside. In a large bowl, whisk together the flour, baking powder, baking soda, salt, sugar, and chives. Using a pastry blender, cut in the butter and cream cheese until the mixture resembles coarse crumbs with a few larger clumps remaining.

Pour in the buttermilk; using a fork, mix in buttermilk until incorporated and the dough just comes together. The dough will be slightly sticky; do not overmix.

Turn out the dough onto a lightly floured work surface. With floured fingers, gently knead about four times, until all the crumbs are incorporated and the dough is smooth. With a lightly floured rolling pin, gently roll out the dough to an 11-by-8-inch rectangle, about 1 inch thick. Using a bench scraper or long offset spatula to lift the ends of the dough, fold the rectangle into thirds (like a business letter). Give the dough a quarter turn. Roll out the dough again (to the same dimensions), and repeat the folding process. Wrap with plastic, and refrigerate for 30 minutes.

Return the dough to the work surface. Roll out as before, and repeat the folding process. Give the dough another quarter turn; roll out the dough one more time, again into a rectangle about 1 inch thick. Using a sharp knife, trim and discard ¼ inch from all sides; divide the rectangle into 12 equal squares or rectangles. Place on the prepared baking sheet about 1½ inches apart. Refrigerate for 1 hour.

Preheat the oven to 425°F. Bake, rotating the sheet halfway through, until the biscuits are golden and flecked with brown spots, 15 to 18 minutes. Transfer the biscuits to a wire rack to cool.

CREAM CHEESE BISCUIT HOW-TO 1. On a lightly floured work surface, dough is rolled into an 11-by-8-inch rectangle. **2.** The top and bottom thirds are folded inward, overlapping at the center. **3.** The dough is given a quarter turn, then the rolling and folding is repeated twice more.

Baking Powder Biscuits (Strawberry Shortcake variation)

Cream Cheese and Chive Biscuits

SPICY CHEESE BISCUITS

MAKES 10 *Sweet smoked paprika is also known as Pimentòn de la Vera. If you prefer foods less spicy, omit it from the biscuit tops.*

2¼ cups all-purpose flour

1¼ teaspoons baking powder

¾ teaspoon baking soda

1 teaspoon salt

2 teaspoons sugar

¾ teaspoon sweet smoked paprika, plus more for dusting

6 tablespoons unsalted butter, cold, cut into pieces

6 ounces manchego cheese, finely grated (about 1 cup)

1½ cups heavy cream

Preheat the oven to 375°F. Line a baking sheet with parchment paper; set aside. In a large bowl, whisk together the flour, baking powder, baking soda, salt, sugar, and paprika. Using a pastry blender, cut the butter into the flour mixture until it resembles coarse meal with a few larger clumps remaining. Stir in the cheese with a fork.

Add the cream; using a rubber spatula, stir until the dough just comes together. The dough will be slightly sticky; do not overmix. Using a ½-cup measure, scoop mounds of dough about 1½ inches apart on the prepared baking sheet. Lightly dust with paprika.

Bake, rotating the sheet halfway through, until golden brown, 15 to 20 minutes. Slide parchment and biscuits onto a wire rack to cool. Serve warm or at room temperature.

muffins

BLUEBERRY MUFFINS

MAKES 1 DOZEN *Try sprinkling granulated sugar over the tops of the unbaked muffins (one tablespoon should cover all twelve) to give them a bit of crunch.*

- 1 stick (½ cup) unsalted butter, room temperature, plus more for pan
- 2 cups all-purpose flour, plus more for pan
- 1½ teaspoons baking powder
- ½ teaspoon salt
- 2 cups fresh blueberries
- 1 cup sugar
- 2 large eggs
- 2 teaspoons pure vanilla extract
- ½ cup milk

Preheat the oven to 375°F. Generously butter a standard 12-cup muffin pan and dust with flour, tapping out excess; set aside. In a medium bowl, whisk together the flour, baking powder, and salt. Working over the bowl, toss the blueberries in a fine sieve with about 1½ teaspoons of the flour mixture to lightly coat; set aside the flour mixture and blueberries.

In the bowl of an electric mixer fitted with the paddle attachment, beat the butter and sugar on medium-high speed until light and fluffy, about 3 minutes. Add the eggs, one at a time, beating until combined. Mix in the vanilla.

With the mixer on low speed, add the reserved flour mixture, beating until just combined. Add milk, beating until just combined; do not overmix. Using a rubber spatula, fold in the blueberries. Divide the batter evenly among the prepared muffin cups.

Bake, rotating the pan halfway through, until the muffins are golden brown and a cake tester inserted in the center of one muffin comes out clean, about 30 minutes. Transfer the pan to a wire rack to cool 10 minutes. Turn the muffins on their sides in their cups, and let cool. Serve warm or at room temperature.

BLUEBERRY MUFFIN HOW-TO Tossing the blueberries with some of the flour mixture helps keep them from sinking to the bottom of the muffins as they bake.

CRANBERRY-ZUCCHINI MUFFINS

MAKES 10 *These muffins offer a nice balance of tart and sweet flavors.*

- Unsalted butter, room temperature, for pan, or nonstick cooking spray
- 1¾ cups all-purpose flour
- ½ teaspoon baking powder
- ½ teaspoon baking soda
- ½ teaspoon ground cinnamon
- ¼ teaspoon salt
- 2 large eggs
- 1 cup sugar
- ½ cup vegetable oil
- ½ teaspoon pure vanilla extract
- 1 cup finely grated zucchini (1 to 2 medium)
- ½ cup fresh or frozen whole cranberries

Preheat the oven to 375°F. Generously butter 10 cups of a standard 12-cup muffin pan; set aside. In a medium bowl, whisk together the flour, baking powder, baking soda, cinnamon, and salt; set aside.

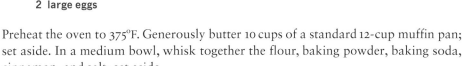

Plum Coffee-Cake Muffins
Cranberry-Zucchini Muffins
Blueberry Muffins
Date-Bran Muffins

In a large bowl, whisk together the eggs, sugar, oil, and vanilla. Stir in the zucchini. Add the flour mixture, and stir to combine; do not overmix. Using a rubber spatula, fold in the cranberries. Divide the batter evenly among the 10 prepared muffin cups.

Bake, rotating the pan halfway through, until the muffins are golden and a cake tester inserted in the center of one muffin comes out clean, 25 to 30 minutes. Transfer the pan to a wire rack to cool for 10 minutes. Turn the muffins on their sides in their cups, and cool. Serve warm or at room temperature.

CRANBERRY-ZUCCHINI QUICK BREAD VARIATION Follow instructions for Cranberry-Zucchini Muffins, transferring batter to a 9-by-5-inch loaf pan coated with butter or nonstick cooking spray. Bake at 375°F, rotating the pan halfway through, until a cake tester inserted into the center comes out clean, 45 to 50 minutes. Transfer to a wire rack to cool before serving.

PLUM COFFEE-CAKE MUFFINS

MAKES 10 *You can substitute an equal amount of chopped peaches or nectarines for the plums. Or use your favorite berries instead—the recipe is very versatile.*

1 stick (½ cup) unsalted butter, melted, plus more for pan	Pinch of ground nutmeg
¾ cup plus 2 tablespoons sugar	2 large eggs, room temperature
¾ teaspoon ground cinnamon	1 teaspoon pure vanilla extract
2 cups all-purpose flour	¾ cup milk
1 tablespoon baking powder	3 ripe red plums (about 1 pound), pitted and cut into small chunks
½ teaspoon salt	

Preheat the oven to 375°F. Generously butter 10 cups of a standard 12-cup muffin tin; set aside. Combine 2 tablespoons sugar and ¼ teaspoon cinnamon in a small bowl; set aside. In a large bowl, whisk together the flour, baking powder, salt, nutmeg, and remaining ¾ cup sugar and ½ teaspoon cinnamon; set aside.

In another large bowl, whisk together the eggs, vanilla, and milk. Whisk in the melted butter. Using a rubber spatula, fold the egg mixture into the flour mixture until just combined. Dividing evenly, fill each of the 10 muffin cups halfway with batter. Smooth the batter with an offset spatula.

Distribute the plum pieces evenly among the cups (about 3 tablespoons per muffin), scattering them over the batter. Spoon the remaining batter on top, dividing evenly. Sprinkle tops with the reserved cinnamon-sugar mixture.

Bake, rotating the pan halfway through, until the muffins are puffed and golden brown and a cake tester inserted in the center of one muffin comes out clean, 16 to 18 minutes. Transfer the pan to a wire rack and let stand 5 to 10 minutes. Turn out the muffins onto the rack to cool a few minutes. Serve warm.

PLUM COFFEE-CAKE MUFFIN HOW-TO To keep the chopped fruit in an even layer, the muffin cups are first partially filled with batter, then topped with fruit and another layer of batter. The tops are sprinkled with cinnamon-sugar before baking.

DATE-BRAN MUFFINS

MAKES 1 DOZEN *Be sure to use unsulfured molasses—not sulfured or blackstrap—in this recipe. Also, buy the freshest, moistest dates you can find.*

1½ sticks (¾ cup) unsalted butter, room temperature, plus more for pan
1½ cups all-purpose flour
1½ teaspoons baking soda
½ teaspoon salt
1½ cups wheat bran
¼ cup plus 2 tablespoons packed light-brown sugar

2 large eggs
1½ cups sour cream
¼ cup unsulfured molasses
1½ cups (8 ounces) pitted, chopped dates
1 teaspoon freshly grated orange zest

Preheat the oven to 375°F. Generously butter a standard 12-cup muffin pan; set aside. In a medium bowl, whisk together the flour, baking soda, salt, and bran; set aside.

In the bowl of an electric mixer fitted with the paddle attachment, beat the butter and brown sugar on medium-high speed until light and fluffy, 2 to 3 minutes, scraping down the sides of the bowl as needed. Beat in the eggs one at a time. Add the sour cream and molasses; mix on low speed until just combined.

Using a rubber spatula, fold in the reserved flour mixture, dates, and orange zest until just combined; do not overmix. Divide the batter evenly among the prepared muffin cups.

Bake, rotating the pan halfway through, until a cake tester inserted in the center of one muffin comes out clean, 22 to 25 minutes. Transfer the pan to a wire rack to cool for 10 minutes. Turn the muffins on their sides in their cups, and let cool completely.

POPOVERS

MAKES 1 DOZEN *Since they will start to deflate as they cool, popovers are best served warm from the oven. Butter and jam are traditional accompaniments.*

Unsalted butter, room temperature, for pan
1½ cups milk
6 large eggs

1½ cups all-purpose flour
¾ teaspoon salt
1½ tablespoons confectioners' sugar

Preheat the oven to 425°F, with the rack in the lower third. Generously butter a 12-cup popover tin; set aside. In a medium bowl, whisk together the milk and eggs. Add the flour, salt, and sugar, and whisk until the mixture is the consistency of heavy cream (some small lumps may remain); do not overmix.

Fill each prepared cup with about 5 tablespoons batter. Bake until the popovers are very puffed and extend over the top of the tin by about 3 inches, about 30 minutes. Immediately invert pan to remove popovers, and serve.

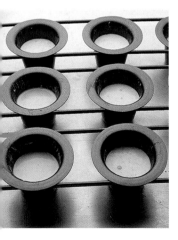

POPOVER HOW-TO Popover batter is thin, with a high proportion of wet ingredients to dry. Some of the liquid evaporates during baking, creating steam that puffs the batter until it "pops" over the tins.

CURRANT SCONES

MAKES 16 *Sanding sugar is coarser than granulated sugar and lends a lovely sparkle when sprinkled over the tops of scones, biscuits, pies, and cookies before baking. It is available at baking-supply stores and many grocery stores.*

$4\frac{1}{2}$ cups all-purpose flour, plus more for dusting

2 tablespoons granulated sugar

2 tablespoons baking powder

1 teaspoon baking soda

1 teaspoon salt

2 sticks (1 cup) unsalted butter, cold, cut into small pieces

1 cup dried currants

$2\frac{1}{4}$ cups heavy cream, plus more if needed

1 large egg yolk

Sanding sugar, for sprinkling (optional)

Line two baking sheets with parchment paper; set aside. In a bowl, whisk together the flour, granulated sugar, baking powder, baking soda, and salt. Using a pastry blender, cut in the butter until the mixture resembles coarse crumbs with a few larger clumps remaining. Fold in the currants. Make a well in the center.

Pour 2 cups cream into the flour mixture. Using your hands, draw the dry ingredients over the cream, gradually gathering and combining the dough until it just comes together. If it is too dry, add more cream, 1 tablespoon at a time.

Turn out the dough onto a lightly floured work surface. With lightly floured hands, gently press and pat the dough into an 11-by-7-inch rectangle, about 1 inch thick. Using a sharp knife or pastry wheel, cut the rectangle into 16 triangles. Place the triangles on the prepared baking sheets; cover with plastic wrap and freeze until the dough is very firm, at least 2 hours or overnight. (At this point, you can freeze the unbaked scones in a resealable plastic bag until ready to bake, up to 3 weeks.)

Preheat the oven to 375°F. In a small bowl, lightly beat the egg yolk with the remaining ¼ cup cream; brush over the tops of the scones and sprinkle generously with sanding sugar, if using. Bake, rotating sheets halfway through, until the tops are golden and flecked with brown spots, 30 to 35 minutes. You can also lift one scone with a spatula to check that the bottom is golden. Transfer to a wire rack to cool. Serve warm or at room temperature. They are best eaten the day they are baked.

LEMON-GINGER SCONES VARIATION Follow instructions for Currant Scones, folding in ¾ cup (about 4 ounces) diced crystallized ginger and the finely grated zest of 2 lemons after cutting in the butter; omit the currants. Pour 2¼ cups heavy cream (instead of 2 cups) into the flour mixture, along with ½ cup freshly squeezed lemon juice. Proceed with the recipe.

OAT AND DRIED APRICOT SCONES

MAKES 8 *Feel free to substitute other dried fruits for the apricots. We particularly like using sour cherries, cranberries, golden raisins, or chopped figs.*

1 cup oats (old-fashioned or quick-cooking)

¾ cup all-purpose flour, plus more for dusting

½ cup whole-wheat flour

¼ cup plus 2 tablespoons granulated sugar

1½ teaspoons baking powder

½ teaspoon baking soda

½ teaspoon salt

1¼ sticks (10 tablespoons) unsalted butter, cold, cut into small pieces

Heaping ½ cup diced dried apricots (¼-inch pieces)

1 large whole egg, plus 1 large egg yolk

½ cup buttermilk

1 tablespoon heavy cream

Sanding sugar, for sprinkling (optional)

Line a baking sheet with parchment paper; set aside. In a large bowl, whisk together the oats, all-purpose and whole-wheat flours, granulated sugar, baking powder, baking soda, and salt. Using a pastry blender, cut in the butter until the mixture resembles coarse crumbs with a few larger clumps remaining. Fold in the apricots.

Whisk together the whole egg and buttermilk. Add egg mixture to the flour mixture; using a rubber spatula, fold in, working in all directions and incorporating crumbs at the bottom of the bowl, until the dough just comes together.

Turn out the dough onto a lightly floured work surface. With lightly floured hands, gently press and pat dough into a rectangle, about 1¼ inches thick. Using a sharp knife or pastry wheel, cut into eight triangles. Place triangles about 2 inches apart on the prepared baking sheet; cover with plastic wrap and freeze until the dough is very firm, at least 1 hour or overnight. (At this point, you can freeze the unbaked scones in a resealable plastic bag until ready to bake, up to 3 weeks.)

Preheat the oven to 375°F. In a small bowl, lightly beat the egg yolk with the cream; brush over the tops of the scones, and sprinkle generously with the sanding sugar, if using. Bake, rotating the sheet halfway through, until the tops are golden, 25 to 30 minutes. Transfer to a wire rack to cool. They are best eaten the day they are baked.

Chocolate Scones

Currant Scones

Oat and Dried
Apricot Scones

CHOCOLATE SCONES

MAKES 6 *These scones are so rich and dense, you may prefer to eat them as an afternoon snack, rather than for breakfast. Either way, they're great with coffee.*

2¼ cups all-purpose flour, plus more for dusting

3 tablespoons Dutch-process cocoa powder

½ cup plus 2 tablespoons granulated sugar

1½ teaspoons baking powder

½ teaspoon baking soda

¼ teaspoon salt

1¼ sticks (10 tablespoons) unsalted butter, cold, cut into small pieces

5 ounces semisweet chocolate, chopped into ⅓-inch to ½-inch pieces (1 cup)

1 large whole egg, plus 1 large egg yolk

½ cup plus 2 tablespoons heavy cream

Sanding sugar, for sprinkling (optional)

Line a baking sheet with parchment; set aside. In a large bowl, whisk together the flour, cocoa, granulated sugar, baking powder, baking soda, and salt. Using a pastry blender, cut in the butter until the mixture resembles coarse crumbs with a few larger clumps remaining. Fold in the chocolate.

Whisk together the whole egg and ½ cup plus 1 tablespoon cream. Add egg mixture to the flour mixture; using a rubber spatula, fold in, working in all directions and incorporating crumbs at the bottom of the bowl, until dough just comes together.

Turn out the dough onto a lightly floured work surface, and gently pat into a 18-by-3-inch rectangle about 1 inch thick. Using a sharp knife or a pastry wheel, cut the rectangle into six 3-inch squares. Place squares about 2 inches apart on the prepared baking sheet. Cover with plastic wrap and freeze until the dough is very firm, at least 1 hour or overnight. (At this point, you can freeze the unbaked scones in a resealable plastic bag until ready to bake, up to 3 weeks.)

Preheat the oven to 375°F. In a small bowl, lightly beat the egg yolk with the remaining tablespoon heavy cream; brush over the tops of the scones and sprinkle generously with sanding sugar, if using. Bake, rotating the sheet halfway through, until the sugar on top of the scones turns golden all over, or a cake tester inserted in the center of a scone comes out clean, 25 to 30 minutes. Transfer to a wire rack to cool. They are best eaten the day they are baked.

FENNEL AND GOLDEN-RAISIN SCONES

MAKES 1 DOZEN *The dough for these savory scones gets its unique texture and flavor from a combination of butter and olive oil. It was inspired by a similarly flavored yeast bread sold at Amy's Bread in New York City.*

3 tablespoons fennel seeds, plus more for sprinkling

4 cups all-purpose flour, plus more for dusting and cutting

2 tablespoons baking powder

1 tablespoon sugar

1 teaspoon baking soda

½ teaspoon salt

1 stick (½ cup) unsalted butter, cold, cut into small pieces

1½ cups golden raisins, coarsely chopped

½ cup plus 1 tablespoon extra-virgin olive oil

1½ cups heavy cream, plus more if needed

1 large egg, lightly beaten

Line a baking sheet with parchment paper; set aside. Place fennel seeds in a spice grinder, and pulse until coarsely ground, 10 times; set aside. (Alternatively, crush the seeds using a mortar and pestle.) In a large bowl, whisk together the flour, baking powder, sugar, baking soda, and salt to combine. Using a pastry blender, cut in the butter until the mixture resembles coarse crumbs, with a few larger clumps remaining.

Add the raisins and reserved fennel seeds, ½ cup olive oil, and the cream; stir until the dough just comes together. If the dough is too dry, add more cream, 1 tablespoon at a time. Turn out the dough onto a lightly floured work surface. With lightly floured hands, gently pat the dough into a round about 1½ inches thick.

Using a floured 2¾-inch cookie cutter, cut out as many rounds as possible, dipping the cutter in flour each time; place on the prepared baking sheet about 2 inches apart. Gently pat the scraps together, and continue cutting out rounds. Cover with plastic wrap and freeze until the dough is very firm, at least 2 hours or overnight. (At this point, you can freeze the unbaked scones in a resealable plastic bag until ready to bake, up to 3 weeks.)

Preheat the oven to 350°F. Whisk together the egg and the remaining tablespoon olive oil; brush over the tops of the rounds, then sprinkle with fennel seeds. Bake, rotating the sheet halfway through, until the tops of the scones are golden and flecked with brown spots, 20 to 25 minutes. Transfer to a wire rack to cool. They are best eaten the day they are baked.

Pumpkin Bread, Banana-Nut Bread, and Fig-Walnut Bread

quick breads

BANANA-NUT BREAD

MAKES TWO 9-BY-5-INCH LOAVES OR SIX 6-BY-2¾-INCH MINILOAVES *If you use miniloaf pans, reduce the baking time to forty-five minutes. The recipe comes from Deanna Caceres Cahn, a former brand manager in the Martha Stewart Signature furniture group.*

3 cups all-purpose flour

1 teaspoon baking soda

¾ teaspoon salt

3 large eggs

2 cups sugar

1⅓ cups vegetable oil

2 tablespoons pure vanilla extract

1½ cups ripe mashed banana (about 3 medium)

1 cup unsweetened shredded coconut

1 cup (about 4 ounces) walnuts or pecans, toasted and finely chopped

½ cup buttermilk

Nonstick cooking spray

Preheat the oven to 350°F. Coat two 9-by-5-inch loaf pans with cooking spray; set aside. In a large bowl, whisk together the flour, baking soda, and salt; set aside.

In the bowl of an electric mixer fitted with the paddle attachment, beat the eggs, sugar, and vegetable oil on medium-low speed until combined. Beat in the flour mixture. Add the vanilla, banana, coconut, nuts, and buttermilk, and beat just to combine.

Divide batter evenly between prepared pans; smooth with an offset spatula. Bake, rotating pans halfway through, until a cake tester inserted in the centers comes out clean, 60 to 65 minutes. Transfer to a wire rack to cool for 10 minutes. Remove loaves from pans and let cool completely. Bread can be kept at room temperature, wrapped well in plastic, for up to 1 week, or frozen for up to 3 months.

PUMPKIN BREAD

MAKES TWO 8½-BY-4½-INCH LOAVES OR SIX 6-BY-2¾-INCH MINILOAVES *If you use miniloaf pans, reduce the baking time to forty-five minutes. This bread is delightful as soon as it cools, but it's even better the next day, when the flavors have had a chance to develop.*

Unsalted butter, room temperature, for pans

3 cups all-purpose flour

2 teaspoons baking powder

2 teaspoons baking soda

2½ teaspoons ground cinnamon

½ teaspoon freshly grated nutmeg

¼ teaspoon ground allspice

¼ teaspoon salt

2 cups canned pumpkin purée

1 cup granulated sugar

1 cup packed dark-brown sugar

4 large eggs

¼ cup vegetable oil

1⅔ cups buttermilk

Preheat the oven to 350°F. Coat two 8½-by-4½-inch loaf pans with butter; set aside. In a large bowl, whisk together the flour, baking powder, baking soda, cinnamon, nutmeg, allspice, and salt; set mixture aside.

In the bowl of an electric mixer fitted with the paddle attachment, combine the pumpkin purée and both sugars; mix on medium speed until well combined, 2 to 3 minutes. Add the eggs and oil; mix until incorporated, about 2 minutes, scraping down the sides of the bowl. With mixer on low, add the flour mixture in two batches, alternating with the buttermilk and beginning and ending with the flour, until just combined.

Divide the batter between the prepared pans; smooth the tops with an offset spatula. Place the pans on a baking sheet. Bake, rotating the sheet halfway through, until a cake tester inserted in the centers comes out clean, 55 to 60 minutes. Transfer pans to a wire rack to cool 10 minutes. Remove loaves from pans and cool completely. Bread can be kept at room temperature, wrapped in plastic, for up to 4 days.

FIG-WALNUT BREAD

MAKES TWO 9-BY-5-INCH LOAVES OR SIX 6-BY-2¾-INCH MINILOAVES *If you use miniloaf pans, reduce the baking time to forty-five minutes. Because this recipe calls for dried figs, it can be made year-round; the figs' seeds give the bread a nice crunch.*

2 sticks (1 cup) unsalted butter, room temperature, plus more for pans	1 pound (about 3 cups) dried figs, stemmed and chopped into ½-inch pieces
3 cups all-purpose flour	1¾ cups packed light-brown sugar
2 teaspoons baking soda	4 large eggs
1 teaspoon baking powder	1 cup sour cream
½ teaspoon ground cinnamon	1 cup (about 3 ounces) walnuts, toasted and coarsely chopped
¼ teaspoon ground allspice	
Pinch of freshly grated nutmeg	
1 teaspoon salt	

Preheat the oven to 325°F. Coat two 9-by-5-inch loaf pans with butter; set aside. In a large bowl, whisk together the flour, baking soda, baking powder, cinnamon, allspice, nutmeg, and salt; set mixture aside.

Bring 1 cup water to a simmer in a medium saucepan. Remove from heat, and add 1½ cups dried figs; let stand until softened, about 10 minutes. Transfer figs and liquid to a food processor. Purée until smooth, about 1 minute; set aside.

In the bowl of an electric mixer fitted with the paddle attachment, beat the butter and brown sugar on medium-high speed until light and fluffy, 2 to 3 minutes. Add the eggs, one at a time, and mix to combine, scraping down the sides of the bowl as needed. Add the flour mixture, and beat until combined, 1 to 2 minutes. Add the sour cream and reserved fig purée; beat until just incorporated, about 1 minute. Using a rubber spatula, stir in the remaining chopped figs and the walnuts.

Divide the batter between the prepared pans; smooth the tops with an offset spatula. Place pans on a baking sheet. Bake, rotating the sheet halfway through, until deep golden brown and a cake tester inserted in the centers comes out clean, about 1 hour. Transfer the pans to a wire rack to cool 10 minutes. Remove loaves from pans and cool completely. Bread can be kept at room temperature, wrapped well in plastic, for up to 4 days.

CORNBREAD

MAKES ONE 8-INCH SQUARE *Sautéed corn moistens this cornbread, but you can omit it if you are using the bread in a traditional stuffing. For a spicy variation, add two medium jalapeños, seeded and finely chopped, to the corn before sautéeing.*

- ⅓ cup vegetable shortening, plus more for pan
- 1 tablespoon unsalted butter
- 1 cup corn kernels, fresh or frozen
- 1 cup all-purpose flour
- ⅓ cup sugar
- 2 teaspoons baking powder
- ¾ teaspoon salt
- 1 cup stone-ground yellow cornmeal
- 1 cup milk
- 1 large egg, lightly beaten

Preheat the oven to 425°F. Coat an 8-inch square baking pan with vegetable shortening; set aside. Melt butter in a medium sauté pan over medium-high heat; add corn. Cook, stirring occasionally, until corn has softened and some of the kernels have begun to turn light golden brown, about 5 minutes. Remove from heat, and set aside to cool slightly.

In a medium bowl, whisk together flour, sugar, baking powder, and salt. Stir in the cornmeal. Using a pastry blender, cut shortening into mixture until it resembles coarse meal. Add milk, egg, and reserved corn; stir to combine. Do not overmix.

Transfer batter to the prepared pan, and bake until the top begins to turn golden and a cake tester inserted in the center comes out clean, 18 to 20 minutes. Transfer to a wire rack to cool completely. Cornbread is best served the day it is baked, but it can be kept at room temperature, wrapped well in plastic, for up to 1 day.

IRISH SODA BREAD

MAKES ONE 8-INCH ROUND LOAF *The addition of raisins, caraway seeds, and egg makes this version richer and even more delicious than traditional Irish soda bread.*

4 cups all-purpose flour	2 cups golden or dark raisins
¼ cup sugar	1 large whole egg, plus 1 large egg yolk
2 tablespoons caraway seeds	
2 teaspoons baking powder	Scant 1½ cups buttermilk
1 teaspoon salt	1 teaspoon baking soda
4 tablespoons unsalted butter, cold, cut into small pieces	1 tablespoon heavy cream

Preheat the oven to 350°F. Line a baking sheet with parchment paper; set aside. In a large bowl, whisk together the flour, sugar, caraway seeds, baking powder, and salt until well combined. Using a pastry blender, cut in the butter until the mixture resembles coarse crumbs with a few larger clumps remaining. Fold in the raisins.

In a bowl, whisk together the whole egg, buttermilk, and baking soda until combined. Pour egg mixture into the flour mixture; using a rubber spatula, fold in, working in all directions and incorporating crumbs at the bottom of the bowl, until the dough just comes together. With your hands, form dough into a round, domed loaf, about 8 inches in diameter. Gently lift dough from the bowl, and place on the prepared sheet.

In a small bowl, lightly beat the egg yolk with the cream; brush over the loaf. With a sharp knife, cut a cross, about ¾ inch deep, in the center of the top of the loaf. Bake, rotating the sheet halfway through, until deep golden brown and a cake tester inserted in the center of the loaf comes out clean, about 1 hour 10 minutes. Transfer the bread to a wire rack to cool completely. Irish Soda Bread is best eaten the day it is baked, but it can be kept at room temperature, wrapped well in plastic, for up to 3 days.

CHERRY-STREUSEL COFFEE CAKE

MAKES ONE 9-INCH TUBE CAKE *Sour cream gives this cake a particularly lovely tang. Tube pans are made with both regular and removable bottoms; either is fine for this recipe.*

1 stick (½ cup) unsalted butter, room temperature, plus more for pan

2 cups all-purpose flour

1 teaspoon baking powder

1 teaspoon baking soda

1 teaspoon salt

1 cup sugar

2 large eggs

1 teaspoon pure vanilla extract

1 cup sour cream

1 cup frozen sour cherries, thawed and drained well

1 cup Streusel (page 394)

Milk Glaze (recipe follows)

COFFEE CAKE HOW-TO
Half the batter is topped with a layer of sour cherries. Then the remaining batter is poured over the top and sprinkled with streusel.

Preheat the oven to 350°F. Butter a 9-inch tube pan; set aside. In a medium bowl, sift together the flour, baking powder, baking soda, and salt; set aside.

In the bowl of an electric mixer fitted with the paddle attachment, beat the butter, sugar, eggs, and vanilla on medium speed until light and fluffy, 2 to 3 minutes. Add the flour mixture in three parts, alternating with the sour cream and beginning and ending with the flour. Beat until just combined, scraping down the sides of the bowl as needed.

Spoon about half the batter into the prepared pan. Arrange the cherries in a single layer on top of the batter; avoid placing any cherries against the pan's edge, as they may stick or burn if not fully encased in batter. Top with the remaining batter, making sure it is evenly distributed, and smooth with an offset spatula. Sprinkle the streusel evenly over the top of the batter.

Bake until the cake is golden brown and springs back when touched, 40 to 45 minutes. Transfer the pan to a wire rack set over a rimmed baking sheet, and let the cake cool 10 to 15 minutes. Invert the cake onto the rack, then reinvert (so streusel side is up), and let cool completely. Spoon the glaze over the cake, letting it drip down the sides. Let the cake sit until the glaze is set, about 5 minutes, before serving. Cake can be kept at room temperature, wrapped well in plastic, for up to 4 days.

MILK GLAZE
MAKES ENOUGH FOR ONE 9-INCH TUBE CAKE

1 cup confectioners' sugar, sifted

2 tablespoons milk

In a medium bowl, whisk together the confectioners' sugar and milk until completely smooth. Immediately drizzle glaze over cake.

CLASSIC CRUMB CAKE

MAKES ONE 13-BY-9-INCH CAKE *This foolproof cake is perfect for beginning bakers.*

1¼ sticks (10 tablespoons) unsalted butter, room temperature, plus more for pan

2½ cups all-purpose flour

1 teaspoon baking soda

1 teaspoon baking powder

½ teaspoon salt

1 cup granulated sugar

3 large eggs

1 teaspoon pure vanilla extract

1¼ cups sour cream

Crumb Topping (page 394)

Confectioners' sugar, for dusting (optional)

Preheat the oven to 350°F. Generously butter a 13-by-9-inch baking pan; set aside. Whisk together flour, baking soda, baking powder, and salt in a bowl; set aside.

In the bowl of an electric mixer fitted with the paddle attachment, beat the butter and sugar until light and fluffy, about 4 minutes, scraping down the sides of the bowl as needed. Add the eggs, one at a time, beating until incorporated after each addition. Mix in the vanilla. Add the flour mixture and sour cream; beat just until combined.

Spoon the batter into the pan, and smooth with an offset spatula. Sprinkle the topping evenly over the batter. Bake, rotating the pan halfway through, until cake is golden brown and a cake tester inserted in the center comes out clean, 40 to 50 minutes. Transfer to a wire rack to cool. Before serving, dust with confectioners' sugar, if using.

PEAR-SPICE BUNDT CAKE

MAKES ONE 10-INCH CAKE *This is a slight twist on applesauce cake, relying instead on a homemade pear sauce. The cake can be made a day ahead. Keep it at room temperature, then glaze it and garnish it with pear chips just before serving.*

- 1/3 cup granulated sugar
- 2 1/2 pounds (about 5) ripe Bartlett pears, peeled, cored, and cut into 1 1/2-inch chunks
- 2 sticks (1 cup) unsalted butter, room temperature, plus more for pan
- 3 cups all-purpose flour, plus more for dusting
- 2 teaspoons baking powder
- 1 teaspoon salt
- 3/4 teaspoon ground cinnamon
- 3/4 teaspoon ground cardamom
- 3/4 teaspoon ground ginger
- 1/2 teaspoon baking soda

- 1/4 teaspoon freshly ground black pepper
- 1/4 teaspoon freshly grated nutmeg
- 1 3/4 cups packed dark-brown sugar
- 1/4 cup honey
- 4 large eggs
- 1/2 cup milk
  Cream Cheese Glaze, for serving (optional; page 60); or Confectioners' sugar, for dusting (optional)
  Pear Chips, for garnish (optional; page 60)

In a saucepan, spread the granulated sugar in an even layer. Cook over medium-high heat, without stirring, until sugar around the edge of the pan melts and begins to turn golden, 3 to 4 minutes. Using a wooden spoon, slowly stir until all sugar has melted and mixture is translucent and golden.

Add pear chunks to caramel, and stir to coat. Cook, covered, over low heat until very soft, 6 to 8 minutes, swirling the pan occasionally. Using a potato masher, mash the pears until they are broken down but still slightly chunky. Continue cooking, uncovered, 5 minutes more, stirring frequently. Remove from heat; let cool completely.

Preheat the oven to 350°F. Butter and flour a 10-inch (12-cup capacity) Bundt pan, tapping out excess. In a medium bowl, sift together the flour, baking powder, salt, cinnamon, cardamom, ginger, baking soda, pepper, and nutmeg; set aside.

In the bowl of an electric mixer fitted with the paddle attachment, beat the butter, brown sugar, and honey on medium-high speed until light and fluffy, 3 to 4 minutes, scraping down the sides of the bowl as needed. Add the eggs, one at a time, beating until combined after each addition. With the mixer on the lowest speed, add the flour mixture in two batches, alternating with the milk and beginning and ending with the flour. Add the reserved pear sauce, and mix to combine, about 1 minute, scraping down the sides of the bowl as needed. Do not overmix.

Spoon the batter into the prepared pan, and smooth with a small offset spatula. Bake, rotating the pan halfway through, until cake is a deep golden brown and a cake tester inserted in the center comes out clean, 35 to 40 minutes. Transfer the pan to a wire rack to cool slightly. Invert the cake onto a wire rack set over a piece of parchment paper and allow to cool 10 minutes. Once cool, pour the glaze over the top, letting some drip down the sides. Alternatively, dust with confectioners' sugar. Garnish with pear chips, if using.

PEAR SAUCE HOW-TO
1. Pear chunks are added to a pan of caramel and cooked over low heat. **2.** After several minutes, a potato masher is used to help break down the pears. **3.** The final consistency of the sauce is thick and somewhat chunky.

Pear-Spice Bundt Cake

PEAR CHIPS HOW-TO 1. A pear is very thinly sliced and coated with lemon juice to keep it from turning brown. **2.** The pear slices briefly cook in simple syrup. **3.** The slices are then baked in a single layer at a low temperature for a little more than 2 hours.

CREAM CHEESE GLAZE
MAKES ENOUGH FOR ONE 9-INCH CAKE

4 ounces cream cheese, room temperature	1 tablespoon freshly squeezed lemon juice
½ cup confectioners' sugar, sifted	3 tablespoons milk, plus more if needed
Pinch of salt	

In the bowl of an electric mixer fitted with the paddle attachment, beat the cream cheese on medium-high speed until light and fluffy, 4 to 5 minutes, scraping down the sides of the bowl as needed. Add the sugar, and beat until combined, about 1 minute. Add the salt, lemon juice, and milk; mix on low speed until smooth. If the glaze is too thick to drizzle, add more milk, 1 tablespoon at a time.

PEAR CHIPS

MAKES ABOUT 18 *For the prettiest chips, use blemish-free pears that are not quite ripe. A mandoline will help make the pear slices perfectly even.*

1 cup sugar	1 lemon, halved
1 small underripe Bartlett pear	

Preheat the oven to 200°F. Line a large baking sheet with parchment paper or a non-stick baking mat (such as a Silpat); set aside.

In a medium saucepan over medium-high heat, combine the sugar with 1 cup water. Bring to a boil; cook, stirring occasionally, until the sugar has dissolved, about 8 minutes. Reduce the heat to medium-low; keep at a simmer as you proceed.

Using a mandoline or a very sharp knife, slice the pear lengthwise as thinly as possible; make sure that each slice remains intact and is uniformly thick. Do not worry about removing seeds or the core (they soften during baking). Squeeze lemon halves over pear slices, coating both sides with juice. Place the slices in the simmering syrup; cook 2 minutes. Remove the slices with a slotted spoon, and place on the prepared baking sheet about 1 inch apart.

Bake the pear slices until they are dry to the touch, about 2 hours. Using a small offset spatula, loosen the edges of the slices; use your hands to peel the pears from the sheet, then flip them over. Return to the oven; bake, checking frequently, until chips are completely dry and crisp (but not browned), about 20 minutes. Chips can be kept in an airtight container at room temperature, layered with parchment paper, up to 2 days.

CLASSIC POUND CAKE

MAKES ONE 9-BY-5-INCH LOAF *This recipe does not contain the traditional pound each of butter, eggs, flour, and sugar, but its proportions produce the most delicious results.*

- 3 sticks (1½ cups) unsalted butter, room temperature, plus more for pan
- 2 cups all-purpose flour
- 1 teaspoon salt
- 1½ cups granulated sugar
- 1 teaspoon pure vanilla extract
- 6 large eggs
- Confectioners' sugar, for dusting (optional)

Preheat the oven to 350°F. Butter a 9-by-5-inch loaf pan; set aside. In a medium bowl, whisk together the flour and salt; set aside.

In the bowl of an electric mixture fitted with the paddle attachment, beat the butter, granulated sugar, and vanilla on medium-low speed until light and fluffy, 3 to 5 minutes, scraping down the sides as needed. Add the eggs, one at a time, beating until combined. With mixer on low speed, add flour mixture; beat until just combined.

Spoon the batter into the prepared pan, and smooth with an offset spatula. Bake until cake is golden and a cake tester inserted in the center comes out clean, 50 to 55 minutes. Transfer to a wire rack to cool, 10 to 15 minutes. Turn out the cake onto the rack to cool completely. Before serving, dust with confectioners' sugar, if using. Cake can be kept at room temperature, wrapped well in plastic, for up to 3 days.

GLAZED LEMON POUND CAKES

MAKES TWO 8½-BY-4½-INCH LOAVES *Poppy seeds give these cakes an interesting texture and appearance, but you can certainly omit them if you prefer.*

- 2 sticks (1 cup) unsalted butter, room temperature, plus more for pans
- 2½ cups plus 2 tablespoons all-purpose flour
- 1 tablespoon baking powder
- 1½ teaspoons salt
- 2 tablespoons poppy seeds
- 1½ cups sugar
- 2 tablespoons finely grated lemon zest (about 2 lemons)
- ½ teaspoon pure lemon extract
- ½ cup sour cream
- 5 large eggs
- ¼ cup vegetable oil
- 2 tablespoons freshly squeezed lemon juice
- 1 cup apricot jam
- ¼ cup Cognac

Preheat the oven to 350°F. Generously butter two 8½-by-4½-inch loaf pans; set aside. In a bowl, sift together the flour, baking powder, and salt. Stir in poppy seeds; set aside.

In the bowl of an electric mixer fitted with the paddle attachment, beat the butter, sugar, lemon zest, lemon extract, and sour cream on medium speed until light and

Brown Sugar Pound Cake

Glazed Lemon Pound Cake

Marble Cake with White-Chocolate Glaze

Classic Pound Cake

fluffy, 2 to 3 minutes. Add the eggs, one at a time, beating to incorporate after each and scraping down the sides of the bowl as needed. Beat in the oil and lemon juice. Add the reserved flour mixture and beat until just combined. Do not overmix.

Divide batter evenly between the prepared pans, and smooth with an offset spatula. Bake until cakes are lightly golden and a cake tester inserted in the centers comes out clean, 50 to 55 minutes. Transfer pans to a wire rack set over a piece of parchment paper to cool 10 minutes. Turn out cakes onto the rack to cool completely.

Combine the apricot jam and Cognac in a small saucepan and place over medium-low heat. Simmer until the jam liquefies, about 3 minutes. Using a rubber spatula, press the jam through a fine sieve set over a small bowl; discard solids. Brush the tops and sides of cakes with the glaze. Let stand at room temperature for 30 minutes. Cakes can be kept at room temperature, wrapped well in plastic, for up to 3 days.

BROWN SUGAR POUND CAKES

MAKES TWO 8½-BY-4½-INCH LOAVES OR SIX 5¾-BY-3¼-INCH MINILOAVES *If you are using the miniloaf pans, place them on a baking sheet, and bake cakes for about forty-five minutes.*

2 sticks (1 cup) unsalted butter, room temperature, plus more for pans	½ teaspoon salt
3 cups sifted all-purpose flour	2¼ cups packed light-brown sugar
2 teaspoons baking powder	5 large eggs
	¾ cup buttermilk

Preheat the oven to 325°F. Butter two 8½-by-4½-inch loaf pans; set aside. In a medium bowl, sift together the flour, baking powder, and salt; set aside.

In the bowl of an electric mixer fitted with the paddle attachment, beat butter and sugar on medium speed until light and fluffy, 2 to 3 minutes, scraping down the sides of the bowl as needed. Add eggs one at a time, beating until combined.

Add the reserved flour mixture in three batches, alternating with the buttermilk and beginning and ending with the flour; beat until combined. Divide the batter between the prepared pans, and smooth with an offset spatula.

Bake, rotating pans halfway through, until cakes are golden brown and a cake tester inserted in the centers comes out clean, about 1 hour. Transfer pans to a wire rack to cool 10 minutes. Turn out cakes onto the rack to cool completely. Cakes can be kept at room temperature, wrapped well in plastic, for up to 3 days.

MARBLE CAKE WITH WHITE-CHOCOLATE GLAZE

MAKES ONE 9-BY-5-INCH LOAF *We like the way this cake looks glazed with white chocolate, but you can substitute semisweet chocolate in the glaze recipe, if you prefer. Be careful not to overswirl the vanilla and chocolate batters when you are running a knife through the two; the marbling won't look as beautiful if you overdo it.*

1 stick (½ cup) unsalted butter, room temperature, plus more for pan

1¾ cups cake flour (not self-rising)

2 teaspoons baking powder

½ teaspoon salt

1 cup sugar

3 large eggs, room temperature

1 teaspoon pure vanilla extract

⅔ cup buttermilk, room temperature

¼ cup plus 1 tablespoon Dutch-process cocoa powder

¼ cup plus 2 tablespoons boiling water

White-Chocolate Glaze (recipe follows)

Preheat the oven to 350°F. Generously butter a 9-by-5-inch loaf pan; set aside. Whisk together the cake flour, baking powder, and salt; set aside.

In the bowl of an electric mixer fitted with the paddle attachment, beat the butter and sugar until light and fluffy, about 5 minutes. Add the eggs one at a time, beating until combined after each addition and scraping down the sides of the bowl as needed. Mix in the vanilla. Add the flour mixture in two batches, alternating with the buttermilk and beginning and ending with the flour. Set aside one-third of the batter.

In a bowl, mix the cocoa and the boiling water with a rubber spatula until smooth. Add the cocoa mixture to the reserved cake batter; stir until well combined.

Spoon the batters into the prepared pan in two layers, alternating spoonfuls of vanilla and chocolate to simulate a checkerboard. To create marbling, run a table knife (or wooden skewer) through the batters in a swirling motion.

Bake, rotating the pan halfway through, until a cake tester comes out clean, 40 to 50 minutes. Transfer pan to a rack to cool 10 minutes. Turn out cake from the pan and cool completely on the rack. Pour glaze over cake, letting it drip down the sides. Cake can be kept in an airtight container at room temperature for up to 3 days.

WHITE-CHOCOLATE GLAZE
MAKES ENOUGH FOR ONE 9-BY-5-INCH LOAF

¾ cup confectioners' sugar, sifted, plus more if needed

2 tablespoons milk, plus more if needed

2¼ ounces best-quality white chocolate, melted and cooled

In a small bowl, whisk together the confectioners' sugar and milk. The mixture should have the consistency of thin sour cream. Add the melted chocolate and whisk until glaze is smooth. If it is too thin, add more sugar, 1 tablespoon at a time; if too thick, add more milk, 1 teaspoon at a time. Use immediately.

MARBLEIZING HOW-TO
1. Spoonfuls of vanilla and chocolate batters are alternated, in two layers, in a checkerboard pattern. **2.** A table knife is run through the batters to create swirls.

COOKIES

recipes

C

It was the most welcoming aroma after a long day at school: the scent of freshly baked cookies, right out of the oven. While you may have finished school long ago, you have probably never outgrown the appeal of cookies.

ookies offer variety, perhaps more so than any other kind of baked good. The dough can be dropped in balls onto baking sheets, rolled out and cut into shapes, or refrigerated in logs that allow you to slice off and bake a batch large enough to serve at a holiday open house (or small enough to satisfy your own late-night craving). Invariably, you'll find that how you handle the dough before it goes into the oven affects the texture and shape of what comes out. This is why it's so important to space drop cookies carefully on the baking sheet, to roll out dough to an even thickness for cutouts, and, when needed, to chill shaped cookies briefly in the freezer before sliding them into the oven. And so it is that Double-Chocolate Brownie Cookies end up crackly and chewy; Gingerbread Men, identical and evenly baked; and Sugar Cookies, thin and smooth as a painter's canvas, ready for a squiggle of icing or sprinkling of sugar.

Not surprisingly, cookies also suit a variety of occasions. Delicately curved Lace Tuiles are sophisticated enough for dessert at a dinner party, just as Peanut Butter Sandwich Cookies are the perfect ending to a paper-bag lunch. Come holidays throughout the year, you'll find that all of these cookies are not only delicious but pretty enough to place in a special tin, tie with a ribbon, and offer as a gift. For all of the flavors, textures, and shapes cookies offer, few things are easier to bake or require so little time. Indeed, many of our cookies are in the oven for less than twenty minutes. They need a few extra moments on the rack to cool, but even as they rest, you can feast on the aroma—which will heighten your anticipation of those first few bites.

Lining cookie sheets with parchment paper or non-stick baking mats eliminates the need for greasing. Liners also make it possible to lift a whole batch of cookies at once—and they make cleanup easy.

If baking cookies in batches, you can reuse a hot baking sheet **by running it under cold water** until it is completely cool, and then dry it thoroughly.

When baked in the lower third of the oven, cookies tend to darken too much on the bottoms. If you are baking many batches at once and must use the lower third, **insulate the bottoms from the heat** by baking the cookies on two stacked baking sheets.

Many kinds of cookie dough can be **frozen raw and baked later.** After the cookies are formed, place them on a parchment-lined baking sheet and chill them in the freezer until firm, about 1 hour. Transfer to resealable bags, and freeze for up to a month, until ready to bake. There is no need to thaw the dough; however, you may need to add a few minutes to the baking time.

Some bar cookie recipes call for prebaking the bottom crust. **Let the crust cool completely** before topping it; otherwise the bottom may become soggy.

If you prefer soft cookies, slightly underbake them. They should be golden around the edges but can remain pale in the center. In most instances, simply substituting brown sugar for some or all of the granulated sugar in a recipe will also produce softer cookies, since it contains more moisture.

If you prefer **crisp cookies,** try using egg whites in place of some of the whole eggs.

Don't overmix cookie dough or brownie batter once the dry ingredients have been added; doing so would overdevelop the gluten, which could hinder tenderness and result in an unpleasant texture.

When **adding raisins or other dried fruits** to cookie dough, try "plumping" them first. Pour just enough boiling water over the ingredient to cover; soak for a couple of minutes, then drain. The fruit will be softer in the finished cookie.

Sift any chopped nuts or chocolate that are used in a light-colored cookie dough. Eliminating the "dust" from these ingredients will help maintain the color of the dough and keep flavors distinct.

Always **rotate baking sheets,** usually once about halfway through the baking time. Turn the sheets front to back, and, if you have one on both the upper and lower racks of the oven, swap the sheets' positions. Most ovens have hot and cold spots, so this will ensure that the cookies bake evenly.

When storing cookies, do not combine crisp and soft cookies in the same container, as this will cause the crisp ones to soften a bit. You can **restore the crisp texture of cookies** that have softened by heating them in a 300-degree oven for about 10 minutes. Let the cookies cool completely before serving.

1 Baking sheet

Look for sheets made of heavy-duty aluminum, a durable material that encourages even browning. Avoid air-insulated sheets or those made of thin metal, both of which tend to warp. A sheet with at least two rimless sides allows for air circulation around cookies. Open sides also make it easy to slide cookies onto a cooling rack.

2 Parchment paper

Parchment paper (brown or white—they're interchangeable) is helpful for baking all kinds of cookies. Nonstick and disposable, the paper can be used to line baking sheets. You can turn parchment over and reuse it several times before discarding it, provided you stick to the same cookie type so as not to mix up flavors. When rolling out dough for cutouts, use parchment to prevent sticking: Place the dough between two sheets, then roll the pin over the top. You can also use parchment to shape and wrap logs of dough or to make cornets for piping icing.

3 Ice cream scoop

A scoop with a release mechanism is a great tool for accurately measuring out small amounts of dense dough (such as the kind used to make drop cookies) and cleanly placing them on sheets. The scoops are available in different sizes.

4 Shaped cookie cutters

An otherwise plain cookie becomes instantly festive when it's cut into a decorative shape. Cookie cutters are available in many sizes and shapes; nesting ones work particularly well for creating a motif or for cutting out the center from a larger cookie of the same shape. To prevent dough from sticking to the cutters, dip cutters in flour between cuts.

5 Baking pan

You'll need square and rectangular pans to make brownies and other kinds of bar cookies. Choose ones made of heavy-duty aluminum. As you read a recipe, make sure you choose a pan the exact size that's called for; even an inch difference can affect results.

6 Metal spatula

A wide spatula with a thin edge is useful for transferring cookie-dough cutouts from a work surface onto a baking sheet without affecting their shapes, as well as for removing hot cookies from sheets.

7 Wooden skewers

Skewers are effective for a variety of small jobs. They can be used to dock shortbread or to poke holes in holiday cookies you plan to hang decoratively. Skewers are useful for cookie-decorating tasks as well: Use them to tint royal icing with food coloring or to create detailed designs by swirling piped lines or dots of icing.

8 Paper cornet

When it comes to piping icing or glaze onto baked cookies, a cornet—a small paper cone—is often preferable to a pastry bag. This is especially true when using a tiny amount of icing, or when piping fine lines or dots. See page 21 for instructions on how to make one. No cleanup is necessary for the cornet; after using, simply discard it.

FORMING DROP COOKIES A mini ice cream scoop is used to shape balls of drop-cookie dough. The uniform-sized balls will bake evenly and result in cookies that look professionally made.

CUTTING LOGS Dough that is shaped into a log is then cut at even intervals. This produces cookies that are equal in size and will bake at the same rate. Depending upon the recipe, the slices are left flat or first rolled into balls.

STORING COOKIES Cookies are layered between waxed or parchment paper. This keeps them from sticking together or losing crispness. Metal tins keep cookies firmer than plastic bins. Let cookies cool before storing.

CUTTING OUT ROLLED COOKIES 1. Cookie dough that is rolled out between two sheets of parchment paper won't stick to the work surface or rolling pin and is easy to transport back and forth from the refrigerator or freezer to chill. **2.** A cookie cutter is dipped into a bowl of flour between cuts so that the dough doesn't stick to it; tapping the cutter on the side of the bowl after dipping will eliminate excess flour. **3.** Room-temperature cookie dough will lose its shape when transferred to baking sheets (left); dough that is chilled until firm (right) will remain sturdy and retain its form.

  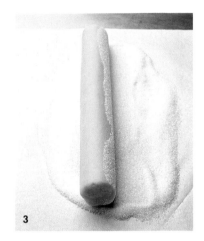

SHAPING REFRIGERATOR COOKIE DOUGH 1. As dough is formed into a log, a straightedge, such as a ruler, is pressed against the edge of the parchment-paper-wrapped dough to form a long, narrow cylinder. **2.** The dough logs can be prepared ahead of time, wrapped first in plastic and then in parchment, labeled for reference, and stored in the freezer until ready to bake. **3.** In some recipes, the dough is brought to room temperature, rolled in sanding sugar, and sliced into rounds before being baked. Rotating the dough as it is being cut prevents the log from flattening and the cookies from being misshapen.

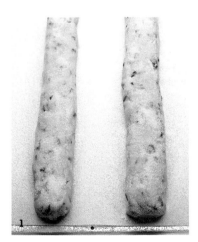  

MAKING BISCOTTI 1. Just after mixing, the dough is shaped by hand into long loaves, then brushed with egg wash and sprinkled with granulated or sanding sugar before the first of two rounds in the oven. **2.** After cooling slightly (about 20 minutes), the once-baked loaves are cut at an angle into thick slices. **3.** The slices are baked on a wire rack set over a baking sheet, which allows air to circulate around the biscotti and eliminates the need to flip them during the second round of baking.

White Chocolate–Butterscotch Cookies, Double-Chocolate Brownie Cookies, and Chocolate Chunk Cookies

drop cookies

CHOCOLATE CHUNK COOKIES

MAKES ABOUT 3 DOZEN *Unlike in recipes for chewy cookies, we used more butter and less brown sugar to produce the ideal thin and crisp cookie.*

- 2 cups all-purpose flour
- 1 teaspoon baking soda
- 1 teaspoon salt
- 2 sticks (1 cup) unsalted butter, room temperature
- 1 cup granulated sugar
- 1/2 cup packed dark-brown sugar
- 2 teaspoons pure vanilla extract
- 1 large whole egg, plus 1 large egg white
- 12 ounces semisweet chocolate chunks (about 2 cups)

Preheat the oven to 375°F, with racks in the upper and lower thirds. Line two large baking sheets with parchment paper; set aside. In a medium bowl, whisk together the flour, baking soda, and salt; set aside. In the bowl of an electric mixer fitted with the paddle attachment, beat the butter and both sugars on medium speed until light and fluffy, about 3 minutes, scraping down the sides of the bowl as needed.

Add the vanilla, whole egg, and egg white. Beat on low speed until well combined, scraping down the sides of the bowl as needed, about 1 minute. Add flour mixture in two batches; mix until just combined. Mix in chocolate.

Shape 2 heaping tablespoons of dough at a time into balls and place about 1½ inches apart on prepared baking sheets. Bake, rotating sheets halfway through, until cookies are golden brown, about 18 minutes. Transfer parchment and cookies to a wire rack to cool completely. Cookies can be kept in an airtight container at room temperature for up to 4 days.

DOUBLE-CHOCOLATE BROWNIE COOKIES

MAKES ABOUT 30 *Like brownies, these cookies are dense and fudgy beneath their crackly exteriors. Use your favorite nuts in place of the walnuts, or omit them altogether. The dough can be shaped into balls and refrigerated for up to two days or frozen for up to three weeks; freeze on a baking sheet until firm, then transfer to a resealable plastic bag.*

- 9 ounces semisweet chocolate, chopped into 1/4-inch chunks
- 3 ounces unsweetened chocolate, coarsely chopped
- 6 tablespoons unsalted butter
- 1 cup sugar
- 3 large eggs
- 1/2 teaspoon pure vanilla extract
- 1 cup sifted all-purpose flour
- 1/4 teaspoon salt
- 3/4 cup (about 3 ounces) chopped walnuts (optional)

Preheat the oven to 375°F. Line two large baking sheets with parchment paper; set aside. In a heatproof bowl set over (but not touching) simmering water, melt 5 ounces semisweet chocolate, the unsweetened chocolate, and the butter. Stir until smooth. Set mixture aside to cool slightly, about 5 minutes.

In the bowl of an electric mixer fitted with the paddle attachment, beat chocolate mixture and sugar on medium speed until well combined, about 3 minutes, scraping down the sides of the bowl as needed. Add eggs, and mix until completely combined. Beat in vanilla. Add the flour and salt, and beat until just incorporated. Stir in remaining 4 ounces semisweet chocolate and the nuts, if using.

Shape 2 tablespoons of dough at a time into 1½-inch balls and place about 1½ inches apart on prepared baking sheets. Bake, rotating sheets halfway through, until edges are set and centers are still a bit soft, 9 to 11 minutes. Transfer parchment and cookies to a wire rack to cool completely. Cookies can be kept in an airtight container at room temperature for up to 4 days.

WHITE CHOCOLATE–BUTTERSCOTCH COOKIES

MAKES ABOUT 2 DOZEN *While still warm, these cookies are crisp on the outside and chewy on the inside. As they cool, they become crisp all the way through.*

1¾ cups all-purpose flour	1¼ cups packed dark-brown sugar
½ teaspoon baking soda	1 large egg
½ teaspoon salt	1 tablespoon pure vanilla extract
2 tablespoons unsalted butter, room temperature	8 ounces best-quality white chocolate, chopped into ¼-inch pieces
¾ cup vegetable shortening, room temperature	

Preheat the oven to 350°F, with racks in the upper and lower thirds. Line two large baking sheets with parchment paper; set aside. In a medium bowl, whisk together the flour, baking soda, and salt; set aside.

In the bowl of an electric mixer fitted with the paddle attachment, beat the butter, shortening, and brown sugar on medium speed until light and fluffy, about 3 minutes, scraping down the sides of the bowl as needed. Beat in the egg and the vanilla until combined. With the mixer on low speed, add the flour mixture in two batches, beating until just combined. Stir in the white chocolate.

Drop 2 tablespoons of dough at a time about 2 inches apart on prepared baking sheets. Bake, rotating sheets halfway through, until lightly golden brown around the edges, about 15 minutes. Let cookies cool on sheets for 2 minutes, then transfer parchment and cookies to a wire rack to cool completely. Cookies can be kept in an airtight container at room temperature for up to 4 days.

OATMEAL-RAISIN COOKIES

MAKES ABOUT 2 DOZEN *These classic drop cookies are large, soft, and chewy. Look for grade B maple syrup, which has a deeper flavor than grade A.*

- 1½ cups all-purpose flour
- 1 teaspoon ground cinnamon
- 1 teaspoon baking soda
- 1 teaspoon salt
- 1 cup sweetened, shredded coconut
- 2 sticks (1 cup) unsalted butter, room temperature
- 1 cup packed light-brown sugar
- ⅓ cup pure maple syrup
- 1 large egg
- 2 teaspoons pure vanilla extract
- 3 cups old-fashioned rolled oats
- 1 cup raisins

Preheat the oven to 325°F, with racks in the upper and lower thirds. Line two baking sheets with parchment paper; set aside. In a medium bowl, whisk together the flour, cinnamon, baking soda, and salt; stir in the coconut. Set aside.

In the bowl of an electric mixer fitted with the paddle attachment, beat the butter and brown sugar on medium speed until light and fluffy, 3 to 4 minutes. Add the maple syrup, and mix to combine. Add the egg and vanilla; beat until well combined, about 1 minute, scraping down the sides of the bowl as needed.

With the mixer on low speed, add the flour mixture in two batches; mix until just combined. Add oats and raisins; mix until combined.

Shape 3 level tablespoons of dough at a time into 1½-inch balls (or use a 2-inch ice-cream scoop) and place 2 inches apart on prepared baking sheets. Bake, rotating sheets halfway through, until golden brown, 15 to 20 minutes. Let cookies cool on sheets for 2 minutes, then transfer parchment and cookies to a wire rack to cool completely. Cookies can be kept in an airtight container at room temperature for up to 4 days.

BLACK AND WHITE COOKIES

MAKES ABOUT 18 *A New York specialty for more than half a century, these cookies taste best the day after they are made. Wrap in plastic and keep overnight at room temperature.*

3 cups all-purpose flour	½ cup vegetable shortening
¼ teaspoon baking powder	1 cup plus 3 tablespoons sugar
¼ teaspoon baking soda	2 large whole eggs, plus 1 large egg yolk
¼ teaspoon salt	1 tablespoon pure vanilla extract
1¼ sticks (10 tablespoons) unsalted butter, room temperature	¼ cup heavy cream
	Black and White Icings (recipe follows)

Preheat the oven to 350°F. Line two large baking sheets with parchment paper; set aside. In a bowl, whisk together the flour, baking powder, baking soda, and salt.

In the bowl of an electric mixer fitted with the paddle attachment, beat the butter, shortening, and sugar on medium speed until light and fluffy, about 3 minutes, scraping down the sides of the bowl as needed. Add whole eggs and egg yolk, one at a time; beat until combined after each addition. Beat in vanilla. Add the flour mixture in two batches, alternating with the cream. Beat until just combined (do not overmix).

Use a ¼-cup measure to scoop dough 3 inches apart onto prepared sheets. Bake, rotating sheets halfway through, until the edges just begin to turn golden and the centers are cakey and tender, 10 to 12 minutes. Transfer parchment and cookies to a wire rack to cool for 10 minutes. Remove cookies from parchment and let cool completely.

On the flat side (bottom) of each cookie, use a small offset spatula to spread chocolate icing over one half of the cookie, creating a line straight down the center. Spread white frosting on the other half. Set cookies aside until icing is set, about 30 minutes.

BLACK AND WHITE ICINGS

MAKES ENOUGH FOR ABOUT 18 COOKIES *If either glaze becomes too firm to spread, place it in a heatproof bowl over simmering water and stir until it's the right consistency.*

1 cup heavy cream	5 tablespoons Dutch-process cocoa powder
3½ cups confectioners' sugar, sifted	6 tablespoons boiling water

Whisk cream into sugar until smooth. Set aside 1¼ cups (for white icing).

Combine cocoa with boiling water, and stir until dissolved. Add to remaining sugar mixture; stir to combine (for black icing). Use immediately.

BLACK AND WHITE COOKIE HOW-TO One half of the flat side of each cookie is carefully covered with chocolate icing using a small offset spatula; white icing is spread on the other half.

GINGERBREAD MEN

MAKES ABOUT 2 DOZEN *These make ideal holiday cookies when festively decorated with icing, but they are also delicious without any adornment.*

- 3½ cups all-purpose flour, plus more for dusting
- 1½ teaspoons baking soda
- ¼ teaspoon salt
- 1¼ teaspoons ground cinnamon
- 1¼ teaspoons ground ginger
- 1¼ teaspoons ground allspice
- ¼ teaspoon ground cloves

- 2 sticks (1 cup) unsalted butter, room temperature
- ¾ cup granulated sugar
- ¾ cup packed dark-brown sugar
- 1 tablespoon plus 1 teaspoon grated, peeled fresh ginger
- 1 large egg
- ¼ cup unsulfured molasses
- Royal Icing (page 389; optional)

GINGERBREAD MEN HOW-TO
A paper cornet or pastry bag filled with Royal Icing is all that's needed to decorate gingerbread cutouts. You can keep the cookies abstract, as pictured, or draw faces on them.

In a large bowl, whisk together flour, baking soda, salt, cinnamon, ground ginger, allspice, and cloves; set aside.

In the bowl of an electric mixer fitted with the paddle attachment, beat butter, both sugars, and fresh ginger on medium speed until light and fluffy, 2 to 3 minutes, scraping down the sides of the bowl as needed. Beat in egg and molasses to combine. With mixer on low speed, gradually add the flour mixture, beating until just incorporated. Turn out the dough onto a clean work surface. Divide in half, and shape into flattened disks; wrap each in plastic. Refrigerate at least 1 hour or overnight.

Preheat the oven to 350°F, with racks in the upper and lower thirds. Line two large baking sheets with parchment paper; set aside. Remove dough from the refrigerator, and let stand until slightly softened. (This will help keep the dough from cracking when rolled.) On a large piece of parchment paper lightly dusted with flour, roll out dough to about ¼ inch thick. To prevent sticking while rolling, occasionally run a large offset spatula under dough, and add more flour. Place parchment paper and dough on another baking sheet; freeze until very firm, about 15 minutes.

Remove dough from freezer; working quickly, cut out with large cookie cutters. (If the dough begins to soften too much, return to the freezer for a few minutes.) Using a wide metal spatula, transfer cutouts to prepared baking sheets; chill until firm, about 15 minutes.

Bake, rotating sheets halfway through, until cookies are crisp but not darkened, 12 to 15 minutes. Transfer parchment and cookies to a wire rack to cool completely. Decorate as desired with Royal Icing, if using. Cookies can be kept in an airtight container at room temperature for up to 5 days.

SUGAR COOKIES

MAKES ABOUT 3 DOZEN *You can garnish these cookies simply with sanding sugar or sprinkles before baking, or bake them first and then cover with Royal Icing.*

4 sticks (1 pound) unsalted butter, room temperature

3 cups sugar

2 large eggs

1 teaspoon pure vanilla extract

1½ teaspoons salt

5 cups all-purpose flour, plus more for dusting

Colored sanding sugar or sprinkles, for decorating (optional)

Royal Icing (page 389; optional)

In the bowl of an electric mixer fitted with the paddle attachment, beat butter and sugar on medium-high speed until light and fluffy, about 5 minutes. Add eggs, vanilla, and salt; mix on medium-high speed until combined. With mixer on low speed, add flour in two batches, mixing until just incorporated.

Turn out the dough onto a clean work surface. Divide in half, and pat into flattened rectangles; wrap each in plastic. Refrigerate for at least 2 hours or up to 1 week.

Preheat the oven to 350°F, with racks in the upper and lower thirds. Line large baking sheets with parchment paper. On a lightly floured work surface, roll out one rectangle of dough to a scant ¼-inch thickness. Using cookie cutters, cut out shapes. Using a small offset spatula, transfer shapes to prepared sheets, placing about 2 inches apart. Chill in freezer or refrigerator until firm, about 15 minutes. Set scraps aside. Repeat process with remaining rectangle of dough. Gather all the scraps, and roll out again. Chill 15 minutes; cut out more shapes, and place on sheets.

Decorate cookies with sanding sugar or sprinkles, if using, before baking. Bake, rotating sheets halfway through, until cookies are golden around the edges and slightly firm to the touch, about 15 minutes. Transfer cookies to a wire rack to cool completely. Decorate with Royal Icing, if using. Top icing with sanding sugar or sprinkles, if using. Cookies can be kept in an airtight container, layered between sheets of waxed or parchment paper, at room temperature for up to 3 days.

SUGAR COOKIE HOW-TO
Royal Icing is best applied by piping it onto cookies, rather than spreading it with a knife or offset spatula. Pipe the outline of the cookie first, then draw tight zigzags within the outlined area to fill it in (this is known as flooding). While the icing is still wet, apply dots or lines in contrasting colors, or decorate with sprinkles or sanding sugar. To stretch polka dots into flourishes (as shown on the letter V, opposite), drag the tip of a toothpick or wooden skewer through the dots.

RUGELACH

MAKES 4 DOZEN *First brought to America by Eastern European immigrants, rugelach are popular on nearly every Jewish holiday table (except at Passover). The rich cream-cheese dough is filled with dried fruit, chocolate, or nuts—or a combination of all three.*

- 2 sticks (1 cup) unsalted butter, room temperature
- 8 ounces cream cheese, room temperature
- ¾ cup granulated sugar
- ¼ teaspoon plus a pinch of salt
- 1 large whole egg, plus 3 large egg yolks
- 2⅓ cups all-purpose flour, plus more for dusting

- 1 teaspoon pure vanilla extract
- 1¼ cups (4 ounces) walnut halves or pieces
- Pinch of ground cinnamon
- 1 cup plus 2 tablespoons (12 ounces) apricot jelly, melted
- 2 cups currants, mini semisweet chocolate chips, or a combination
- Fine sanding sugar (or granulated sugar), for sprinkling

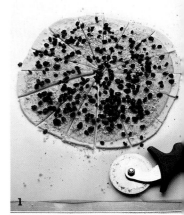

RUGELACH HOW-TO
1. Rounds of cookie dough are covered with melted apricot jelly, ground walnuts, and currants, then cut into even wedges. **2.** The wedges are rolled up around the filling before baking.

In the bowl of an electric mixer fitted with the paddle attachment, beat the butter and cream cheese on medium speed until light and fluffy, 3 to 4 minutes, scraping down the sides of the bowl. Add ½ cup granulated sugar and ¼ teaspoon salt; beat until combined and fluffy, about 3 minutes. Add the egg yolks, one at a time, beating to combine after each. With the mixer on low speed, beat in flour to combine. Mix in vanilla.

Turn out the dough onto a lightly floured work surface. Divide into three equal pieces, and shape into flattened disks; wrap each in plastic. Refrigerate at least 1 hour or overnight.

Preheat the oven to 325°F, with racks in the upper and lower thirds. Line three baking sheets with parchment paper; set aside. In a food processor, pulse together the walnuts, remaining ¼ cup granulated sugar, the cinnamon, and pinch of salt until finely ground; set aside. On a lightly floured work surface, roll out one disk of dough into a 10-inch round about ¼ inch thick. Brush the top evenly with melted jelly. Sprinkle with a third of the walnut mixture and a third of the currants. Using the rolling pin, gently roll over the round to press the filling into the dough.

Using a pizza cutter or sharp knife, cut the round into 16 equal wedges. Beginning with the outside edge of each wedge, roll up to enclose filling. Place about 1 inch apart on the prepared baking sheets. Repeat with remaining dough and filling ingredients. Lightly beat the whole egg; brush over tops, and sprinkle with sanding sugar.

Bake two sheets, rotating halfway through, until the cookies are golden brown, 20 to 25 minutes. Transfer to a wire rack to cool completely. Repeat with remaining baking sheet. Rugelach can be kept in an airtight container at room temperature for up to 4 days.

BRETON BISCUITS

MAKES ABOUT 2 DOZEN *These shortbread-like cookies hail from Brittany, a region of France renowned for its delicious butter. Be sure not to underbake them or they will not be crisp enough. Scoring the lattice pattern on the top takes a bit of time, but it's easy to do and the end result is well worth the effort.*

1½ cups all-purpose flour, plus more for dusting

1 cup cake flour (not self-rising)

1½ teaspoons baking powder

½ teaspoon salt

1 large whole egg, plus 4 large egg yolks

1 cup sugar

2 sticks (1 cup) unsalted butter, room temperature

Sift both flours, baking powder, and salt into a large bowl; set aside.

In the bowl of an electric mixer fitted with the paddle attachment, beat the egg yolks and sugar on medium-high speed until doubled in volume and pale yellow, 2 to 3 minutes, scraping down the sides of the bowl as needed. Add the butter in four parts, beating until completely combined after each, 1 to 2 minutes total. With the mixer on low speed, add flour mixture, beating until combined.

Turn out the dough onto a lightly floured surface. Divide in half, and flatten into disks; wrap each in plastic. Refrigerate at least 30 minutes or up to 1 day.

BRETON BISCUIT HOW-TO
After each round of dough is brushed with egg wash, a sharp paring knife is used to score a decorative diamond pattern on the top.

Preheat the oven to 325°F, with racks in the upper and lower thirds. Line two large baking sheets with parchment paper; set aside. Generously dust a large piece of parchment paper with flour. Place one disk of dough in the center, and roll out to slightly thicker than ¼ inch. To prevent sticking while rolling, occasionally run a large offset spatula under dough, and add more flour to the top or bottom. Transfer parchment and dough to a baking sheet; chill until firm, about 15 minutes. Repeat with remaining disk. (You can stack sheets of dough in the freezer.)

Remove one sheet of dough and parchment from the freezer, and transfer to a clean work surface. Using a 2½-inch round cookie cutter, cut out rounds and place about 1½ inches apart on prepared baking sheets. Gather the scraps; roll out again and cut out more rounds. In a small bowl, whisk together the whole egg and 1 tablespoon water; brush over tops of rounds. Let stand 5 minutes and brush again. Using a paring knife, score each round in a shallow lattice pattern, making sure not to cut all the way through the dough. Repeat with remaining dough.

Bake, rotating sheets halfway through, until cookies are amber on top and deeply golden around the edges, 18 to 22 minutes. Transfer parchment and cookies to a wire rack to cool completely. Cookies can be kept in an airtight container at room temperature for up to 4 days.

SEVILLE OLIVE-OIL WAFERS

MAKES ABOUT 18 *These light, crisp cookies are inspired by the Spanish biscuits sold in Olivier Baussan's store, O&Co., in New York City. They are perfect in the morning with tea or coffee, as a snack anytime, or for dessert, served with ice cream or fresh fruit. You will need to bake them in batches, using two baking sheets each time. Run the sheets under cold water to cool completely, dry thoroughly, then proceed with the next batch.*

1½ cups plus 2 tablespoons all-purpose flour	1 teaspoon baking powder
¼ cup unhulled sesame seeds	½ teaspoon salt
3 tablespoons sugar, plus more for sprinkling	½ cup extra-virgin olive oil
1 tablespoon anise seeds	¼ cup plus 2 tablespoons ice water
	2 large egg whites, beaten until foamy

Preheat the oven to 400°F, with racks in the upper and lower thirds. In the bowl of an electric mixer fitted with the paddle attachment, mix flour, sesame seeds, sugar, anise seeds, baking powder, and salt on low speed until just combined. In a small bowl, combine the olive oil and water; add to flour mixture. Beat on low speed until just combined, scraping down the sides of the bowl as needed.

Shape a 1½ tablespoon of dough into a ball. Place two balls at a time on a piece of parchment paper, at least 5 inches apart, and cover with another piece of parchment. Roll out into very thin 8-by-4-inch ovals. Transfer dough and parchment to a baking sheet. Lift off top piece of parchment. Generously brush ovals with egg white, and generously sprinkle with sugar. Repeat with two more balls of dough.

Bake, rotating sheets halfway through, until cookies are brown around the edges and in spots on top, 6 to 8 minutes. Transfer parchment and cookies to a wire rack to cool completely. Repeat with remaining balls of dough. Cookies can be kept, stacked between layers of parchment paper, in an airtight container at room temperature for up to 4 days.

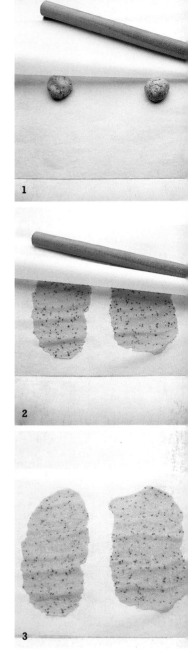

SEVILLE WAFER HOW-TO
1. The cookie dough—which is made with olive oil rather than butter—is shaped into balls, then placed between sheets of parchment for rolling. **2.** To achieve the proper texture, the rolled pieces of dough should be very thin. **3.** Just before baking, the dough is brushed with beaten egg white and sprinkled liberally with sugar.

SAVORY CARAWAY-CHEESE CRISPS

MAKES ABOUT 5 DOZEN *These cookies are surprisingly rich and light at the same time. Served with cheese and grapes, they are the perfect ending to a multicourse dinner.*

2¾ cups sifted all-purpose flour, plus more for dusting

½ teaspoon baking soda

½ teaspoon table salt

¼ cup sugar

2 sticks (1 cup) unsalted butter, room temperature, cut into pieces

8 ounces mascarpone cheese

1 large egg

2 tablespoons caraway seeds, for sprinkling

1 tablespoon coarse salt, for sprinkling

In the bowl of an electric mixer fitted with the paddle attachment, mix the flour, baking soda, table salt, and sugar on low speed to combine. Add the butter, one piece at a time, beating until the mixture resembles coarse meal. Add the mascarpone, and beat just until a soft dough forms, scraping down the sides of the bowl as needed.

Turn out the dough onto a clean work surface. Divide in half, and shape each into a flattened square; wrap each in plastic. Refrigerate at least 1 hour or overnight.

On a well-floured work surface, roll out each piece of dough into a 13-inch square about ⅛ inch thick. Stack squares between parchment paper, and place on a baking sheet; chill in freezer until firm, about 25 minutes.

Preheat the oven to 350°F. Line two large baking sheets with parchment paper; set aside. In a small bowl, whisk together the egg and 1 tablespoon water. Remove one dough square from the freezer, and brush the entire surface with egg wash. Using a pizza wheel or sharp knife, cut the dough into triangles. (They should be roughly the same size, but the shapes don't have to be uniform.) Repeat with remaining dough square.

Transfer the dough pieces to the prepared baking sheets, about ½ inch apart. Sprinkle with caraway seeds and coarse salt. Bake, rotating sheets halfway through, until crisps are golden brown, 15 to 18 minutes. Transfer to a wire rack to cool completely. Crisps can be kept in an airtight container at room temperature for up to 3 days.

SAVORY CARAWAY-CHEESE CRISP HOW-TO 1. After the dough has been rolled out very thin, it is cut into irregular triangles using a pizza wheel. **2.** The triangles are brushed with egg wash and sprinkled with caraway seeds and salt before baking.

GRAHAM CRACKERS

MAKES 4 DOZEN *The dough for these cookies can also be used to make a delicious crust for pies and tarts, such as the Key Lime Tart on page 261; try it for cheesecake, as well.*

1½ cups all-purpose flour, plus more for dusting

1½ cups graham flour

1 teaspoon baking soda

1 teaspoon ground cinnamon

½ teaspoon salt

2 sticks (1 cup) unsalted butter, room temperature

¾ cup packed light-brown sugar

2 tablespoons honey

Preheat the oven to 350°F. In a medium bowl, whisk together both flours, baking soda, cinnamon, and salt; set aside. In the bowl of an electric mixer fitted with the paddle, beat butter, brown sugar, and honey on medium speed until light and fluffy, 2 to 3

minutes, scraping down the sides of the bowl as needed. With mixer on low, add the flour mixture; beat until just combined.

Turn out the dough onto a lightly floured surface. With a knife or bench scraper, cut dough into four equal pieces. Roll out each piece between two sheets of parchment paper into rectangles a bit larger than 9 by 6 inches, about ⅛ inch thick. Using a fluted pastry wheel, trim the outermost edges of each rectangle, and divide into three 6-by-3-inch rectangles. Pressing lightly, so as not to cut all the way through, score each piece in half lengthwise and crosswise, to form four 3-by-1½-inch crackers. Stack parchment and dough on a baking sheet and chill in freezer until firm, about 20 minutes.

Remove two sheets of dough from freezer. Using a fork, pierce each piece in a decorative pattern. Transfer dough (on parchment) to a large baking sheet. Bake, rotating halfway through, until crackers are deep golden brown, 15 to 18 minutes. Repeat with remaining dough. Transfer to a wire rack to cool completely before breaking crackers along perforated lines. Crackers can be kept in an airtight container at room temperature for up to 5 days.

PIGNOLI COOKIES

MAKES ABOUT 18 *Pine nuts are known as pignoli in Italy. Almond paste is available in specialty food stores and most supermarkets; do not substitute marzipan.*

- 7 ounces almond paste
- ½ cup granulated sugar
- ½ cup confectioners' sugar, plus more for dusting
- 2 large egg whites
- ½ teaspoon pure vanilla extract
- 3 tablespoons all-purpose flour
- ⅛ teaspoon salt
- ¾ cup pine nuts

Preheat the oven to 350°F, with racks in the center and lower third. Line two large baking sheets with parchment paper; set aside.

In the bowl of an electric mixer fitted with the paddle attachment, beat almond paste and both sugars on medium speed until mixture resembles coarse crumbs, about 2 minutes. Add egg whites and vanilla, and beat on medium-high speed until a smooth paste forms, 3 to 4 minutes. Add flour and salt; beat until combined, about 1 minute. Dough will be very soft and tacky.

Place pine nuts in a small bowl. Scoop out a tablespoon of dough; using dampened fingers, drop dough into pine nuts, coating one side. Transfer rounds, coated side up, to prepared baking sheet, about 2 inches apart. Repeat with remaining dough. Fill in any bare spots on rounds with remaining pine nuts.

Bake, rotating sheets halfway through, until edges of cookies and pine nuts have turned golden brown, 13 to 15 minutes. Transfer cookies on parchment to a wire rack to cool completely. Using an offset spatula, carefully loosen from parchment paper. Using a fine sieve, dust cookies with confectioners' sugar. Cookies can be kept, stacked between layers of waxed or parchment paper, in an airtight container at room temperature for up to 4 days.

PIGNOLI COOKIE HOW-TO
Balls of almond-rich dough are dropped into a bowl of pine nuts to coat the tops before baking.

LEMON SUGAR SNAPS

MAKES ABOUT 4 DOZEN *These cookies have a delicate texture and light, fresh taste.*

- 1¾ cups all-purpose flour
- 1 teaspoon baking soda
- 1 teaspoon cream of tartar
- ½ teaspoon salt
- 2 sticks (1 cup) unsalted butter, room temperature
- 1 cup sugar, plus more for coating
- 1 large egg
- Freshly grated zest of 3 lemons
- 1 tablespoon freshly squeezed lemon juice

In a bowl, whisk together flour, baking soda, cream of tartar, and salt; set aside. In the bowl of an electric mixer fitted with the paddle attachment, beat the butter and sugar on medium speed until light and fluffy, about 2 minutes. Add the egg and lemon zest and juice; beat until combined. Add the flour mixture; beat until just combined,

Pignoli Cookies

Lemon Sugar Snaps

Gingersnaps

Nut Crescents

scraping down the sides of the bowl as needed. Transfer dough to a bowl, cover with plastic wrap, and refrigerate for at least 2 hours or overnight.

Preheat oven to 350°F. Line two large baking sheets with parchment paper. Place sugar in a shallow bowl. Shape leveled tablespoons of dough into 1-inch balls. Roll balls in sugar to coat completely, and place about 3 inches apart on the prepared baking sheets. Bake, rotating sheets halfway through, until the edges just begin to turn golden brown, 12 to 15 minutes. Transfer cookies to a wire rack to cool completely. Cookies can be kept in an airtight container at room temperature for up to 5 days.

NUT CRESCENTS

MAKES ABOUT 30 *It's important to shape the dough properly; be sure the ends are not too thin, or they will brown too quickly before the cookies are baked through.*

½ cup walnut halves	1½ sticks (¾ cup) unsalted butter, room temperature
¾ cup blanched almonds	
1½ cups all-purpose flour	1½ cups confectioners' sugar
¼ teaspoon salt	1 teaspoon pure vanilla extract

Preheat the oven to 350°F. Spread walnuts and almonds in a single layer on a rimmed baking sheet, and toast until light golden and fragrant, about 8 minutes. Transfer to a plate, and let cool completely. Line two baking sheets with parchment paper.

In a food processor, combine ½ cup flour with the toasted nuts, and pulse until the nuts are finely ground. In a medium bowl, whisk together the flour-nut mixture and the remaining 1 cup flour and the salt; set aside.

In the bowl of an electric mixer fitted with the paddle attachment, beat the butter and ½ cup sugar until light and fluffy, about 2 minutes. Beat in vanilla. With the mixer on low speed, add the flour mixture in two batches, and beat until combined.

Roll 1 tablespoon of dough into a 3-inch log. Using your fingers, shape log into a crescent, tapering the ends slightly so that the center is the widest part. Repeat with remaining dough, placing crescents about 1 inch apart on prepared sheets. Freeze or refrigerate until crescents are very firm, about 30 minutes.

Bake, rotating sheets halfway through, until the edges of the cookies begin to turn golden, 16 to 18 minutes. Transfer sheets to a wire rack to cool, 5 minutes. Transfer cookies to the rack to cool completely. Place the remaining 1 cup sugar in a shallow bowl and roll cookies in it to coat completely. Cookies can be kept in an airtight container at room temperature for up to 5 days.

SPELT CRESCENTS VARIATION Follow instructions for Nut Crescents, replacing all-purpose flour with 1½ cups spelt flour and substituting ½ cup blanched (about 2½ ounces) hazelnuts for the walnuts.

NUT CRESCENT HOW-TO
The dough is first rolled into logs, then curved into tapered crescents before baking.

GINGERSNAPS

MAKES ABOUT 5 DOZEN *These old-fashioned favorites are crunchy all the way through; using fresh ginger gives them a distinctive sweet-spicy flavor. When crushed and mixed with melted butter, the cookies make an excellent crust for cheesecake.*

2 cups all-purpose flour	1¼ cups packed dark-brown sugar
2 teaspoons baking soda	¼ cup unsulfured molasses
¾ teaspoon ground cinnamon	1½ tablespoons finely grated, peeled ginger (one 3-inch piece)
¼ teaspoon ground cloves	
¼ teaspoon freshly ground pepper	1 large egg
½ teaspoon salt	¼ cup granulated sugar
1½ sticks (¾ cup) unsalted butter, room temperature	

In a large bowl, whisk together the flour, baking soda, cinnamon, cloves, pepper, and salt; set aside.

In the bowl of an electric mixer fitted with the paddle attachment, beat butter, brown sugar, molasses, and ginger on medium-high speed until light and fluffy, 2 to 3 minutes, scraping down the sides of the bowl as needed. Beat in the egg until smooth and combined, about 1 minute. Add flour mixture, and beat on low speed until just combined. Transfer dough to a bowl and wrap in plastic; refrigerate until well chilled, about 1 hour or overnight.

Preheat the oven to 350°F, with racks in the center and lower third. Line two large baking sheets with parchment paper. Shape dough into 1-inch balls. Place granulated sugar in a shallow bowl; roll balls in sugar to coat completely, and place about 2 inches apart on the prepared sheets.

Bake, rotating sheets halfway through, until cookies are deep golden all over and centers are firm, 15 to 18 minutes. Transfer cookies to a wire rack to cool completely. Cookies can be kept in an airtight container at room temperature for up to 4 days.

MEXICAN WEDDING COOKIES

MAKES ABOUT 6 DOZEN *Our method for preparing these classic cookies differs from most recipes. Rather than rolling them in sugar while they're still warm, we let them cool first; this keeps the sugar from becoming pasty while preserving the cookie's characteristic texture. The result is a cookie that truly melts in your mouth.*

1 cup (3¾ ounces) pecan halves	2 sticks (1 cup) unsalted butter, room temperature
2 cups confectioners' sugar	
2 cups all-purpose flour	1 teaspoon pure vanilla extract
¼ teaspoon salt	½ teaspoon pure almond extract

Preheat the oven to 350°F, with racks in the upper and lower thirds. Line two large baking sheets with parchment paper; set aside. In a food processor, combine pecans with ¼ cup confectioners' sugar; pulse until nuts are finely ground. In a large bowl, whisk together the sugar-nut mixture, flour, and salt; set aside.

Mexican Wedding Cookies

In the bowl of an electric mixer fitted with the paddle attachment, beat the butter and ¾ cup confectioners' sugar on medium speed until light and fluffy, about 4 minutes, scraping down sides of bowl as needed. Beat in the vanilla and almond extracts. Add the flour mixture, and beat on low speed until the dough just comes together.

Roll dough into ¾-inch balls; place about 2 inches apart on prepared baking sheets. Bake, rotating sheets halfway through, until cookies are pale on top and lightly browned on the bottom (lift with a spatula to check), 10 to 12 minutes. Transfer the cookies to a wire rack to cool completely.

Place remaining 1 cup confectioners' sugar in a shallow bowl, and roll cookies in it to coat completely. Cookies can be kept in an airtight container, layered between sheets of waxed or parchment paper, at room temperature for up to 4 days.

TORTA SBRISOLONA

MAKES ONE 10-INCH COOKIE *This giant round of crisp cookie topped with large clumps of streusel is a specialty of Mantua, Italy. It's perfect served with a bunch of grapes at the end of a dinner party. Set it in the center of the table and let guests break off pieces.*

1¾ sticks (14 tablespoons) unsalted butter, room temperature, plus more for pan	¾ cup sugar
1¾ cups all-purpose flour	¼ teaspoon salt
1½ cups (about 5 ounces) blanched almonds, finely ground	1½ teaspoons pure vanilla extract

Preheat the oven to 350°F. Butter a 10-inch springform pan; set aside. In a large bowl, whisk together flour, ground almonds, sugar, salt, and vanilla. Cut in the butter with a pastry blender until it is completely incorporated and there are no dry crumbs. Squeeze the mixture to form pea-size to 1-inch clumps.

Gently press three-quarters of the mixture into the prepared pan, and sprinkle evenly with remaining crumbs. Bake until cookie begins to turn golden, about 25 minutes. Reduce oven temperature to 300°F, and continue to bake until golden brown and fairly dry, about 10 minutes more.

Transfer pan to a wire rack to cool completely. Remove sides of pan to unmold. Cookie can be kept, wrapped well in aluminum foil, at room temperature for up to 3 days.

ICEBOX BUTTER COOKIES

MAKES ABOUT 5 DOZEN *Since you slice and bake only what you need, these logs of dough are great to keep on hand for when guests drop by or for when you're in the mood for just a few cookies. They can be kept in the freezer, wrapped well in plastic and parchment, for up to three weeks; let dough sit at room temperature for thirty minutes before slicing. To help logs hold their shape, chill them first in empty paper-towel tubes.*

2 sticks (1 cup) unsalted butter, room temperature

¾ cup granulated sugar

1 large egg

1 teaspoon pure vanilla extract

2½ cups plus 2 tablespoons sifted all-purpose flour

1 teaspoon salt

½ cup sanding sugar (or granulated sugar), for rolling

In the bowl of an electric mixer fitted with the paddle attachment, beat the butter and granulated sugar on medium speed until light and fluffy, about 3 minutes, scraping down the sides of the bowl as needed. Add the egg and vanilla, and beat to combine. Add the flour and salt; mix on low speed until combined.

Turn out the dough onto a clean work surface. Divide in half and roll each piece into a log about 1½ inches in diameter. Wrap in parchment paper, making sure to cover ends completely, and place in empty paper-towel tubes, if using. Refrigerate until firm, at least 1 hour or overnight.

Preheat the oven to 350°F, with racks in the upper and lower thirds. Line two large baking sheets with parchment paper. Let dough stand at room temperature until soft enough to slice, about 15 minutes. Roll dough logs in sanding sugar, coating them evenly, and slice into ¼-inch-thick rounds. Place about 1 inch apart on prepared sheets. Bake, rotating sheets halfway through, until golden brown around the edges, 15 to 20 minutes. Transfer cookies to a wire rack to cool completely.

ICEBOX CHOCOLATE-FLAKE COOKIES VARIATION Finely chop 4 ounces bittersweet chocolate (¾ cup). Sift out fine dust and discard. Follow instructions for the Icebox Butter Cookies, adding chopped chocolate along with the flour.

ICEBOX CHOPPED-NUT COOKIES VARIATION Finely chop 4 ounces (½ cup) lightly toasted pecans or pistachios. Sift out fine dust and discard. Follow instructions for the Icebox Butter Cookies, adding chopped nuts along with the flour.

LIME-GLAZED COOKIES

MAKES ABOUT 3 DOZEN *To keep these cookies flaky and light, do not overmix the butter and sugars; the dough must not become too soft before adding the remaining ingredients.*

1½ sticks (¾ cup) unsalted butter,
   room temperature

¼ cup granulated sugar

¼ cup confectioners' sugar

2 tablespoons finely grated lime zest
   (2 medium limes)

2 tablespoons freshly squeezed
   lime juice

¼ teaspoon salt

1½ cups all-purpose flour

   Lime Glaze (recipe follows)

In the bowl of an electric mixer fitted with the paddle attachment, beat the butter and both sugars on medium-high speed until light and fluffy, 3 to 4 minutes, scraping down the sides of the bowl as needed. Add lime zest and juice, and salt; beat until combined. Add flour; beat until just combined.

Turn out the dough onto a large piece of parchment or waxed paper. Using your hands, shape dough into an 8-inch log; flatten into a rectangle (1½ inches high and

2½ inches wide). Fold paper over log; flatten sides against work surface. Freeze or refrigerate dough until firm, at least 1 hour or overnight.

Preheat the oven to 350°F, with racks in the upper and lower thirds. Line two large baking sheets with parchment paper. Using a sharp knife, cut dough into ¼-inch-thick slices. Place about 2 inches apart on prepared sheets. Bake, rotating sheets halfway through, until cookies are puffed and barely golden, about 15 minutes. Transfer to a wire rack to cool completely. Using the back of a spoon, spread about 1 teaspoon Lime Glaze on each cookie. Unglazed cookies can be kept in an airtight container at room temperature for up to 4 days; they should be eaten the same day they are glazed.

LIME GLAZE

MAKES ENOUGH FOR ABOUT 3 DOZEN COOKIES *Speckles of grated lime zest in this pretty soft-green icing give the finished cookies a fresh citrus flavor.*

- ¾ cup confectioners' sugar
- 1 tablespoon plus 2 teaspoons freshly squeezed lime juice
- 1 teaspoon finely grated lime zest

In a small bowl, whisk together all ingredients until spreadable. Use immediately.

COCONUT–MACADAMIA NUT COOKIES

MAKES ABOUT 44 *For a more pronounced coconut flavor, lightly toast the coconut along with the nuts before adding the coconut to the dough.*

- ½ cup plus 2 tablespoons salted macadamia nuts
- 2 cups all-purpose flour
- 1 teaspoon baking powder
- ½ teaspoon salt
- 1 stick (½ cup) unsalted butter, room temperature
- ½ cup vegetable shortening
- 1 cup sugar
- 3 large eggs
- ½ teaspoon pure vanilla extract
- ½ cup unsweetened shredded coconut, plus more for sprinkling

Preheat the oven to 325°F. Spread the macadamia nuts in a single layer on a rimmed baking sheet. Toast until lightly golden and fragrant, about 10 minutes. Let cool, then slice 22 nuts in half. Finely grind the remaining nuts, and set aside. In a medium bowl, whisk together flour, baking powder, and salt; set aside.

In the bowl of an electric mixer fitted with the paddle attachment, beat the butter, shortening, and sugar on medium speed until light and fluffy, 3 to 4 minutes, scraping down the sides of the bowl as needed. Beat in 2 eggs and the vanilla to combine. Add the flour mixture, ground macadamia nuts, and coconut; mix on low speed until just incorporated.

Turn out the dough onto a clean work surface. Shape into an 11-inch log, 2 inches in diameter. Wrap in plastic, and refrigerate until firm, at least 2 hours or overnight.

Preheat oven to 350°F, with racks in the upper and lower thirds. Line two large baking sheets with parchment paper. Remove log from refrigerator. Using a sharp knife, cut into ⅓-inch-thick slices. Place slices about 1½ inches apart on prepared baking sheets. In a small bowl, whisk together the remaining egg with 1 tablespoon water. Using a pastry brush, lightly brush the top of each cookie with egg wash. Sprinkle with coconut, and press a macadamia half into the center.

Bake, rotating sheets halfway through, until the edges are golden and the coconut on top is lightly toasted, 14 to 16 minutes. Transfer to a wire rack to cool completely. Cookies can be kept in an airtight container at room temperature for up to 5 days.

SPICE SANDWICH COOKIES

MAKES ABOUT 1 DOZEN SANDWICH COOKIES *These cookies get their flavor from freshly ground whole spices. Be sure to make the cookies at least a day before serving; they will soften a bit and the flavors of the cookie and the filling will have a chance to meld. You can also omit the filling and serve these cookies on their own.*

3 whole allspice berries	1½ sticks (¾ cup) unsalted butter, room temperature
3 whole black peppercorns	½ cup packed light-brown sugar
2 whole green cardamom pods	½ cup granulated sugar, plus more for rolling
1 whole clove	⅓ cup unsulfured molasses
½ whole star anise	1 large egg
2 cups all-purpose flour	Apple–Cream Cheese Filling (recipe follows)
½ teaspoon salt	¼ cup apple butter (not unsweetened)
½ teaspoon baking soda	
⅛ teaspoon freshly grated nutmeg	

Line two large baking sheets with parchment paper; set aside. In a clean electric spice or coffee grinder, combine allspice, peppercorns, cardamom, clove, and star anise; grind to a fine powder. Transfer spices to a large bowl, and add flour, salt, baking soda, and nutmeg; whisk to combine, and set aside.

In the bowl of an electric mixer fitted with the paddle attachment, beat butter and both sugars on medium-high speed until light and fluffy, 3 to 4 minutes. Add molasses and egg; beat to combine, about 1 minute. With mixer on low speed, add flour mixture; beat until just combined.

Shape a ½ tablespoon of dough at a time into balls, and roll in granulated sugar. Place balls about 1 inch apart on the prepared sheets; press down to flatten slightly. Freeze or refrigerate until firm, at least 30 minutes or overnight.

Preheat the oven to 350°F. Let cookies come to room temperature. Bake, rotating sheets halfway through, until cookies are golden brown, 15 to 18 minutes. Transfer parchment and cookies to a wire rack to cool completely.

Using an offset spatula, spread 2 teaspoons of Apple–Cream Cheese Filling onto the flat sides of half of the cookies. Spread 1 teaspoon apple butter over filling. Sandwich with remaining cookies, keeping flat sides down. Once filled, cookies can be kept in an airtight container in the refrigerator for up to 4 days.

Spice Sandwich Cookies

Chocolate Wafer Sandwich Cookies

Grapefruit Sandwich Cookies

Peanut Butter Sandwich Cookies

APPLE–CREAM CHEESE FILLING
MAKES ENOUGH TO FILL 1 DOZEN SANDWICH COOKIES

8 ounces cream cheese, room temperature

½ cup apple butter (not unsweetened)

In the bowl of an electric mixer fitted with the paddle attachment, beat cream cheese and apple butter on medium speed until well combined, about 3 minutes. Use immediately, or cover tightly with plastic wrap and refrigerate overnight. If refrigerated, let stand at room temperature for 20 minutes to soften slightly before using.

CHOCOLATE WAFER SANDWICH COOKIES

MAKES ABOUT 2 DOZEN SANDWICH COOKIES *These crisp cookies can be sandwiched with Vanilla or Chocolate Cream Filling, freshly whipped cream, or your favorite ice cream.*

1¼ cups all-purpose flour, plus more for dusting

¼ cup plus 2 tablespoons Dutch-process cocoa powder

½ teaspoon baking powder

½ teaspoon baking soda

¼ teaspoon salt

1 stick (½ cup) unsalted butter, room temperature

⅔ cup packed light-brown sugar

⅓ cup granulated sugar

1 large egg

1 teaspoon pure vanilla extract

Vanilla Cream Filling or Chocolate Cream Filling (recipes follow)

Line two large baking sheets with parchment paper; set aside. In a large bowl, whisk together flour, cocoa, baking powder, baking soda, and salt; set aside. In the bowl of an electric mixer fitted with the paddle attachment, beat the butter and both sugars on medium speed until light and fluffy, 2 to 3 minutes. Add the egg and vanilla; beat to combine. With mixer on low speed, add flour mixture, and beat to combine, scraping down the sides of the bowl as needed.

Turn out the dough onto a piece of plastic wrap, and divide in half. With floured hands, shape each piece into a flattened rectangle, wrap with plastic, and refrigerate until firm, about 30 minutes.

Place one rectangle of dough on a lightly floured work surface. Roll out dough to a scant ⅛-inch thickness, stopping every so often to release the dough by running an offset spatula underneath. You should end up with a rectangle that's about 14 by 11 inches. Transfer dough to a prepared baking sheet, and freeze until very firm, about 30 minutes. Repeat with remaining dough.

Preheat the oven to 350°F. Place one rectangle of dough on a clean work surface. Working quickly, cut out rounds using a 2-inch cookie cutter. (If the dough begins to soften too much, return to the freezer for a few minutes.) Using a wide metal spatula, transfer rounds to parchment-lined baking sheets, about 1½ inches apart. Gather together remaining scraps, reroll, and cut out more rounds. Freeze until firm, about 15 minutes. Repeat with the remaining rectangle of dough.

Bake, rotating sheets halfway through, until the centers of the cookies feel firm when lightly pressed, 12 to 14 minutes. Transfer to a wire rack to cool completely.

Using an offset spatula, spread 1 tablespoon desired filling onto the flat sides of half the cookies. Sandwich with remaining cookies, keeping the flat sides down. Unfilled cookies can be kept in an airtight container at room temperature for up to 1 week. Once filled, cookies are best eaten the day they are made, but they can be kept in an airtight container in the refrigerator for up to 3 days.

VANILLA CREAM FILLING
MAKES ENOUGH TO FILL 2 DOZEN SANDWICH COOKIES

$1\frac{1}{3}$ cups confectioners' sugar

$\frac{1}{3}$ cup vegetable shortening

$\frac{1}{3}$ cup unsalted butter, room temperature

$\frac{1}{2}$ teaspoon pure vanilla extract

Pinch of salt

In the bowl of an electric mixer fitted with the paddle attachment, combine all ingredients. Beat on medium-high speed until fluffy and light, 3 to 4 minutes. Use immediately or refrigerate in an airtight container for up to 3 days. Let soften at room temperature before using.

CHOCOLATE CREAM FILLING

MAKES ENOUGH TO FILL 2 DOZEN SANDWICH COOKIES *You can transform the flavor of this filling into chocolate-mint or mocha by substituting ¼ teaspoon pure peppermint extract or ½ teaspoon pure coffee extract for the vanilla.*

$4\frac{1}{2}$ ounces semisweet chocolate, chopped (1 cup)

$\frac{3}{4}$ ounce unsweetened chocolate, chopped

$\frac{2}{3}$ cup (half of one 14-ounce can) sweetened condensed milk

1 tablespoon unsalted butter

1 teaspoon pure vanilla extract

Melt chocolates in a heatproof bowl set over (but not touching) simmering water, stirring occasionally. Add condensed milk, butter, and extract; stir to combine. Continue to stir over simmering water until all ingredients are smooth, 2 minutes. Remove from heat, and set aside to cool slightly.

GRAPEFRUIT SANDWICH COOKIES

MAKES 15 SANDWICH COOKIES *You can bake the cookies and make the filling a day ahead.*

Grated zest of 1 ruby red grapefruit, plus ¼ cup freshly squeezed juice

1 cup sugar

1 cup all-purpose flour, plus more for dusting

¾ cup cake flour (not self-rising)

1 teaspoon baking powder

½ teaspoon salt

1 stick (½ cup) unsalted butter, room temperature

2 large egg yolks

Grapefruit Cream Filling (recipe follows)

Preheat the oven to 350°F. Line a large baking sheet with parchment paper; set aside. In a small bowl, combine the grapefruit zest with 1 tablespoon sugar; set aside. In a medium bowl, whisk together both flours, baking powder, and salt; set aside.

In the bowl of an electric mixer fitted with the paddle attachment, beat the butter and remaining sugar on medium-high speed until light and fluffy, about 2 minutes, scraping down the sides of the bowl as needed. Add the egg yolks, and beat until combined, scraping down the sides of the bowl as needed. Beat in the reserved zest-sugar mixture. Add flour mixture in two batches, alternating with the juice, and beat to combine.

Turn out the dough onto a piece of plastic wrap, and shape into a 1-inch-thick disk. Wrap in plastic and refrigerate until firm, about 30 minutes.

On a lightly floured work surface, roll out the disk to ⅛ inch thick. Using a 2-inch round cookie cutter, cut out rounds and place about 1 inch apart on the prepared sheet. Bake, rotating the sheet halfway through, until the edges are golden, 18 to 20 minutes. Transfer sheet to a wire rack to cool 5 minutes. Transfer parchment paper and cookies to rack to cool completely.

Using an offset spatula, spread 1 tablespoon filling onto the flat sides of half the cookies. Sandwich with remaining cookies, keeping the flat sides down. Once filled, cookies can be kept in an airtight container in the refrigerator for up to 3 days.

GRAPEFRUIT CREAM FILLING

MAKES ENOUGH TO FILL 15 SANDWICH COOKIES *You can refrigerate the filling, covered, for up to one day; let it soften at room temperature before using.*

1 stick (½ cup) unsalted butter, room temperature

2 cups confectioners' sugar

1 tablespoon honey

3 tablespoons freshly squeezed ruby red grapefruit juice

In the bowl of an electric mixer fitted with the paddle attachment, beat the butter and sugar until light and fluffy, about 4 minutes. Beat in the honey. Add juice, 1 tablespoon at a time, until filling holds together and is smooth and creamy, about 2 minutes. Transfer to a small bowl, cover, and set aside until ready to use.

PEANUT BUTTER SANDWICH COOKIES

MAKES ABOUT 3 DOZEN SANDWICH COOKIES *These lunchbox favorites are equally delicious when sandwiched with jam—use any flavor you like.*

2 cups all-purpose flour, plus more for dusting

½ teaspoon baking soda

¼ teaspoon salt

1½ sticks (¾ cup) unsalted butter, room temperature

¾ cup smooth peanut butter, preferably natural

½ cup granulated sugar

½ cup packed light-brown sugar

1 large egg

1 teaspoon pure vanilla extract

Peanut Butter Filling (recipe follows)

In a bowl, whisk together flour, baking soda, and salt; set aside. Place butter, peanut butter, and both sugars in the bowl of an electric mixer fitted with the paddle attachment; beat on medium-high speed until light and fluffy, 2 to 3 minutes. Add the egg and vanilla, and beat to combine, scraping down the sides of the bowl. With mixer on low, add reserved flour mixture and beat until incorporated, about 1 minute.

Divide dough in half, and shape into two flattened disks. Wrap in plastic and refrigerate at least 30 minutes or overnight.

Preheat the oven to 325°F. Line two large baking sheets with parchment paper. (If refrigerated overnight, let dough stand at room temperature to soften slightly.) On a lightly floured work surface, roll out dough to a scant ¼-inch thickness. Using a sharp knife, cut dough into 2½-by-1-inch rectangles. Using the floured tines of a fork, score the top of each cookie. Transfer cookies to prepared baking sheets, placing 1½ inches apart, and refrigerate until firm, about 15 minutes.

Bake, rotating sheets halfway through, until lightly golden around the edges and firm in the center, 15 to 20 minutes. Transfer to a wire rack to cool completely.

Using an offset spatula, spread 1 tablespoon filling onto the flat sides of half of the cookies. Sandwich with remaining cookies, keeping the flat sides down. Unfilled cookies can be kept in an airtight container at room temperature for up to 1 week. Once filled, cookies are best eaten the same day, but can be kept in the refrigerator for up to 3 days.

PEANUT BUTTER FILLING
MAKES ENOUGH TO FILL 3 DOZEN SANDWICH COOKIES

6 tablespoons unsalted butter, room temperature

¾ cup confectioners' sugar

¾ cup smooth peanut butter, preferably natural

3 tablespoons heavy cream

In the bowl of an electric mixer fitted with the paddle attachment, combine all ingredients. Beat on medium-high speed until light and fluffy, about 5 minutes, scraping down the sides of the bowl as needed. Use immediately, or transfer to an airtight container and refrigerate up to 3 days. If refrigerated, let filling stand at room temperature to soften before using.

CHEESECAKE THUMBPRINTS

MAKES ABOUT 30 *These cookies are best eaten after they have been refrigerated overnight. Allow them to sit at room temperature for twenty minutes before serving.*

4 ounces cream cheese, room temperature	1½ teaspoons sour cream
½ cup sugar	⅛ teaspoon pure vanilla extract
¼ teaspoon salt, plus a pinch	2 sticks (1 cup) unsalted butter, room temperature
2 large egg yolks	2 cups all-purpose flour

In the bowl of an electric mixer fitted with the paddle attachment, beat cream cheese on medium speed until light and fluffy, about 3 minutes, scraping down the sides of the bowl as needed. Add ¼ cup sugar and a pinch of salt, and beat until smooth, about 3 minutes. Add 1 egg yolk, sour cream, and vanilla; beat until smooth. Transfer to a small bowl, and refrigerate for about 30 minutes.

Preheat the oven to 350°F, with racks in the upper and lower thirds. Line two large baking sheets with parchment paper; set aside. In the bowl of an electric mixer fitted with the paddle attachment, beat the butter and remaining ¼ cup sugar on medium speed until well combined, 1 to 2 minutes, scraping down the sides of the bowl as needed. Add remaining ¼ teaspoon salt and egg yolk; beat to combine. With mixer on low speed, gradually add the flour, mixing until just combined.

Shape level tablespoons of dough into balls, and place on prepared baking sheets about 1 inch apart. Using the lightly floured end of a thick wooden spoon handle (or your thumb), make an indentation in the center of each ball.

Bake 10 minutes; remove from oven and make indentations again. Rotate sheets, return to oven, and bake until edges of cookies begin to turn golden, 7 to 9 minutes more. Transfer cookies to a wire rack to cool completely.

Using a small teaspoon, fill the center of each cookie with about 1 teaspoon cream-cheese filling, mounding it slightly. Return cookies to the oven, and bake until the filling is firm, 7 to 8 minutes. Transfer cookies to a wire rack to cool completely. Refrigerate in an airtight container, layered between waxed or parchment paper, at least 4 hours before serving (cookies can be refrigerated overnight).

CHEESECAKE-FILLED CHOCOLATE THUMBPRINTS VARIATION In a heatproof bowl set over (but not touching) simmering water, melt 2 ounces semisweet chocolate; let cool. Follow instructions for Cheesecake Thumbprints, adding melted chocolate to butter mixture along with the egg yolk and salt. Reduce the flour by 3 tablespoons, and whisk with 3 tablespoons Dutch-process cocoa powder before adding to the dough. (The edges of these cookies will be firm to the touch when baked.)

CHEESECAKE THUMBPRINT HOW-TO **1.** The floured handle of a wooden spoon is pressed into each ball of cookie dough to make an indentation. **2.** A rich cheesecake filling is added to the centers after the cookies are partially baked.

COCONUT-PECAN-CARAMEL SANDWICH COOKIES

MAKES ABOUT 3 DOZEN SANDWICH COOKIES *These shortbread sandwiches are laced with chopped pecans and toasted coconut and filled with buttery caramel. Be sure to let cookies cool completely before filling, or bake them a day in advance and fill the next day.*

¼ cup sweetened shredded coconut	1 teaspoon pure vanilla extract
½ cup (about 2 ounces) pecans	2 cups all-purpose flour, plus more for dusting
2 sticks (1 cup) unsalted butter, room temperature	½ teaspoon salt
½ cup sugar	Caramel Filling (recipe follows)

Preheat the oven to 350°F. Spread the coconut in an even layer on one half of a rimmed baking sheet and the pecans on the other. Toast, stirring coconut halfway through, until nuts are fragrant and coconut is light golden, 5 to 7 minutes. Place coconut and pecans in a food processor, and pulse until finely chopped.

In the bowl of an electric mixer fitted with the paddle attachment, beat the butter and sugar on medium speed until light and fluffy, about 4 minutes, scraping down the sides of the bowl as needed. Beat in vanilla. With mixer on low speed, add the flour and salt; beat until combined. Beat in chopped coconut-nut mixture until combined. Turn out the dough onto a piece of plastic wrap and shape into a flattened disk. Wrap in plastic. Chill dough until firm, 30 to 45 minutes.

Line two large baking sheets with parchment paper; set aside. On a lightly floured piece of parchment paper, roll out the dough to ⅛-inch thickness. Transfer to another baking sheet, and freeze until firm, 5 to 10 minutes. Using a 2-inch flower cookie cutter, cut out shapes, and place 1 inch apart on prepared baking sheets. Freeze until firm, 5 to 10 minutes.

Remove from freezer. Using a ¾-inch round cookie cutter (or the wide end of a pastry tip) cut out and remove the centers from half of the cookies.

Bake, rotating sheets halfway through, until golden brown, about 12 minutes. Transfer parchment and cookies to a wire rack to cool completely. Cookies can be made 1 day ahead and kept in an airtight container at room temperature.

Spoon or pipe about 1 teaspoon Caramel Filling onto the flat side of each of the whole cookies. Top with cut cookies, keeping flat sides down. Drizzle the remaining caramel over the tops. Let caramel set at least 2 hours, or overnight, at room temperature. Cookies can be kept, layered between sheets of parchment paper, in an airtight container at room temperature for up to 5 days.

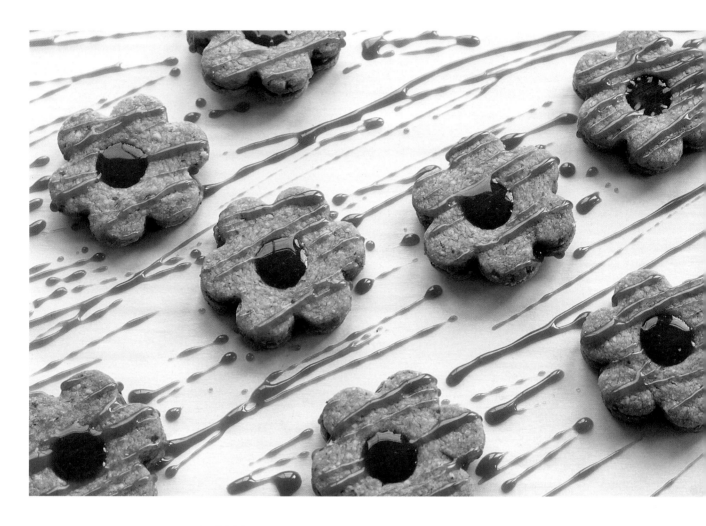

CARAMEL FILLING

MAKES ENOUGH TO FILL ABOUT 3 DOZEN SANDWICH COOKIES

1⅓ cups sugar

½ cup heavy cream

4 tablespoons unsalted butter, cut into small pieces

Place the sugar and ¼ cup plus 2 tablespoons water in a medium heavy-bottom saucepan. Set over medium-high heat, and stir to combine. Without stirring, bring the mixture to a boil, and cook until dark amber in color, about 5 minutes, washing down the sides of the pan with a wet pastry brush to prevent crystals from forming.

Remove from heat. Carefully pour the cream down the side of the pan (it will spatter), stirring constantly, until fully combined. Add the butter and stir to combine. Transfer filling to a heatproof bowl, and let cool slightly before filling cookies.

LINZER HEARTS

MAKES ABOUT 1 DOZEN SANDWICH COOKIES *Hazelnuts impart an unmistakable flavor to these cookies, but feel free to substitute the same amount of almonds, pecans, or walnuts. You will need two sizes of heart-shaped cookie cutters (three inches and two inches).*

- 2 cups all-purpose flour, plus more for dusting
- 1 teaspoon baking powder
- ½ teaspoon ground cinnamon
- ¼ teaspoon salt
- 1 cup (4½ ounces) blanched hazelnuts
- 2 sticks (1 cup) unsalted butter, room temperature
- ⅔ cup granulated sugar
- 2 large egg yolks
- ½ teaspoon pure vanilla extract
- ½ teaspoon freshly grated lemon zest
- ½ cup raspberry jam, for filling
- ¼ cup confectioners' sugar, for dusting

In a large bowl, sift together flour, baking powder, cinnamon, and salt. In a food processor, pulse hazelnuts until finely ground. Whisk the ground hazelnuts into the flour mixture; set aside.

In the bowl of an electric mixer fitted with the paddle attachment, beat butter and granulated sugar on medium-high speed until light and fluffy, 2 to 3 minutes. Add the egg yolks, vanilla, and lemon zest; beat to combine, scraping down the sides of the bowl as needed. With mixer on low speed, add hazelnut-flour mixture, and beat until just combined, 10 to 15 seconds.

Turn out the dough onto a lightly floured work surface, divide in half, and shape into flattened disks. Wrap in plastic and refrigerate at least 1 hour or overnight.

Remove one disk of dough from the refrigerator, and let stand until softened slightly. (This will help keep the dough from cracking when rolled.) On a large piece of parchment paper lightly dusted with flour, roll dough to ⅛-inch thickness. To prevent sticking while rolling, occasionally run a large offset spatula under dough, and add more flour to the top or bottom of dough. Transfer parchment paper and dough to a baking sheet; freeze until firm, about 20 minutes. Repeat with remaining dough. (You can stack the parchment and dough.)

Preheat the oven to 325°F. Line two large baking sheets with parchment paper. Remove one sheet of dough and parchment from freezer; working quickly, cut into heart shapes with a 3-inch cookie cutter. Cut out center from half the shapes with a 2-inch cutter. (If the dough begins to soften too much, return to the freezer for a few minutes.) Using a wide metal spatula, transfer open hearts to prepared baking sheets, about 1½ inches apart; freeze until firm, about 15 minutes. (You can either bake the cutout centers for bite-size cookies, or reroll them to make the larger hearts.)

Bake, rotating sheets halfway through, until cookies are crisp and lightly golden all over, about 15 minutes. Transfer cookies to a wire rack to cool completely. (Cooled cookies can be stored overnight in an airtight container at room temperature before filling.) Spread the flat sides of the whole hearts with about 1½ teaspoons jam. Sift confectioners' sugar over the open hearts. Just before serving, top open hearts with jam. Cookies should be eaten the day they're filled.

LINZER HEART HOW-TO
Heart shapes are cut from chilled linzer cookie dough, then the centers of half the hearts are cut out. Once baked and cooled, the whole hearts are spread with raspberry jam, then topped with open hearts dusted with confectioners' sugar. The smaller heart shapes can also be baked and dusted with confectioners' sugar; the baking time will be the same.

FUDGY CHOCOLATE BROWNIES

MAKES 16 *Some people prefer their brownies cakey. We developed this recipe to satisfy our craving for a bar that was just the opposite: dense, fudgy, and full of deep chocolate flavor.*

1 stick (½ cup) unsalted butter, plus more for pan

8 ounces bittersweet chocolate, coarsely chopped

1½ cups sugar

4 large eggs

1 teaspoon pure vanilla extract

¾ cup all-purpose flour

½ teaspoon salt

Preheat the oven to 350°F. Butter an 8-inch square baking pan or heatproof glass dish. Line the pan with parchment paper, leaving a 1-inch overhang on two sides. Set aside. Place butter and chocolate in a large heatproof bowl set over (but not touching) simmering water; stir frequently until chocolate and butter are melted, about 7 minutes. Remove bowl from heat; let cool to room temperature, 10 to 15 minutes.

Stir sugar into cooled chocolate mixture until combined. Whisk in eggs one at a time, whisking until smooth after each addition. Whisk in vanilla. Gently fold in flour and salt.

Pour batter into prepared pan, and smooth top with an offset spatula. Bake until a cake tester inserted in the center comes out with only a few moist crumbs attached, 40 to 45 minutes. Transfer pan to a wire rack to cool completely.

Run a knife or offset spatula around the edges of the pan. Using parchment, lift brownies out of pan and onto the rack. Transfer to a cutting board; cut into 2-inch squares. Brownies can be kept in an airtight container at room temperature for up to 3 days.

NUTTY CHOCOLATE BROWNIES VARIATION Follow instructions for Fudgy Chocolate Brownies, folding in 1½ cups (4½ ounces) walnut halves, finely chopped, after the flour and salt. Proceed with the recipe.

FUDGY CHOCOLATE BROWNIE HOW-TO Dusting the bottoms of the cooled brownies with sugar prevents them from sticking together when stacking; you can also place a piece of parchment or waxed paper between them.

CARAMEL-NUT BARS

MAKES 25 *Salted nuts balance the sweetness of caramel in these candy-like cookies. These bars are quite rich, so feel free to cut them in half.*

2¼ sticks unsalted butter, room temperature, plus more for pan

1½ cups (6 ounces) pecans

1 cup (4½ ounces) salted cashews

1 cup (5 ounces) salted peanuts

¾ cup packed light-brown sugar

2¼ cups all-purpose flour

2½ teaspoons plus a pinch of salt

4 cups granulated sugar

½ teaspoon cream of tartar

1 cup heavy cream

Preheat the oven to 350°F. Butter a 15-by-10-inch rimmed baking sheet, and line with parchment paper, leaving a 1-inch overhang on long sides; set aside. Spread nuts on another rimmed baking sheet. Toast until nuts are fragrant and lightly golden around

Caramel-Nut Bars, Citrus Bars, and Jam Crumb Bars

the edges, about 10 minutes. Transfer nuts to a clean surface; spread evenly, and let cool completely. Coarsely chop, and set aside.

In the bowl of an electric mixer fitted with the paddle attachment, beat 2 sticks of butter with the brown sugar on medium speed until light and fluffy, about 3 minutes, scraping down the sides of the bowl as needed. With mixer on low speed, add flour and a pinch of salt; mix until just combined.

Transfer dough to prepared baking sheet, and cover with parchment paper. Using a wine bottle or small rolling pin, roll along the length of pan to smooth dough. (Alternatively, press the dough into the pan with the back of a large spoon.) Bake until lightly golden, 10 to 12 minutes. Transfer to a wire rack to cool completely.

Combine granulated sugar, cream of tartar, remaining 2½ teaspoons salt, and 1 cup water in a wide, heavy-bottom saucepan. Cook over high heat, without stirring, until some sugar begins to melt and turn golden, 5 to 7 minutes. Reduce heat to medium; continue to cook, stirring occasionally with a wooden spoon, until sugar is completely melted, mixture is deep golden, and a candy thermometer registers 300°F (hard-crack stage). Stirring constantly, carefully pour cream slowly down the side of the pan (it will spatter) until fully combined. Remove from heat; add remaining ¼ stick butter and stir to combine. Transfer caramel to a heatproof bowl to cool for 10 minutes.

Stir in nuts; spread caramel mixture over cooled crust. Bake until caramel is set, about 10 minutes. Transfer to a wire rack to cool. Cut into 3-by-2-inch bars. Bars can be kept in an airtight container at room temperature for up to 1 week.

CHOCOLATE CARAMEL-NUT BARS VARIATION Follow instructions for Caramel-Nut Bars, reducing salt in the caramel to 1 teaspoon and adding 8 ounces melted semisweet chocolate and 2 tablespoons Dutch-process cocoa powder to the caramel along with the ¼ stick butter. Proceed with the recipe.

CARAMEL-NUT BAR HOW-TO
1. A combination of salted nuts is stirred into a bowl of freshly cooked caramel. 2. The caramel-nut mixture is spread atop a cooled cookie base before the bars are baked a second time to set.

CITRUS BARS

MAKES 30 *Classic lemon bars get a couple of twists: wheat germ adds texture to the shortbread crust, and lime juice and zest flavor the filling.*

3½ cups plus ⅔ cup all-purpose flour	8 large eggs
½ cup wheat germ	4 cups granulated sugar
½ cup confectioners' sugar, plus more for dusting	¾ cup freshly squeezed lemon juice
1½ teaspoons salt	¾ cup freshly squeezed lime juice
4 sticks (1 pound) unsalted butter, cold, cut into pieces	1 tablespoon finely grated lemon zest
	1 tablespoon finely grated lime zest

Preheat the oven to 350°F. In a large bowl, whisk together 3½ cups flour, wheat germ, confectioners' sugar, and ½ teaspoon salt. Using a pastry blender, cut in the butter until the largest pieces are the size of peas.

Press mixture into bottom and up sides of an ungreased 17½-by-12½-inch rimmed baking pan. Bake until golden, 20 to 30 minutes. Transfer to a wire rack to cool.

In a medium bowl, whisk together the eggs, granulated sugar, and remaining ⅔ cup flour until combined. Whisk in lemon and lime juices, zests, and remaining 1 teaspoon salt until combined. Pour filling onto crust.

Bake, rotating pan halfway through, until center is set, about 30 minutes. Transfer to a wire rack to cool completely. Dust with confectioners' sugar, and cut into bars approximately 3 by 2 inches. Bars can be stored at room temperature for up to 1 day, then kept in an airtight container in the refrigerator for up to 3 days.

JAM CRUMB BARS

MAKES 25 *These bars provide the perfect contrast of crisp and gooey. For a chocolate variation, omit the jam and evenly scatter fourteen ounces of finely chopped semisweet chocolate over the cooled crust before proceeding.*

3 sticks (1½ cups) unsalted butter, room temperature, cut into pieces, plus more for pan

2¼ cups (11 ounces) blanched almonds, very finely ground

3 cups all-purpose flour

1¼ cups sugar

½ teaspoon salt

1¾ cups raspberry, apricot, or strawberry jam

Preheat the oven to 350°F. Butter a 15-by-10-inch rimmed baking sheet. Line with parchment paper, leaving a 1-inch overhang on the long sides. Set aside.

In a large bowl, whisk together ground almonds, flour, sugar, and salt. Cut in the butter with a pastry blender until the mixture resembles coarse crumbs. Using your fingers, squeeze the mixture together to create pea-size crumbs with a few larger clumps.

Transfer half of crumb mixture (about 4½ cups) to prepared baking sheet; set aside remaining mixture. Cover with a sheet of parchment paper. Using the back of a large spoon, press dough evenly into pan, lifting the parchment occasionally to ensure it doesn't stick. With a wine bottle or small rolling pin, roll along the length of the pan to smooth dough. Dough should be firmly packed, with no holes or cracks. Bake, rotating the pan halfway through, until lightly golden all over, 15 to 20 minutes. Transfer pan to a wire rack to cool completely.

Evenly spread jam over cooled crust. Scatter with remaining crumb mixture, squeezing some of the mixture so that large clumps are visible and evenly distributed over the top of the jam. Bake, rotating the pan halfway through, until the topping begins to turn light golden brown (the jam should not be too dark), 20 to 22 minutes. Transfer pan to a wire rack to cool completely.

Run a knife around the edges of the pan to loosen; using two wide spatulas, transfer to a cutting board and cut into 3-by-2-inch bars. Bars can be kept in an airtight container at room temperature for up to 4 days.

CARAMEL CRUMB BARS VARIATION Follow instructions for Jam Crumb Bars, omitting jam. While crust cools, prepare Basic Caramel (page 389); let cool slightly. Pour warm caramel evenly over the crust, smoothing with a spatula, and proceed with the recipe.

JAM CRUMB BAR HOW-TO
1. An empty wine bottle is used to roll out the cookie-dough base in the pan.
2. Raspberry jam and an almond-crumb mixture are layered on top of the partially baked crust.

SHORTBREAD FINGERS

MAKES 22 *These are best the same day they are baked, when they're still nice and crisp, especially around the edges. After that, they will be softer but still delicious.*

3 sticks (1½ cups) unsalted butter, room temperature, plus more for pan

2½ cups all-purpose flour

¼ teaspoon salt

¾ cup plus 2 tablespoons confectioners' sugar

Granulated sugar, for sprinkling

Preheat the oven to 325°F. Butter a 12-by-8-inch rimmed baking sheet and line with parchment paper, leaving a 1-inch overhang on long sides. Whisk together flour and salt in a small bowl; set aside.

In the bowl of an electric mixer fitted with the paddle attachment, beat butter until fluffy on medium speed, 3 to 4 minutes. Add confectioners' sugar; continue to beat until very light and fluffy, about 2 minutes, scraping down the sides of the bowl as needed. Add flour mixture, and beat on low speed, scraping down sides occasionally, until just incorporated. (It should have the consistency of soft cookie dough.)

Using a small offset spatula, evenly spread dough in prepared baking sheet. Chill in the freezer or refrigerator until dough is firm, about 15 minutes.

Prick dough all over with a fork. Bake, rotating sheet halfway through, until shortbread is golden brown, 40 to 45 minutes. Transfer to a wire rack and immediately sprinkle with granulated sugar. While still hot, use a large knife to cut shortbread into 4-by-1-inch pieces. Cool completely in the pan. Shortbread can be kept in an airtight container at room temperature for up to 1 week.

WHEATMEAL SHORTBREAD WEDGES

MAKES 8 *Be sure to sprinkle the shortbread with granulated sugar as soon as it comes out of the oven; this will help the sugar adhere to the cookie.*

1 cup all-purpose flour, plus more for dusting

¾ cup whole-wheat flour

¼ cup wheat bran

¾ teaspoon salt

1¾ sticks (14 tablespoons) unsalted butter, room temperature

½ cup packed light-brown sugar

Granulated sugar, for sprinkling

Preheat the oven to 325°F. Have ready a 10-inch springform pan or a 10-inch tart pan with a removable bottom. In the bowl of an electric mixer fitted with the paddle attachment, mix both flours, the bran, and salt on low speed just to combine. Add the butter and brown sugar, and beat until all the ingredients come together and form a smooth dough, about 3 minutes, scraping down the sides of the bowl as needed.

Turn out dough into the pan. Using your fingers, spread out the dough evenly while pressing it firmly into the pan.

WHEATMEAL SHORTBREAD HOW-TO After partially baking, the shortbread is scored into wedges using a bench scraper, then decoratively pierced with a wooden skewer.

Shortbread Fingers

Place pan in oven, and reduce temperature to 300°F. Bake until the edges just begin to turn golden, about 30 minutes. Remove pan from oven; using a bench scraper or long, sharp knife, score the cookie into 8 wedges. Using the tip of a wooden skewer or the tines of a fork, prick the shortbread all over in a decorative pattern, if desired. Return pan to oven, and bake until golden all over, about 15 minutes more. Transfer pan to a wire rack. Sprinkle shortbread with granulated sugar. Remove the sides of the pan. Let stand until completely cool before cutting into wedges. Shortbread can be kept in an airtight container at room temperature for up to 1 week.

CHOCOLATE SHORTBREAD FINGERS

MAKES 22 *The combination of cocoa and ground cinnamon is commonly found in Mexican chocolate and hot drinks; we've used it here to flavor a traditional Scottish cookie.*

- 3 sticks (1½ cups) unsalted butter, room temperature, plus more for pan
- 2½ cups plus 2 tablespoons all-purpose flour
- 4½ tablespoons Dutch-process cocoa powder

- Heaping ½ teaspoon ground cinnamon
- ½ teaspoon salt
- ¼ teaspoon baking soda
- 1 cup superfine sugar
- Granulated sugar, for sprinkling

Preheat the oven to 325°F. Butter a 12-by-8-inch rimmed baking sheet, and line with parchment paper, leaving a 1-inch overhang on long sides; set aside. In a medium bowl, whisk together flour, cocoa, cinnamon, salt, and baking soda until combined.

In an electric mixer fitted with the paddle attachment, beat the butter and superfine sugar on medium-high speed until light and fluffy, 3 to 4 minutes, scraping down the sides of the bowl. Add flour mixture, and beat on medium speed until just combined.

Using a small offset spatula, evenly spread dough in prepared baking sheet. Chill in the freezer or refrigerator until dough is firm, about 15 minutes. Prick dough all over with a fork; bake until just firm to the touch, about 20 minutes. Transfer to a wire rack. While still hot, use a large knife to cut shortbread into 4-by-1-inch pieces. Sprinkle with granulated sugar. Cool completely in the pan. Shortbread can be kept in an airtight container at room temperature for up to 1 week.

biscotti

CRANBERRY-PISTACHIO BISCOTTI

MAKES ABOUT 4 DOZEN *These red-and-green-flecked cookies are particularly festive at Christmas; Martha likes to bake several batches to give away as gifts.*

½ cup dried cranberries

½ cup boiling water

3 cups all-purpose flour, plus more for dusting

2 teaspoons baking powder

¼ teaspoon salt

4 tablespoons unsalted butter, room temperature

1 cup sugar, plus more for sprinkling

3 large eggs, plus 1 large egg, lightly beaten

2 teaspoons pure vanilla extract

½ cup shelled unsalted pistachios, coarsely chopped (2½ ounces)

Preheat the oven to 375°F. Line a large baking sheet with parchment paper; set aside. Place cranberries in a small bowl, and add boiling water. Let stand until plump, about

15 minutes. Drain and set aside. Sift together flour, baking powder, and salt into a medium bowl; set aside.

In the bowl of an electric mixer fitted with the paddle attachment, beat the butter and sugar on medium speed until light and fluffy, about 2 minutes. Add 3 eggs, one at a time, beating to incorporate after each addition and scraping down the sides of the bowl as needed. Beat in vanilla. Add the flour mixture, and mix on low speed until combined. Mix in the drained cranberries and the pistachios.

Turn out dough onto a lightly floured surface; divide in half. Shape each piece into a 16-by-2-inch log, and transfer to prepared baking sheet, about 3 inches apart. With the palm of your hand, flatten logs slightly. Brush beaten egg over the surface of the dough logs, and sprinkle generously with sugar.

Bake, rotating sheet halfway through, until logs are slightly firm to the touch, about 25 minutes. Transfer logs on parchment paper to a wire rack to cool slightly, about 20 minutes. Reduce oven temperature to 300°F.

Place logs on a cutting board. Using a serrated knife, cut the logs crosswise on the diagonal into ½-inch-thick slices. Place a wire rack on a large rimmed baking sheet. Arrange slices, cut sides down, on the rack. Bake until firm to the touch, about 30 minutes. Remove pan from oven; let biscotti cool completely on the rack. Biscotti can be kept in an airtight container at room temperature for up to 1 week.

ANISE-ALMOND BISCOTTI

MAKES ABOUT 4 DOZEN *The traditional Italian flavors of almond and anise are delicate enough for teatime yet equally good with strong coffee or espresso.*

1½ cups (7½ ounces) unblanched almonds	1 cup granulated sugar
2½ cups all-purpose flour, plus more for dusting	1 teaspoon pure anise extract
½ cup yellow cornmeal	3 large eggs, plus 1 large egg, lightly beaten
2 teaspoons baking powder	1 tablespoon anise seeds
½ teaspoon salt	Sanding sugar (or granulated sugar), for sprinkling (optional)
4 tablespoons unsalted butter, room temperature	

Preheat the oven to 375°F. Line a large baking sheet with parchment paper; set aside. Spread the almonds in a single layer on a rimmed baking sheet. Toast in the oven until fragrant and just beginning to turn light golden, 6 to 8 minutes. Transfer nuts to a clean surface; spread evenly, and let cool completely. Sift together flour, cornmeal, baking powder, and salt into a medium bowl; set aside.

In the bowl of an electric mixer fitted with the paddle attachment, beat the butter and granulated sugar on medium-high speed until light and fluffy, about 3 minutes. Beat in the anise extract. Add 3 eggs, one at a time, beating to incorporate after each addition and scraping down the sides of the bowl as needed. Add the flour mixture, and beat on low speed until combined. Mix in anise seeds and toasted almonds.

Turn out the dough onto a lightly floured surface, and knead to evenly distribute the nuts and seeds. Divide in half. Shape each piece into an 18-inch log, and transfer to the prepared baking sheet, about 3 inches apart. Brush beaten egg over the surface of the logs, and sprinkle generously with sanding sugar, if using.

Bake, rotating pan halfway through, until logs are lightly browned and firm to the touch, about 30 minutes. Transfer parchment and logs to a wire rack to cool slightly, about 20 minutes. Reduce oven temperature to 300°F.

Place logs on a cutting board. Using a serrated knife, cut the logs crosswise on the diagonal into ½-inch-thick slices. Place a wire rack on a rimmed baking sheet. Arrange slices cut side down on the rack. Bake until firm to the touch, about 30 minutes. Remove pan from oven; let biscotti cool completely on the rack. Biscotti can be kept in an airtight container at room temperature for up to 1 week.

CHOCOLATE-HAZELNUT BISCOTTI
MAKES ABOUT 4 DOZEN

2¼ cups all-purpose flour, plus more for dusting	1½ cups (about 8 ounces) blanched hazelnuts
¼ cup Dutch-process cocoa powder	4 large whole eggs, plus 1 large egg white, lightly beaten
1 teaspoon baking soda	1½ cups granulated sugar
1 teaspoon salt	Sanding sugar (or granulated sugar), for sprinkling (optional)
12 ounces (about 2 cups) semisweet chocolate chunks	

Preheat the oven to 350°F. Line a large baking sheet with parchment paper; set aside. In a food processor, pulse the flour, cocoa, baking soda, salt, 1 cup chocolate chunks, and hazelnuts until chips and hazelnuts are the size of peas.

In the bowl of an electric mixer fitted with the whisk attachment, beat the whole eggs and granulated sugar until the mixture holds a ribbon-like trail on the surface for a few seconds when you raise the whisk. Switch to the paddle attachment. With mixer on low speed, add the flour mixture and remaining 1 cup chocolate chunks, and beat until just combined.

Turn out the dough onto a lightly floured work surface, and divide into three equal pieces. Shape each piece into an 18-inch log. Transfer to prepared baking sheet. With the palm of your hand, gently press the logs to flatten slightly. Brush egg white over logs. Sprinkle with sanding sugar, if using.

Bake, rotating pan halfway through, until logs are just firm to the touch, 20 to 24 minutes. Transfer sheet to a wire rack to cool slightly, about 20 minutes.

Place logs on a cutting board. Using a serrated knife, cut ¾-inch-thick slices on the diagonal. Place a wire rack on a large rimmed baking sheet. Arrange slices, cut sides down, on the rack. Bake until biscotti are firm to the touch and completely dry, 10 to 12 minutes. Remove pan from oven; let biscotti cool completely on the rack. Biscotti can be kept in an airtight container at room temperature for up to 1 week.

PALMIERS

MAKES ABOUT 40 *If you wish to make these with store-bought puff pastry, increase the sugar to one cup. Thaw and unfold the dough on the sugared work surface, then trim each piece into a ten-inch square, about ⅛ inch thick. Proceed with the recipe, sprinkling and rolling as directed. (Standard packages contain about one pound of dough, so the yield will be slightly greater than for our homemade version.)*

| ¾ cup sugar | 12½ ounces Puff Pastry (page 359) |

Sprinkle half of the sugar evenly on a clean work surface. Place dough on top, and sprinkle evenly with remaining sugar.

Gently roll out dough into a 17-by-13-inch rectangle, about ⅛ inch thick, continually coating both sides with sugar and being careful not to press too hard around the edges. Using a pastry wheel or sharp knife, trim the outermost edges.

With your fingers, roll up one long side as tightly as possible into a cylinder, being careful not to stretch out the dough and stopping when you reach the middle. Repeat on the opposite side until you have two tight cylinders that meet in the middle. Wrap tightly in plastic and freeze until firm, about 15 minutes.

Using a sharp knife, cut dough crosswise into ⅜-inch-thick slices. Place slices on ungreased baking sheets, about 2 inches apart, and flatten firmly with the palm of your hand. Cover with plastic wrap, and refrigerate for 1 hour. Meanwhile, preheat the oven to 375°F.

Bake for 5 minutes; reduce oven temperature to 350°F. Using an offset spatula, flip the palmiers over; bake until pastry is golden brown and well caramelized, about 10 minutes more. Using the spatula, immediately transfer to a wire rack to cool completely, shiny side up. Palmiers are best eaten the same day they are baked, but they can be kept in an airtight container at room temperature for up to 3 days.

COCONUT-LIME LACE TUILES

MAKES ABOUT 30 *It's best to bake these cookies on cool, dry days so they can form and retain a curved shape. Because they are fragile, first line airtight containers with several layers of paper towels, then lay tuiles on top, in one layer, without crowding.*

3 tablespoons unsalted butter	1 cup unsweetened shredded coconut
⅓ cup packed light-brown sugar	Pinch of salt
¼ cup light corn syrup	Freshly grated zest of 1 lime
2 tablespoons all-purpose flour	

Preheat the oven to 350°F. Line two large baking sheets with nonstick baking mats (such as Silpats) or parchment paper; set aside. In a small saucepan, combine butter, sugar, and corn syrup; cook over medium heat, stirring constantly, until the butter is melted and the sugar has liquefied, about 3 minutes. Remove from heat.

PALMIER HOW-TO 1. A large piece of puff pastry dough is generously sprinkled with sugar, then trimmed and tightly rolled lengthwise from both ends. **2.** Once both sides have been rolled up and meet in the middle, the dough is sliced crosswise and flattened firmly before baking.

In a bowl, whisk together flour, coconut, and salt. Add to the butter mixture. Add zest; stir until combined. Drop rounds of batter (about 1½ teaspoons each) 2 inches apart onto the prepared baking sheets. (You should be able to fit six per sheet.)

Bake, rotating sheets halfway through, until cookies are golden, 8 to 9 minutes. Have a rolling pin ready. As soon as the cookies come out of the oven, use an offset spatula to lift cookies, one at a time, and drape them over the rolling pin. Let stand until set. Repeat with remaining batter. (If you cannot shape all six cookies before they start to harden, return them to the oven for 1 or 2 minutes to soften, and try baking fewer cookies next time.) For flat cookies, transfer mat and cookies straight from the oven to a wire rack to cool completely. Cookies can be kept in an airtight container at room temperature for up to 3 days.

CHOCOLATE FLORENTINES

MAKES 5 DOZEN *Nonstick baking mats will help these crunchy cookies bake evenly and hold their shape. Once the batter is made, it can be kept in the refrigerator, covered with plastic, for up to five days. Bring it to room temperature before using.*

1¾ cups (about 5 ounces) sliced almonds	¾ cup sugar
3 tablespoons Dutch-process cocoa powder	2 tablespoons light corn syrup
2 tablespoons milk	7 tablespoons unsalted butter, room temperature
	¼ teaspoon salt

Preheat the oven to 350°F. Line two baking sheets with nonstick baking mats (such as Silpats) or parchment paper; set aside. Spread almonds in a single layer on a rimmed baking sheet; toast in oven until lightly golden and fragrant, about 10 minutes. Transfer to a clean work surface. While the nuts are still warm, roll a rolling pin back and forth over nuts to finely crush them. Let cool completely, then place in a bowl. Add cocoa, and whisk to combine; set aside.

In a small saucepan, combine milk, sugar, corn syrup, butter, and salt. Bring to a boil, stirring occasionally with a wooden spoon, and cook until mixture registers 220°F on a candy thermometer. Add reserved almond-cocoa mixture, and stir to combine. Transfer mixture to a medium bowl to cool slightly.

Drop batter by rounded teaspoons, about 3 inches apart, onto prepared baking sheets. Bake, rotating sheets halfway through, until cookies are fragrant and small, tight bubbles emerge from the center, 15 to 20 minutes. Have a rolling pin ready. As soon as the cookies come out of the oven, use an offset spatula to lift cookies, one at a time, and drape them over the rolling pin. Let stand until set. Repeat with the remaining batter. For flat cookies, transfer mats and cookies straight from the oven to a wire rack to cool completely. Cookies can be kept in an airtight container, between layers of waxed or parchment paper, at room temperature for up to 3 days.

Chocolate Florentines and
Coconut-Lime Lace Tuiles

FRENCH ALMOND MACAROONS

MAKES ABOUT 30 SANDWICH COOKIES *These elegant cookies, found in nearly every pastry shop in Paris, have a crisp exterior and a slightly chewy center.*

1¼ cups confectioners' sugar

1½ cups (4 ounces) sliced almonds, finely ground, or almond flour

All-purpose flour, for dipping

3 large egg whites

Pinch of salt

¼ cup granulated sugar

¼ teaspoon pure vanilla extract

½ recipe Swiss Meringue Buttercream (page 386; increase vanilla to 2½ teaspoons)

Preheat the oven to 300°F. Sift confectioners' sugar into a bowl. Whisk in ground almonds; set aside. Line two baking sheets with parchment paper or nonstick baking mats (such as Silpats), and mark circles using a 1½-inch cookie cutter dipped in flour.

In the bowl of an electric mixer fitted with the whisk attachment, beat egg whites on medium speed until foamy; add salt. Gradually add granulated sugar, 1 teaspoon at a time, until the whites reach medium-soft peaks. Transfer to a large bowl.

Sprinkle half of the sugar-almond mixture over the egg-white mixture. Using a large rubber spatula, fold until just incorporated. Add ¼ teaspoon vanilla and remaining sugar-almond mixture, folding until just incorporated. Firmly tap the bottom of the bowl on a counter or work surface to eliminate any air pockets.

Transfer mixture to a large pastry bag fitted with a ½-inch plain tip (such as an Ateco #806). Pipe mixture into marked circles on prepared baking sheet.

Bake, rotating sheets halfway through, until macaroons feel slightly firm to the touch and can be gently lifted off the parchment (the bottoms will be dry), 20 to 25 minutes. Let cool on the baking sheets for 5 minutes, then transfer parchment and macaroons to a wire rack to cool completely. Using a small offset spatula, carefully remove macaroons from parchment. Spread 2 teaspoons buttercream on the flat sides of half the macaroons; sandwich with the other halves, keeping flat sides down. Refrigerate until firm, about 20 minutes, before serving. Filled cookies can be kept in an airtight container in the refrigerator for up to 2 days.

STRAWBERRY MACAROONS VARIATION Follow instructions for French Almond Macaroons, adding 4 drops of red food coloring to the egg whites just before you add the sugar-almond mixture (batter will be pink). For the filling, do not increase vanilla, and fold ⅓ cup strained strawberry preserves (3½ ounces) into Swiss Meringue Buttercream after butter has been incorporated. Proceed with the recipe.

CHOCOLATE MACAROONS VARIATION Follow instructions for French Almond Macaroons, sifting 2 tablespoons Dutch-process cocoa powder with the confectioners' sugar. For the filling, place 5 ounces finely chopped semisweet chocolate in a bowl. In a small saucepan, heat ½ cup heavy cream until it just starts to simmer; pour over chocolate. Let sit for 1 minute; stir until melted. Let ganache stand at room temperature until thick enough to spread. Proceed with the recipe.

chapter three

CAKES

recipes

A

Whether for a birthday, anniversary, or other joyful occasion, you've probably had a cake baked just for you—and you no doubt remember how special it made you feel.

LL KINDS OF CAKES—especially those topped with swirls of frosting, piped decorations, and flickering candles—are used to mark celebrations. No wonder. Whether it's a regal Mocha-Pistachio Wedding Cake or a small fluted Cannelé, a cake can be as striking as sculpture. And just as a sculptor uses scrapers and rasps for detail work, a baker has pastry tips, brushes, and offset spatulas to add flourishes and dimension: piped curlicues of royal icing decorate Petits Fours; thin chocolate leaves adorn Devil's Food Cake; swoops of frosting blanket Coconut Cake.

Then there is the cake itself, a creative interplay of textures and flavors. With the nine-layer Dobos Torte, a single bite holds soft cake, creamy chocolate frosting, and crunchy caramel. For Martha's Birthday Cake, a dome-shaped dessert is filled with alternate layers of apricot jam and almond buttercream before being covered with peaks of meringue. Even a simple cake is irresistible. New York–Style Cheesecake, say, is pleasingly no-nonsense—just a cookie-dough crust and a cool, creamy filling.

Cakes, though impressive, are not difficult to make. The key is to take your time and mind the details: Cream butter and sugar until fluffy; spread batter evenly in the pan; bake until a cake tester comes out clean; beat buttercream until it's smooth and spreadable. These steps and others will eventually seem intuitive. But no matter how familiar the process becomes, a homemade cake will always be something to celebrate.

Always **use the pan size specified** in the recipe. A pan with a different diameter or depth won't be appropriate for the amount of batter you've made. Some cakes—angel food, for example—require a specialized pan in order to bake properly.

When **greasing cake pans,** use softened butter instead of melted (the latter actually makes cakes more likely to stick). Use a pastry brush to apply the butter, and coat the pan's interior completely.

Prepare cake pans after you preheat the oven but before you start to make the batter. This way, the batter can go immediately into the pan, and the pan can go directly into the oven.

Take time to cream butter and sugar. This initial step in many cake recipes is an important one because it aerates the batter and gives the cake volume.

Adding eggs one at a time and beating after each addition adds volume to a cake batter. Don't rush this step by putting all the eggs in at once.

Remember to occasionally **scrape down the sides of the bowl** when mixing.

When adding dry and wet ingredients to most batters, do so in **alternating additions,** beginning and ending with the dry ingredients. Adding the flour or milk all at once will deflate the batter.

Once all of the dry ingredients have been added, be careful **not to overmix the batter.** A good rule of thumb is to stop the mixer about 30 seconds after the last bit of flour has been incorporated.

Fold beaten egg whites into a batter carefully. This will prevent the delicate whites from deflating and ensure that the cake rises properly. First lighten the batter by folding in a small amount of the beaten whites. Then fold in the remainder of the whites, stopping as soon as you no longer see traces of them. Use a long-handled rubber spatula for the job, and fold using large strokes—sweeping down, then across the bottom, then back up and over.

Bring **cheesecake ingredients to room temperature** before working with them. This will ensure that the batter is smooth, with no lumps of cream cheese. If you do find lumps, strain the cheesecake batter before pouring it into the prepared pan.

For even baking, always **rotate cake pans** in the oven halfway through the baking time.

After removing a cake from the oven, let it rest in the pan for about 15 minutes. This way, it will be cool enough to handle and **less likely to crack** when unmolded. Then transfer the cake to a wire rack to cool completely: Invert the cake onto the rack, and reinvert so it cools top side up.

A cake is easier to trim and split when it's cold. Before cutting and frosting a cooled cake, wrap it tightly in plastic and refrigerate until chilled.

1 Madeleine pan

The small French cakes baked in these pans are now common in the United States, and they are widely available. Look for 12-mold pans with deep shell imprints; the deeper the grooves in the molds, the more pronounced the design will look on the cakes.

2 Tube pan

For angel food cakes, a straight-sided tube pan is essential. The pan is often constructed of two pieces: an outer ring, and a piece made up of the bottom and the center tube. The pan's construction allows it to distribute heat from the inside out and the outside in, evenly baking the feathery-light batter and preventing it from collapsing. In some pans, the central tube is higher than the sides; other pans have legs. Both of these designs allow you to invert the delicate cake to cool without compressing it.

3 Graduated cake pans

For layer cakes, the most often used pans are 8 or 9 inches in diameter and 2 inches deep. (There are a handful of cakes in this chapter, however, that call for other dimensions.) If you bake frequently, it's worth buying a set of graduated cake pans, preferably light-colored metal and straight-sided.

4 Cannelé mold

This small fluted pan is used to make cannelés, mini French cakes with crenulated sides. The molds are not especially common in the United States, but they can be found at specialty baking shops. Season copper cannelé molds by rubbing the insides with solid vegetable shortening, and then heating them in a 300-degree oven for 1 hour. Never wash copper molds with soap and water; instead, wipe them out with a damp cloth after each use.

5 Tartlet pans

These miniature pans are available in a range of shapes at cooking-supply stores. Buy them by the dozen and you'll have a good number of pans to work with when making multiples. To bake Financiers (small brown-butter cakes; see page 188), we used a barquette mold (top) instead of the traditional choice, a minirectangle pan (bottom).

6 Springform pan

This pan has two parts: a bottom piece and an outer ring with a buckle. The ring springs open when unhinged, a feature that lets you unmold a cake without inverting it or disturbing the sides. Springform pans are often used for cheesecakes.

7 Tart ring

This bottomless ring is popular with French bakers. The ring is positioned on a lined baking sheet, and then batter is poured into it. A cake that is baked in a bottomless tart ring does not have to be inverted or unmolded; the ring is simply lifted away.

1 Pastry bag
Pastry bags are essential for decorating cakes, but they also serve other functions. Use them to neatly pipe batter for individual cakes (such as Madeleines) into molds. Small jobs can be achieved with a paper cornet, or even a plastic bag with a corner snipped off. But for a wide variety of tasks, nothing beats a set of plastic-coated, easy-to-clean pastry bags.

2 Plastic coupler
Some cake recipes call for frosting to be applied with different decorative tips. Without a coupler, switching pastry tips is a challenge (you either have to reach for a new pastry bag or empty the frosting from the pastry bag you're using). A coupler makes the job easy: Before filling a pastry bag with frosting, drop the base (the larger piece) into the bag. Fit the pastry tip over the base, and secure with the coupler ring. To change tips, remove the ring.

3 Pastry tips
Consider purchasing a starter set of basic pastry tips, available at baking-supply stores and online retailers. As you become a more experienced decorator, you can add specialty tips to the collection.

4 Cardboard round
A set of rounds in graduated sizes is a wise purchase. Use them to support cakes as they are being frosted, to transport cakes from one surface to another, and to carefully slide one layer on top of another. Look for rounds at specialty baking-supply stores.

5 Parchment round
Line the bottoms of cake pans with rounds before baking. To do this, trace the circumference of the pan on parchment, then cut out the round. Precut rounds are available at baking-supply stores.

6 Decorating turntable
Similar in construction to a lazy Susan, a cake turntable spins on its stand, providing convenient access to all sides. This makes it much easier to do cake-decorating work: frosting sides evenly; running a decorating comb around layers; and piping flourishes around a cake's edge. If you decorate cakes frequently, a turntable is worth the expense.

7 Toothpicks
Insert a toothpick into the center of a cake to judge doneness. The sticks can also be used as markers on cakes that need to be split into layers or as minitools for working with marzipan.

8 Paper liners
Use paper cup liners when you bake cupcakes and you won't need to grease or flour the pan.

9 Offset metal spatulas
These tools have endless uses in the kitchen, but they are crucial for cake decorating. The thin blade gives you control over the frosting—how much is applied and how evenly or decoratively it goes on. The spatulas can also smooth out cake batter in the pan before it's baked. Depending upon the task and the size of the cake, you might prefer a long spatula or a short one, so it's a good idea to have both.

10 Candy thermometer
Use a thermometer to gauge the temperature of egg-based frostings, which should reach 160 degrees.

11 Serrated knife
A long serrated knife is the best tool for trimming and splitting cake layers without compressing them. Look for a blade that's at least 10 inches long.

TESTING FOR DONENESS A wooden skewer or toothpick is inserted into the center of a cake layer; it should come out clean. The cake should spring back when lightly touched and be just pulling away from the sides of the pan.

SECURING A CAKE A sprinkling of sugar and a dab of frosting will secure a cake on a turntable or cake stand. Place the dab in the center, and then place the cake on top. Refrigerate 10 minutes before proceeding.

TRIMMING LAYERS A long serrated knife is used to trim a cake, giving it a level top. Hold the cake steady with one hand, and insert the knife horizontally just below the dome. Using a sawing motion, cut all the way through.

CREATING LAYERS Toothpicks are inserted at intervals around the cake to mark two equal halves. Afterward, a long serrated knife is positioned just above the toothpicks, and the cake is cut into two uniform layers.

FILLING THE CAKE After it has been trimmed and halved, the cake is filled with frosting. The stand is covered with parchment to keep it clean. Place frosting in the middle of the cake layer, and spread evenly with an offset spatula.

MAKING A CRUMB COAT Stacked layers are covered by a thin, initial coat of frosting to seal in stray crumbs. Frosting on the sides can be smoothed with a bench scraper. Chill cake for 30 minutes before applying the next coat.

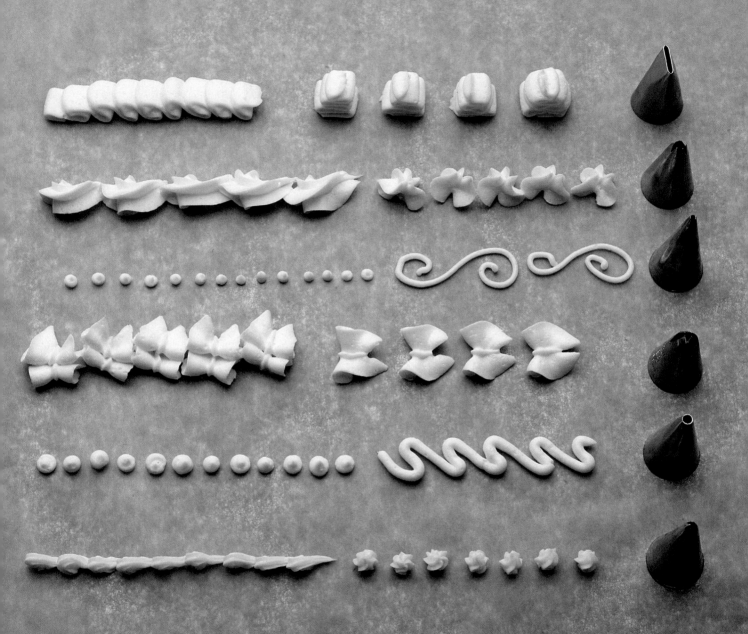

PASTRY TIPS Decorating tips come in a wide range of shapes and sizes. Having a variety of tips on hand will allow you to decorate cakes to suit any style or occasion. Ateco is a widely available brand. Some of its most useful tips include (from top): a standard tip (#44) used to make ruffle borders or straight, flat lines; an open star tip (#75), for piping shell borders or individual stars; a small plain round tip (#4), for making dots and beaded borders, or for writing names and messages; a leaf tip (#69), for piping leaves; a medium plain round tip (#7), for slightly larger dots, lines, and squiggles than the #4; and a small open star tip (#15), for miniature stars or shell borders.

layer cakes and cupcakes

YELLOW BUTTER CAKE WITH CHOCOLATE FROSTING

MAKES ONE 9-INCH LAYER CAKE *This is the kind of classic, all-American layer cake that birthday memories are made of. It's guaranteed to please a crowd.*

2 sticks (1 cup) unsalted butter, room temperature, plus more for pans

1½ cups all-purpose flour, plus more for pans

1½ cups cake flour (not self-rising)

1 tablespoon baking powder

½ teaspoon salt

1¾ cups sugar

4 large eggs

2 teaspoons pure vanilla extract

1¼ cups milk

Dark Chocolate Frosting (page 388)

Preheat the oven to 350°F. Butter two 9-by-2-inch round cake pans; line the bottoms with parchment paper. Butter parchment, and dust with flour, tapping out excess; set aside. Into a medium bowl, sift together flours, baking powder, and salt; set aside.

In the bowl of an electric mixer fitted with the paddle attachment, beat the butter and sugar until light and fluffy, 3 to 4 minutes, scraping down the sides of the bowl as needed. Beat in eggs, one at a time, then beat in vanilla. With the mixer on low speed, add the flour mixture in three parts, alternating with the milk and beginning and ending with the flour; beat until combined after each addition.

Divide the batter between the prepared pans, and smooth with an offset spatula. Bake, rotating the pans halfway through, until cakes are golden brown and a cake tester inserted in the centers comes out clean, 30 to 35 minutes. Transfer pans to a wire rack to cool 20 minutes. Invert cakes onto the rack; peel off the parchment. Reinvert cakes and let them cool completely, top sides up.

Using a serrated knife, trim the tops of the cakes to make level. Place one layer on a cake plate, and spread top with ¾ cup Dark Chocolate Frosting. Place the other cake layer on top. Spread the entire cake with remaining frosting, swirling to coat in a decorative fashion. Cake can be kept in the refrigerator, covered with a cake dome, for up to 3 days. Let cake sit at room temperature for 20 minutes before serving.

CUPCAKE VARIATION Line two standard 12-cup muffin pans with paper liners; set aside. Follow instructions for Yellow Butter Cake, dividing the batter evenly among the prepared cups so that each is about two-thirds full. Bake, rotating pans halfway through, until cupcakes are golden brown and a cake tester inserted in the center of a cupcake comes out clean, about 20 minutes. Transfer pans to a wire rack to cool. Invert cupcakes onto the rack; reinvert and let cool completely, top sides up. Spread about ¼ cup frosting on top of each cupcake. They can be kept in an airtight container at room temperature for up to 3 days. Makes 2 dozen.

COCONUT CAKE

MAKES ONE 9-INCH SQUARE LAYER CAKE *Martha loves the combination of fluffy white frosting and fresh coconut curls that adorn this cake. You can also top the cake with more sweetened or unsweetened coconut, toasted or not. If you don't have square cake pans, use 9-inch round ones; the baking time will be the same.*

- 3 sticks (1½ cups) unsalted butter, room temperature, plus more for pans
- 3½ cups all-purpose flour, plus more for pans
- 1 tablespoon plus 1 teaspoon baking powder
- 1 teaspoon salt
- 1 cup packed sweetened, shredded coconut
- 2⅔ cups sugar
- 4 large whole eggs, plus 4 large egg whites
- 1 tablespoon pure vanilla extract
- 1½ cups unsweetened coconut milk
- Seven-Minute Frosting (page 387)
- Coconut Curls, for garnish (page 395)

Preheat the oven to 350°F. Butter two 9-by-9-by-2-inch cake pans; line the bottoms with parchment paper. Butter parchment, and dust with flour, tapping out excess; set aside. Into a large bowl, sift together the flour, baking powder, and salt. Pulse shredded coconut in a food processor until finely chopped. Stir chopped coconut into the flour mixture until combined; set aside.

In the bowl of an electric mixer fitted with the paddle attachment, beat the butter and sugar until light and fluffy, about 4 minutes, scraping down the sides of the bowl as needed. Add the whole eggs, egg whites, and vanilla; beat until fully incorporated. With the mixer on low speed, add the flour mixture in two parts, alternating with the coconut milk and beginning and ending with the flour; beat until combined after each addition.

Divide batter between prepared pans, and smooth with an offset spatula. Bake, rotating pans halfway through, until cakes are golden brown and a cake tester inserted in the centers comes out clean, about 55 minutes. Transfer pans to a wire rack to cool 30 minutes. Invert cakes onto the rack; peel off the parchment. Reinvert cakes and let them cool completely, top sides up.

Using a serrated knife, trim the tops of the cake layers to make level. Place one layer on a cake plate, and spread top with 1½ cups Seven-Minute Frosting. Place other cake layer on top, cut side down. Using an offset spatula, spread remaining frosting over entire cake, swirling to cover in a decorative fashion. Sprinkle entire cake with Coconut Curls, bending and curling as desired. Cake can be kept in the refrigerator, covered with a cake dome, for up to 3 days.

LEMON CURD CAKE

MAKES ONE 9-INCH LAYER CAKE *The combination of cake flour and all-purpose flour produces a very tender crumb. You will need a paper cornet to pipe the dots and lines of lemon curd that top the buttercream frosting. Fully decorated, the cake looks fresh and whimsical—a perfect choice for a birthday party, baby shower, or other celebration.*

- 2 sticks (1 cup) unsalted butter, room temperature, plus more for pans
- 1½ cups all-purpose flour, plus more for pans
- 1½ cups cake flour (not self-rising)
- 1 tablespoon baking powder
- ½ teaspoon salt
- 1 cup sour cream or crème fraîche

- Finely grated zest of 2 lemons (about 2 tablespoons)
- 2 tablespoons freshly squeezed lemon juice (about ½ lemon)
- 2 cups sugar
- 4 large eggs
- 2 recipes Lemon Curd (page 390), ¾ cup reserved for piping
- Lemon Swiss Meringue Buttercream (page 386)

Preheat the oven to 350°F. Butter two 9-by-2-inch round cake pans; line the bottoms with parchment paper. Butter parchment, and dust with flour, tapping out excess; set aside. Into a medium bowl, sift together the flours, baking powder, and salt; set aside. In a small bowl, combine sour cream with lemon zest and juice; set aside.

In the bowl of an electric mixer fitted with the paddle attachment, beat the butter on medium-high speed until fluffy, about 1 minute. Add sugar, and continue beating until light and fluffy, 4 to 5 minutes, scraping down the sides of the bowl as needed. Add eggs, one at a time, beating for 1 minute after each addition.

With the mixer on lowest speed, add the flour mixture in four parts, alternating with the sour cream mixture and beginning and ending with the flour mixture; beat until just combined, being careful not to overmix.

Divide batter between prepared pans, and smooth with an offset spatula. Bake, rotating pans halfway through, until cakes are golden and pull away from sides of pan, and a cake tester inserted in the centers comes out clean, 30 to 35 minutes. Transfer pans to a wire rack to cool 20 minutes. Run a knife or thin metal spatula around edges of the pans. Invert cakes onto the rack; peel off the parchment. Reinvert cakes and let them cool completely, top sides up.

Using a serrated knife, trim tops of the cakes to make level. Slice each layer in half horizontally into two layers. Place one of the bottom layers on a cake plate, and spread ½ cup Lemon Curd over the top. Repeat with remaining cake layers and curd, leaving final cake layer uncoated. Spread a thin layer of Lemon Swiss Meringue Buttercream over the entire cake to seal in crumbs; refrigerate until well chilled, about 30 minutes.

Using an offset spatula, spread entire cake with remaining buttercream. Refrigerate 30 minutes before decorating with Lemon Curd: Using a paper cornet filled with curd, pipe dots of varying sizes on top of the cake. Starting at the bottom, pipe vertical lines of varying lengths up the side of the cake. Cake can be kept in the refrigerator, covered with a cake dome, for up to 3 days.

OLD-FASHIONED BERRY LAYER CAKE

MAKES ONE 9-INCH LAYER CAKE *You can assemble this showstopping dessert up to eight hours ahead of serving; leave off the last layer of cream and fruit, and refrigerate along with the partially assembled cake. Just before serving, top the cake with the remaining cream and berries, and garnish with the mint leaves. If you can't find beautiful small strawberries, halve or quarter larger ones.*

Unsalted butter, for pans

1 cup all-purpose flour

1/4 cup cornstarch

6 large whole eggs, plus 4 large egg yolks, room temperature

1 cup granulated sugar

1/4 teaspoon salt

2 teaspoons pure vanilla extract

3/4 cup vegetable oil

1 quart (4 cups) heavy cream

1/2 cup confectioners' sugar

1 vanilla bean, split lengthwise (optional)

1 pint small strawberries, hulled

1/2 pint blackberries

1/2 pint red raspberries

1/2 pint golden raspberries

1/2 pint blueberries

Fresh mint leaves, for garnish (optional)

Preheat the oven to 350°F. Butter two 9-by-2-inch round cake pans; set aside. Into a large bowl, sift together flour and cornstarch; set aside.

In the bowl of an electric mixer fitted with the whisk attachment, combine the whole eggs, egg yolks, granulated sugar, salt, and 1 teaspoon vanilla extract. Beat on high speed until thick and pale (it should hold a ribbon-like trail on the surface when the whisk is raised), about 5 minutes; scrape down the sides of the bowl as needed.

Add flour mixture to egg mixture. With mixer on low speed, beat until just combined. Add oil in a steady stream, mixing until just combined. Remove bowl from mixer. Using the whisk, fold mixture several times.

Divide batter between pans, and smooth with an offset spatula. Bake, rotating pans halfway through, until the cakes are springy to the touch and a cake tester inserted in the centers comes out clean, about 30 minutes.

Immediately invert cakes onto a wire rack. Then reinvert cakes, and let them cool completely, top sides up.

In the bowl of an electric mixer fitted with the whisk attachment, combine cream, confectioners' sugar, and remaining teaspoon vanilla extract. Scrape in vanilla seeds, if using. Starting on low speed and gradually increasing to medium-high, whip until stiff peaks form, about 2 minutes.

Using a serrated knife, trim the tops of the cakes to make level. Slice each cake in half horizontally into two layers. Place one of the bottom layers on a serving plate. Spread a quarter of the whipped cream over the layer; arrange a quarter of the mixed berries on top. Repeat with remaining cake layers, cream, and berries; garnish top with mint leaves, if using. Serve immediately; slice with a serrated knife.

BANANA-CARAMEL CAKE

MAKES ONE 9-INCH LAYER CAKE *Bananas vary greatly in size. The six bananas called for in this recipe should weigh a total of about four pounds. Once cut, bananas will discolor rapidly, so it's best to slice them just before using.*

1½ sticks (¾ cup) plus 3 tablespoons unsalted butter, room temperature, plus more for pans

2¾ cups all-purpose flour, plus more for pans

1½ teaspoons baking powder

1 teaspoon baking soda

½ teaspoon salt

3 very ripe bananas, mashed, plus 3 ripe bananas, sliced lengthwise, for filling

¼ cup sour cream or crème fraîche

1 teaspoon pure vanilla extract

1⅔ cups plus ¼ cup sugar

4 large eggs

Mascarpone Frosting (recipe follows)

Caramel Sauce (recipe follows)

Preheat the oven to 350°F. Butter two 9-by-2-inch round cake pans; line bottoms with parchment. Butter parchment and dust with flour, tapping out excess; set aside. Into a medium bowl, sift together flour, baking powder, baking soda, and salt. In a small bowl, stir together mashed bananas, sour cream, and vanilla; set aside.

In the bowl of an electric mixer fitted with the paddle attachment, beat 1½ sticks butter and 1⅔ cups sugar on medium-high speed until light and fluffy, 3 to 4 minutes, scraping down the sides of the bowl as needed. Add the eggs, one at a time, beating well after each addition. With mixer on low speed, add the flour mixture in two parts, beating until combined after each, 2 to 3 minutes. Using a rubber spatula, fold in the reserved banana mixture, being careful not to overmix.

Divide the batter between the prepared pans. Bake, rotating the pans halfway through, until cakes are golden brown and a cake tester inserted in the centers comes out clean, 30 to 35 minutes. Transfer pans to a wire rack to cool 20 minutes. Invert cakes onto the rack; peel off the parchment. Reinvert cakes, and let them cool completely, top sides up.

Sprinkle remaining ¼ cup sugar into a large skillet; cook over high heat, shaking the pan occasionally, until sugar is caramelized. Remove from heat; stir in remaining 3 tablespoons butter until melted. Return pan to medium heat. Add the sliced bananas; cook until slices start to brown, 1 to 2 minutes. Gently turn the bananas, and cook over medium-high heat until browned, about 2 minutes more.

Using a serrated knife, trim tops of layers to make level. Place one layer on a cake plate; arrange caramelized banana slices on top. Place remaining layer on top. Using a large offset spatula, spread Mascarpone Frosting over entire cake, swirling to completely cover. Drizzle Caramel Sauce over the top of the cake, or serve some alongside each slice. Serve immediately, or refrigerate, covered with a cake dome, for up to 3 days.

BANANA-CARAMEL CAKE HOW-TO 1. Long slices of banana are added to a skillet of caramel, then browned on both sides. **2.** The caramelized bananas are arranged on the bottom layer of banana cake, then covered with the top layer of cake.

MASCARPONE FROSTING
MAKES ENOUGH FOR ONE 9-INCH LAYER CAKE (ABOUT 4 CUPS)

1 pound mascarpone cheese

1¼ cups heavy cream

½ cup confectioners' sugar

In the bowl of an electric mixer fitted with the paddle attachment, beat the mascarpone, cream, and confectioners' sugar until medium-soft peaks form, 1 to 2 minutes. Be careful not to overbeat. Use immediately.

CARAMEL SAUCE
MAKES ENOUGH FOR ONE 9-INCH LAYER CAKE

½ cup sugar

½ cup heavy cream

Prepare an ice bath; set aside. Cook sugar in a medium saucepan over medium-high heat until it starts to melt around edges; then shake pan to melt remaining sugar. Continue to cook, stirring with a wooden spoon, until golden amber, about 3 minutes. Remove from heat. Stirring constantly, add cream in a slow, steady stream (it will spatter). If necessary, return pan to heat for a few seconds, stirring until mixture is smooth. Place caramel in a bowl in the ice bath; let stand until cold, stirring frequently.

DEVIL'S FOOD CAKE WITH MINT-CHOCOLATE GANACHE

MAKES ONE 9-INCH LAYER CAKE *Half of the ganache is used for the glaze, which should be cool to the touch but pourable. If necessary, warm it over a pan of simmering water.*

3 sticks (1½ cups) unsalted butter, room temperature, plus more for pans

¾ cup Dutch-process cocoa powder, sifted, plus more for pans

¾ cup hot water

¾ cup sour cream

3 cups cake flour (not self-rising), sifted

1 teaspoon baking soda

½ teaspoon salt

2¼ cups sugar

4 large eggs

1 tablespoon pure vanilla extract

Mint-Chocolate Ganache (page 388)

Chocolate Mint Leaves (recipe follows)

DEVIL'S FOOD CAKE HOW-TO When pans are prepared for baking chocolate cakes, they are dusted with cocoa powder rather than flour, which may leave white streaks on the finished dark cake.

Preheat the oven to 350°F. Butter two 9-by-2-inch round cake pans; line bottoms with parchment paper. Butter parchment; dust with cocoa powder, tapping out excess. In a medium bowl, whisk cocoa with hot water until smooth. Whisk in sour cream; let cool. Into a medium bowl, sift together flour, baking soda, and salt; set aside.

In the bowl of an electric mixer fitted with the paddle attachment, beat butter and sugar on medium speed until light and fluffy, 3 to 4 minutes. Add eggs, one at a time, beating to combine after each; scrape down sides of bowl as needed. Beat in vanilla. With mixer on low speed, add flour mixture in two parts, alternating with the cocoa mixture and beginning and ending with the flour; beat until combined.

Divide batter between prepared pans; smooth with an offset spatula. Bake until a cake tester inserted in centers comes out clean, 45 to 50 minutes. Transfer pans to a wire rack to cool 15 minutes. Invert cakes onto rack; peel off parchment. Reinvert cakes; let cool completely, top sides up. Transfer half of Mint-Chocolate Ganache (3½ cups) to clean bowl of an electric mixer; set aside remaining. Let cool completely, stirring frequently, about 40 minutes. Attach bowl to mixer fitted with whisk attachment. Beat on medium-high speed until ganache holds soft peaks, 5 to 7 minutes.

Using a serrated knife, trim tops of cake layers to make level. Transfer one of the layers to a cake turntable or platter, and spread top with 1½ cups whipped ganache. Top with remaining layer, cut side down, and spread remaining whipped ganache in a thin layer over entire cake, covering completely. Refrigerate until set, about 30 minutes.

Transfer cake to a wire rack set over a rimmed baking sheet. Pour the reserved ganache over the top, letting it run down the sides. If necessary, use a large offset spatula to spread from the center toward the edges, so that the cake is evenly and completely covered. Refrigerate until the ganache has just begun to set, about 30 minutes. Transfer cake to a serving plate, and garnish with Chocolate Mint Leaves. Serve immediately, or refrigerate, covered with a cake dome, for up to 2 days.

CHOCOLATE MINT LEAVES

MAKES ENOUGH FOR ONE 9-INCH LAYER CAKE *The heat from your hands will melt the chocolate, so use tweezers to hold the chocolate leaf as you peel back the mint with your fingers.*

18 fresh mint leaves, ¼ inch of each stem intact	2 ounces semisweet chocolate, melted and cooled

Using a small pastry brush, coat underside of each leaf with a thick layer of chocolate. (If chocolate drips onto the top of the leaf, gently wipe it away with your finger.)

Drape the leaves, chocolate sides up, over the handle of a wooden spoon set on a parchment-lined baking sheet. Refrigerate until set, about 10 minutes.

Gently grasp the chocolate layer of each leaf with kitchen tweezers. Holding the stem, peel off mint leaf. Chocolate leaves can be kept in an airtight container in the refrigerator for up to 2 days.

CHOCOLATE MINT LEAVES HOW-TO 1. Fresh mint leaves are coated on one side with melted semisweet chocolate. While still wet, the leaves are draped over a spoon handle to curve slightly. **2.** After being chilled briefly, the chocolate is separated from the leaf with a pair of kitchen tweezers.

APPLE-SPICE LAYER CAKE

MAKES ONE 6-INCH LAYER CAKE *The applesauce in this cake makes it exceptionally moist. Although homemade applesauce is best, you could also substitute an all-natural store-bought variety. If you would prefer a larger cake, prepare the batter as directed and bake in two nine-inch pans for forty to forty-five minutes.*

1¾ cups plus ⅓ cup sugar

1½ pounds (about 4) McIntosh apples, peeled, cored, and cut into chunks

2 teaspoons fresh lemon juice

2 sticks (1 cup) unsalted butter, room temperature, plus more for pans

3¼ cups all-purpose flour, plus more for pans

2 teaspoons baking powder

½ teaspoon baking soda

½ teaspoon salt

½ teaspoon ground cinnamon

¼ teaspoon ground allspice

¼ teaspoon ground ginger

⅛ teaspoon freshly grated nutmeg

½ cup milk

1 teaspoon pure vanilla extract

¼ cup honey

4 large eggs

Creamy Goat Cheese Frosting (recipe follows)

Caramelized Lady Apples, for garnish (recipe follows; optional)

In a medium saucepan, spread ⅓ cup sugar in an even layer. Cook over medium-high heat, without stirring, until sugar begins to turn golden and melt around the edges, 3 to 4 minutes. Using a wooden spoon, slowly stir until melted and mixture is a translucent golden amber. Add apple chunks and lemon juice, and stir to coat apple pieces with caramel. Cover, and cook over low heat until apples fall apart, 6 to 8 minutes. Continue cooking, stirring frequently, until mixture reaches the consistency of applesauce and generously coats the back of the spoon, about 5 minutes more. (You should have about 1½ cups applesauce.) Remove from heat; let cool completely.

Preheat the oven to 350°F. Butter three 6-by-2-inch round cake pans; line the bottoms with parchment paper. Butter parchment, and dust with flour, tapping out excess; set aside. Into a medium bowl, sift together flour, baking powder, baking soda, salt, cinnamon, allspice, ginger, and nutmeg; set aside. In a small bowl, combine milk and vanilla; set aside.

In the bowl of an electric mixer fitted with the paddle attachment, beat the butter, remaining 1¾ cups sugar, and honey on medium-high speed until light and fluffy, 3 to 4 minutes, scraping down the sides of the bowl as needed. Add eggs, one at a time, beating for 1 minute after each addition, until smooth.

With mixer on low speed, add flour mixture in three parts, alternating with the milk mixture and beginning and ending with flour; beat until just combined after each, being careful not to overmix. Add cooled applesauce; mix to combine, about 1 minute.

Divide the batter among prepared pans. Bake, rotating pans halfway through, until cakes pull away from the sides of the pans and a cake tester inserted in the centers comes out clean, 35 to 40 minutes. Transfer pans to a wire rack to cool 20 minutes. Run a knife or offset spatula around the edges. Invert cakes onto the rack; peel off the parchment. Reinvert cakes and let them cool completely, top sides up.

Using a serrated knife, trim tops of cakes to make level. Place one layer on a cake plate. Spread top with a third of the Creamy Goat Cheese Frosting. Repeat with remaining cake layers and frosting. Refrigerate cake, at least 30 minutes or up to 3 days, covered with a cake dome. Before serving, garnish with Caramelized Lady Apples.

CREAMY GOAT CHEESE FROSTING

MAKES ENOUGH FOR ONE 6-INCH LAYER CAKE *If you would rather make this frosting with only cream cheese, replace the goat cheese with an equal amount of whipped cream cheese, for a total of eighteen ounces.*

- 12 ounces fresh goat cheese, room temperature
- 6 ounces whipped cream cheese, room temperature
- ½ cup confectioners' sugar

In the bowl of an electric mixer fitted with the paddle attachment, beat the goat cheese and cream cheese on medium-high speed until fluffy, about 4 minutes, scraping down the sides of the bowl as needed. Add sugar, and beat until well-combined and fluffy, about 4 minutes. The frosting can be refrigerated, covered, up to 3 days; bring to room temperature, and beat about 3 minutes before using.

CARAMELIZED LADY APPLES

MAKES ENOUGH FOR ONE 6-INCH LAYER CAKE

- 3 tablespoons sugar
- 1 teaspoon unsalted butter
- 2 lady apples, halved

In a small saucepan, cook the sugar over medium-high heat, stirring often with a wooden spoon, until sugar is melted and turns golden amber, about 3 minutes. Stir in the butter. Place apples in the pan, cut sides down. Cook until the apples are coated with the caramel and have softened, about 2 minutes. Transfer them to a parchment-lined baking sheet to cool completely.

MAPLE-WALNUT CUPCAKES

MAKES 2 DOZEN *Maple Buttercream is the perfect complement to these walnut cupcakes, but you can also frost them with Brown Sugar Buttercream (page 386).*

2¾ cups all-purpose flour, sifted

1 tablespoon baking powder

¼ teaspoon salt

1 teaspoon ground cinnamon

2 sticks (1 cup) unsalted butter, room temperature

1½ cups sugar

3 large eggs

1 teaspoon pure vanilla extract

1 cup milk

1½ cups (5½ ounces) walnuts, chopped medium-fine

Maple Buttercream (recipe follows)

Candied Walnuts (page 394; optional)

Preheat the oven to 350°F. Line two standard 12-cup muffin pans with paper liners. Into a large bowl, sift together flour, baking powder, salt, and cinnamon; set aside.

In the bowl of an electric mixer fitted with the paddle attachment, beat the butter and sugar on medium speed until creamy, about 3 minutes. Add the eggs and vanilla, and beat until combined. With the mixer still on medium speed, add the flour mixture in two parts, alternating with the milk and beginning and ending with the flour. Stir in the walnuts with a wooden spoon.

Divide the batter evenly among the muffin cups, adding about ⅓ cup to each. Bake, rotating pans halfway through, until cupcakes are golden and a cake tester inserted in the center of a cupcake comes out clean, 18 to 20 minutes. Transfer the pans to a wire rack to cool slightly. Invert cupcakes onto the rack; then reinvert and let them cool completely, top sides up. Frost tops with Maple Buttercream and garnish with Candied Walnuts, if using. Cupcakes can be refrigerated in an airtight container for up to 3 days.

MAPLE BUTTERCREAM

MAKES ENOUGH FOR 2 DOZEN CUPCAKES (ABOUT 2 CUPS) *This frosting can be refrigerated in an airtight container for up to three days. Bring to room temperature before using.*

3 large egg yolks

1 cup pure maple syrup, best quality

2 sticks (1 cup) unsalted butter, cold, cut into small pieces

In the bowl of an electric mixer fitted with the whisk attachment, beat the egg yolks on high speed until light and fluffy, about 5 minutes; set aside. In a small saucepan set over medium-high heat, bring the maple syrup to a boil, and cook until it registers 240°F on a candy thermometer, about 15 minutes. Remove from heat.

With the mixer running, slowly pour syrup down the side of the bowl in a slow, steady stream, until completely incorporated, about 1 minute. Continue beating until bowl is just slightly warm to the touch, 4 to 5 minutes. Add butter, one piece at a time, until thoroughly incorporated and the frosting is fluffy, about 4 minutes more.

CARROT-GINGER CUPCAKES

MAKES 2 DOZEN *An abundance of grated carrots makes these cupcakes moist, while granulated sugar, instead of the traditional brown, keeps them light.*

1 cup (3 ounces) pecan halves	1 teaspoon pure vanilla extract
3 cups all-purpose flour, plus more for pans	2 cups sugar
2 teaspoons baking powder	1½ cups vegetable oil
1 teaspoon baking soda	1 tablespoon grated, peeled fresh ginger
1 teaspoon salt	Orange Cream-Cheese Frosting (recipe follows)
¾ teaspoon ground cinnamon	Mini Marzipan Carrots (recipe follows)
1 pound large carrots, peeled, green tops reserved for Mini Marzipan Carrots	
3 large eggs, room temperature	
⅓ cup buttermilk	

Preheat the oven to 350°F. Line two standard 12-cup muffin pans with paper liners. Spread pecans in a single layer on a rimmed baking sheet; toast until fragrant, about 10 minutes. Transfer to a plate; let cool completely. Chop pecans finely, and set aside.

In a medium bowl, whisk together the flour, baking powder, baking soda, salt, and cinnamon; set aside. Using the smallest holes of a box grater, grate carrots. (You will need a total of 2½ cups.) Place grated carrots, eggs, buttermilk, vanilla, sugar, vegetable oil, and ginger in a large bowl; whisk until combined. Using a rubber spatula, fold the flour mixture into the carrot mixture until combined. Fold in the chopped pecans.

Divide batter evenly among the muffin cups. Bake, rotating pans halfway through, until a cake tester inserted in the center of a cupcake comes out clean, 20 to 25 minutes. Transfer pans to a wire rack. Invert cupcakes onto the rack; then reinvert and let them cool completely, top sides up. Spread tops with Orange Cream-Cheese Frosting, swirling to coat, and garnish with Mini Marzipan Carrots. Cupcakes can be kept in an airtight container in the refrigerator for up to 3 days.

CARROT-GINGER LAYER CAKE VARIATION Butter two 8-by-2-inch round cake pans; line the bottoms with parchment paper. Butter parchment, and dust with flour, tapping out excess; set aside. Follow instructions for Carrot-Ginger Cupcakes, dividing batter between the prepared pans. Bake until a cake tester inserted in the centers comes out clean, 35 to 40 minutes. Transfer cakes to a wire rack to cool 15 minutes. Run a knife or an offset spatula around the edges. Invert cakes onto the rack; peel off the parchment. Reinvert cakes and let them cool completely, top sides up.

Using a serrated knife, trim tops of cakes to make level. Slice each cake in half horizontally into two layers. Place one of the bottom layers on a cake plate, and spread ¾ cup frosting over the top. Repeat with the remaining layers and more frosting. Spread entire cake with remaining frosting and refrigerate until well-chilled, at least 4 hours or up to 4 days, covered with a cake dome. When ready to serve, place Marzipan Carrots on top and around the edge of the cake.

ORANGE CREAM-CHEESE FROSTING
MAKES ENOUGH FOR 2 DOZEN CUPCAKES OR ONE 8-INCH LAYER CAKE (ABOUT 5½ CUPS)

1½ sticks (¾ cup) unsalted butter, room temperature

3 packages (8 ounces each) cream cheese, room temperature

2 cups confectioners' sugar, sifted

¾ teaspoon finely grated orange zest

1 tablespoon plus 1 teaspoon grated, peeled fresh ginger

Pinch of salt

In the bowl of an electric mixer fitted with the paddle attachment, beat butter on medium-high speed until light and fluffy, about 2 minutes. Add cream cheese, and beat until combined and fluffy, about 2 minutes, scraping down the sides of the bowl as needed. Add the remaining ingredients, and beat 5 minutes. Frosting can be kept at room temperature, covered with plastic wrap, for up to 2 hours.

MINI MARZIPAN CARROTS

MAKES 2 DOZEN *Marzipan comes in plastic-wrapped seven-ounce logs and is available in baking-supply shops and most supermarkets. If you find the marzipan too sticky to shape, dust the work surface with a bit of confectioners' sugar. If you're preparing the Carrot-Ginger Layer Cake, make slightly larger carrots.*

7 ounces marzipan

Orange gel-paste food coloring

5 chocolate wafer cookies, very finely ground

Fresh carrot greens (reserved from Carrot-Ginger Cupcakes) or fresh dill

With a toothpick, add a dab of food coloring to the marzipan and knead with fingers to combine; continue until desired shade is achieved.

Shape mounded ½ teaspoons of marzipan into 24 balls, and place on a clean work surface. Using your hands, roll each piece back and forth to form a 2-inch log. Using your fingers, shape one end of each log into a tapered point to form a carrot shape. (It needn't be perfect; garden carrots have lumps and bumps.) Use the tip of a skewer or toothpick to make a small hole at the top of the carrot. Using a paring knife, make small grooves across the surface of each carrot in a random design. Carrots can be kept at room temperature, in an airtight container, for up to 1 week.

When ready to serve, roll carrots in cookie crumbs, lightly brushing off excess, and insert carrot greens into the holes.

MINI MARZIPAN CARROTS HOW-TO Orange-tinted marzipan balls are rolled into carrot shapes on a work surface, then scored with a knife. The marzipan carrots are then rolled in chocolate cookie crumbs and topped with carrot greens or dill to make them look like they're fresh from the garden.

ONE-BOWL CHOCOLATE CUPCAKES

MAKES 2 DOZEN *This recipe is extremely versatile. We love to use it for cupcakes, but it makes an equally impressive layer or sheet cake; either is a perfect choice for kids' birthday parties, swirled with Swiss Meringue Buttercream. For a more grown-up flavor, try icing the cupcakes with Mocha Buttercream (page 213).*

2½ cups all-purpose flour

1¼ cups Dutch-process cocoa powder

2½ cups sugar

2½ teaspoons baking soda

1¼ teaspoons baking powder

1¼ teaspoons salt

2 large whole eggs,
plus 1 large egg yolk

1¼ cups milk

½ cup plus 2 tablespoons vegetable oil

1¼ teaspoons pure vanilla extract

1¼ cups warm water

Swiss Meringue Buttercream
(page 386)

Chocolate Curls, for garnish
(page 395; optional)

Preheat the oven to 350°F. Line two standard 12-cup muffin pans with paper liners. Into the bowl of an electric mixer, sift together flour, cocoa, sugar, baking soda, baking powder, and salt. Attach bowl to mixer fitted with the paddle attachment; add the eggs and yolk, the milk, oil, vanilla, and warm water. Beat on low speed until smooth and combined, about 3 minutes; scrape down the sides of the bowl as needed.

Divide batter evenly among the muffin cups, filling each about two-thirds full. Bake, rotating pans halfway through, until a cake tester inserted in the center of a cupcake comes out clean, 20 to 25 minutes. Transfer pans to a wire rack to cool slightly. Invert cupcakes onto the rack; then reinvert and let them cool completely, top sides up. Frost cupcakes with Swiss Meringue Buttercream, swirling to cover, and garnish with Chocolate Curls. Cupcakes can be refrigerated in an airtight container for up to 3 days.

LAYER CAKE VARIATION Coat two 8-by-2-inch round cake pans with nonstick cooking spray. Line bottoms with parchment paper; spray parchment. Set aside. **Follow instructions for One-Bowl Chocolate Cupcakes, dividing batter** between the prepared pans. Bake, rotating pans halfway through, until a cake tester inserted in the centers comes out clean, about 45 minutes. Transfer pans to a wire rack to cool 30 minutes. Invert cakes onto the rack; peel off the parchment. Reinvert cakes, and let them cool completely, top sides up.

Using a serrated knife, trim the tops of the cake layers to make level. Place one layer on a cake plate, and spread ⅔ cup buttercream on top. Place other cake layer on top. Spread entire cake with remaining buttercream, swirling to cover completely.

SHEET CAKE VARIATION Butter a 13-by-9-inch pan and dust with cocoa powder, tapping out excess. Follow instructions for One-Bowl Chocolate Cupcakes, transferring batter to the prepared pan. Bake, rotating pan halfway through, until a cake tester inserted in the center comes out clean, 45 to 50 minutes. Frost as desired.

WHITE CUPCAKES WITH STRAWBERRY BUTTERCREAM

MAKES 2 DOZEN *Using only cake flour produces a cupcake that has a pure-white crumb.*

3 cups cake flour (not self-rising)

2 teaspoons baking powder

1 teaspoon salt

3 sticks (1½ cups) unsalted butter, room temperature

2¼ cups sugar

½ teaspoon pure vanilla extract

1 cup milk

8 large egg whites

Strawberry Meringue Buttercream (page 387)

24 small fresh strawberries, washed (hulls intact), for garnish

Preheat the oven to 350°F. Line two standard 12-cup muffin pans with paper liners. Into a medium bowl, sift together the flour, baking powder, and salt; set aside.

In the bowl of an electric mixer fitted with the paddle attachment, beat the butter and 2 cups sugar until light and fluffy, 3 to 4 minutes, scraping down the sides of the bowl as needed. Beat in the vanilla. With mixer on low speed, add flour mixture in three parts, alternating with the milk and beginning and ending with the flour; beat until just combined. Transfer mixture to a large bowl; set aside.

In the clean bowl of an electric mixer fitted with the whisk attachment, beat egg whites on low speed until foamy. With mixer running, gradually add remaining ¼ cup sugar; beat on high speed until stiff, glossy peaks form, about 4 minutes. Do not overbeat. Gently fold a third of the egg-white mixture into the butter-flour mixture until combined. Gently fold in the remaining whites.

Divide batter evenly among the muffin cups, filling each with a heaping ¼ cup batter. Bake, rotating pans halfway through, until the cupcakes are golden brown and a cake tester inserted in the center of a cupcake comes out clean, 20 to 25 minutes. Transfer pans to a wire rack. Invert cupcakes onto the rack; then reinvert and let them cool completely, top sides up. Frost the cupcakes with Strawberry Meringue Buttercream, swirling to cover. Cupcakes can be kept in an airtight container in the refrigerator for up to 3 days. Garnish with strawberries just before serving.

LAYER CAKE VARIATION Butter two 9-by-2-inch round cake pans; line the bottoms with parchment paper. Butter parchment, and dust with flour, tapping out excess; set aside. Follow instructions for White Cupcakes, dividing the batter between prepared pans and smoothing with an offset spatula. Bake, rotating pans halfway through, until cakes are golden brown and a cake tester inserted in centers comes out clean, 30 to 35 minutes. Transfer pans to a wire rack to cool 20 minutes. Invert cakes onto the rack; peel off parchment. Reinvert cakes and let them cool completely, top sides up.

Using a serrated knife, trim tops of cake layers to make level. Place one layer on a plate, and spread with ¾ cup buttercream. Place other cake layer on top, cut side down. Spread the entire cake with remaining frosting, swirling to cover.

SHEET CAKE VARIATION Butter a 13-by-9-inch cake pan, and dust with flour, tapping out excess. Follow instructions for White Cupcakes, transferring batter to the prepared pan. Bake until cake is golden brown and a cake tester inserted in the center comes out clean, about 35 minutes. Frost as desired.

LINZERTORTE

MAKES ONE 9-INCH CAKE *This torte is best eaten the day it is baked, when the crust is still crisp. You will need a nine-inch bottomless tart ring; a springform pan will also work. Instead of making the jam, you can use 1¼ cups store-bought raspberry jam.*

- ½ cup (about 2½ ounces) hazelnuts
- 1 cup (about 5 ounces) blanched almonds
- 1⅓ cups all-purpose flour, plus more for dusting
- ¾ teaspoon baking powder
- ¾ teaspoon ground cinnamon
- ¼ teaspoon salt
- 1½ sticks (¾ cup) unsalted butter, room temperature
- 1 cup granulated sugar
- 1 large egg yolk
- Raspberry Jam (page 393)
- Confectioners' sugar, for dusting (optional)

Preheat the oven to 350°F. Spread the hazelnuts in a single layer on a rimmed baking sheet; toast, stirring occasionally, until skins begin to split, about 15 minutes. Immediately rub hazelnuts vigorously in a clean kitchen towel to remove skins (as much as will come off easily). Let cool.

In a food processor, pulse the hazelnuts and almonds until finely ground. (Be careful not to overprocess; you don't want the mixture to become a paste.) Transfer to a small bowl; set aside. In a medium bowl, whisk together the flour, baking powder, cinnamon, and salt; set aside.

In the bowl of an electric mixer fitted with the paddle attachment, beat the butter and granulated sugar until light and fluffy, about 3 minutes. Add the egg yolk and beat 1 minute to combine. With mixer on low speed, add ground nuts and the flour mixture all at once; beat until just combined.

Divide dough in half. Set a 9-inch bottomless tart ring on a parchment-lined baking sheet. Using your fingers, press one dough half into the ring to form the bottom and continue ¾ inch up the sides of pan. Chill until firm, about 30 minutes. Meanwhile, lightly dust a piece of parchment paper with flour, and roll out the other dough half to a 13-inch round; place on a baking sheet, and chill until firm, about 30 minutes.

Using an offset spatula, spread the Raspberry Jam evenly over the chilled dough in ring; set aside. Using a fluted pastry wheel, cut ¾-inch-wide strips from chilled round of dough. Arrange strips on top of the jam in a lattice pattern. Freeze until firm, about 30 minutes. Meanwhile, preheat the oven to 350°F.

Bake, rotating pan halfway through, until torte is golden brown all over, about 40 minutes. Transfer to a wire rack to cool 20 minutes. Remove ring and cool torte completely. Torte can be kept at room temperature, loosely covered in plastic wrap, for up to 3 days. When ready to serve, dust with confectioners' sugar, if using.

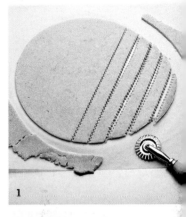

LINZERTORTE HOW-TO
1. A round of linzer dough, richly flavored with ground nuts and a hint of cinnamon, is cut into wide strips with a fluted pastry wheel. **2.** The strips are laid—not woven—in a simple lattice pattern across the traditional raspberry jam filling.

PECAN-APRICOT TORTE

MAKES ONE 9-INCH CAKE *This rustic cake has the flavor and texture of an old-fashioned Eastern European dessert. Use either a nut grinder or food processor to grind pecans.*

Unsalted butter, room temperature, for pan

¾ cup plus 1 tablespoon sifted cake flour (not self-rising), plus more for pan

1½ cups (5½ ounces) pecans

1½ teaspoons baking powder

½ teaspoon ground cinnamon

¼ teaspoon salt

6 large eggs, separated, room temperature

½ cup plus 2 tablespoons granulated sugar

1 teaspoon pure vanilla extract

1½ cups chunky apricot preserves

½ cup (3 ounces) dried apricots

Confectioners' sugar, for dusting

Whipped cream, for serving (optional)

Preheat the oven to 350°F. Butter a 9-inch springform pan, and dust with flour, tapping out excess; set aside. Spread pecans in a single layer on a rimmed baking sheet, and toast until fragrant, 5 to 6 minutes. Transfer to a bowl to cool, then grind into a fine powder. Place ground nuts in a large bowl; add flour, baking powder, cinnamon, and salt, and whisk to combine; set aside.

In the bowl of an electric mixer fitted with the whisk attachment, beat the egg yolks with half of the granulated sugar (¼ cup plus 1 tablespoon) until the mixture is thick and pale and holds a ribbon-like trail on the surface for 1 second when you raise the whisk. Beat in the vanilla, and set aside.

Using a clean bowl and whisk, whip egg whites until they just hold stiff peaks. Add the remaining ¼ cup plus 1 tablespoon granulated sugar; beat until stiff peaks form again.

Stir 1 cup egg-white mixture into egg-yolk mixture. Place a quarter of the remaining egg whites on top, then sprinkle with a quarter of the flour mixture. Fold in quickly. Repeat, adding whites and flour in this way until both have been incorporated.

Pour the batter into the prepared pan, and bake until a cake tester inserted in the center comes out clean, about 35 minutes. Transfer to a wire rack to cool 10 minutes. Remove the sides of the pan, and set cake on the rack to cool completely.

Heat the apricot preserves in a medium saucepan over low heat until warm to the touch. Place the dried apricots in another saucepan and add water to cover; bring to a simmer, and cook until softened, about 3 minutes. Using a slotted spoon, transfer the rehydrated apricots to the warm preserves; stir to combine.

Using a serrated knife, slice cake horizontally into two layers. Place bottom layer on a serving platter; spoon warm preserves and apricots over top, letting some drip down the sides. Then dust top layer with confectioners' sugar, and place on bottom layer. Serve immediately with whipped cream, if desired.

cheesecakes

NEW YORK–STYLE CHEESECAKE

MAKES ONE 10-INCH CAKE *Once chilled, this cake can be covered with plastic wrap and refrigerated for up to three days. In fact, it actually tastes best after being chilled overnight. Let it stand at room temperature for twenty minutes before serving.*

Unsalted butter, room temperature, for pans

1/2 recipe Chocolate Wafer Sandwich Cookie dough (page 108)

3 1/2 pounds (seven 8-ounce packages) cream cheese, room temperature

2 1/4 cups sugar

1/2 cup all-purpose flour

1 cup sour cream, room temperature

1 1/2 teaspoons pure vanilla extract

5 large eggs

Preheat the oven to 350°F. Butter the sides of a 10-inch springform pan. Press the dough into the bottom of the pan, patting it into an even layer. Wrap exterior of pan (including base) in a double layer of foil. Freeze the dough in the pan, about 15 minutes.

Place pan on a baking sheet. Bake until the crust is firm to the touch, 12 to 15 minutes. Transfer pan to a wire rack to cool completely.

In the bowl of an electric mixer fitted with the paddle attachment, beat the cream cheese on medium speed until fluffy, about 3 minutes, scraping down sides as needed. In a large bowl, whisk together sugar and flour. With mixer on low speed, gradually add sugar mixture to cream cheese; mix until smooth. Add sour cream and vanilla; mix until smooth. Add eggs, one at a time, beating until just combined; do not overmix.

Pour cream cheese filling into the prepared pan. Set pan inside a large, shallow roasting pan. Carefully ladle boiling water into roasting pan to reach halfway up sides of springform pan. Bake 45 minutes; reduce oven temperature to 325°F. Continue baking until cake is set but still slightly wobbly in the center, about 30 minutes more. Turn off oven; leave cake in oven with the door slightly ajar, 1 hour. Transfer pan to a wire rack; let cake cool completely. Refrigerate, uncovered, at least 6 hours or overnight. Before unmolding, run a knife around the edge of the cake.

VANILLA COOKIE CRUST VARIATION In the bowl of an electric mixer fitted with the paddle attachment, beat 1 stick butter and 1/4 cup sugar on medium speed until light and fluffy, 3 to 4 minutes. Beat in 1 large egg yolk and 1 teaspoon pure vanilla extract. Add 3/4 cup all-purpose flour and a pinch of salt, and beat until the dough just comes together. Shape dough into a disk, and wrap in plastic. Refrigerate until firm, at least 30 minutes or up to 1 day. Press dough into pan; bake at 350°F until golden, 15 to 18 minutes; cool completely. Proceed with recipe for New York–Style Cheesecake.

RICOTTA CHEESECAKE

MAKES ONE 9-INCH CAKE *This is about the easiest cheesecake you can make—it takes only fifteen minutes to assemble and one hour to bake. Although rich, this cake is lighter than traditional cheesecakes because it calls for ricotta instead of cream cheese.*

Unsalted butter, room temperature, for pan

¾ cup sugar, plus more for pan

1½ pounds fresh whole-milk ricotta cheese, puréed in a food processor until smooth

6 large eggs, separated

¼ cup all-purpose flour

Finely grated zest of 1 orange or 2 lemons

¼ teaspoon salt

Preheat the oven to 375°F. Generously butter and sugar a 9-inch springform pan. In a large bowl, whisk together the ricotta, egg yolks, flour, half the sugar (6 tablespoons), zest, and salt until combined; set aside.

Place the egg whites in the bowl of an electric mixer fitted with the whisk attachment; beat on low speed until foamy. With the mixer on high speed, gradually add the remaining 6 tablespoons sugar, beating until whites are stiff and glossy, 3 to 4 minutes.

Using a rubber spatula, fold a third of the egg-white mixture into the ricotta mixture until combined. Gently fold in the remaining egg-white mixture until just combined. Pour into the prepared pan, and bake until the center is firm and the top is a deep golden brown, about 1 hour.

Transfer to a wire rack to cool 10 minutes. Place another wire rack on top of the pan, and invert the cake onto the rack to remove from pan. Reinvert cake and cool completely, top side up. This cheesecake is best eaten the day it is baked but can be refrigerated, covered loosely with plastic wrap, for up to 3 days. Let sit at room temperature for 20 minutes before serving.

angel food cake

CLASSIC ANGEL FOOD CAKE

MAKES ONE 10-INCH CAKE *Sifting together the flour and sugar four times is essential to achieve the light, airy texture of this cake. You should also be very gentle when folding and transferring the batter so that the egg whites do not deflate. If your tube pan doesn't have legs, invert it over the neck of a wine, or similarly shaped, bottle to cool.*

1 cup cake flour (not self-rising)	1 tablespoon warm water
1½ cups superfine sugar	½ teaspoon salt
1¾ cups large egg whites (about 13 large eggs), room temperature	1 teaspoon cream of tartar
	1 teaspoon pure vanilla extract

ANGEL FOOD CAKE HOW-TO
Once the batter is transferred to the pan, run a knife through it to help release any air bubbles. This will result in a cake with a very fine crumb.

Preheat the oven to 350°F, with the rack in the center. Into a medium bowl, sift together flour and ¾ cup sugar four times; set aside.

In the bowl of an electric mixer fitted with the whisk attachment, beat egg whites and the warm water on low speed until foamy. Add salt, cream of tartar, and vanilla; beat on medium-high speed until soft peaks form, about 3 minutes. While beating, gradually add the remaining ¾ cup sugar, 1 tablespoon at a time. Beat on high speed until peaks are stiff and glossy but not dry, about 2 minutes (do not overmix).

Transfer mixture to a large bowl. Sift flour mixture over egg-white mixture in six parts, quickly but gently folding it in with a rubber spatula after each addition.

Gently transfer batter to an ungreased 10-inch tube pan. Run a knife through the batter to release any air bubbles, and smooth with a small offset spatula. Bake until cake is golden brown and springs back when touched, 35 to 40 minutes.

Invert pan onto its legs and let cool completely, about 1 hour. Carefully run a large offset spatula around the sides of the cake to loosen, then invert onto a wire rack. Cake can be kept in an airtight container at room temperature for up to 4 days.

CHOCOLATE ANGEL FOOD CAKE VARIATION Follow instructions for Classic Angel Food Cake, sifting ¼ cup Dutch-process cocoa powder and 1 teaspoon baking powder along with the flour and ¾ cup sugar. Once cake is completely cool, place on a wire rack set over a parchment-lined baking sheet. Slowly pour Mocha Glaze (page 389) evenly over the top of the cake, guiding it with a spoon and letting some drip down the sides.

upside-down cakes

APRICOT-CHERRY UPSIDE-DOWN CAKE

MAKES ONE 8-INCH CAKE *In traditional upside-down cake recipes, the fruit is first caramelized in a skillet. In our simplified version, the butter and sugar are creamed and spread into the cake pan; then the fruit is layered over the mixture and topped with cake batter.*

1 stick (½ cup) unsalted butter, room temperature, plus more for pan	¼ cup plus 2 tablespoons fine yellow cornmeal
1¼ cups sugar	1 teaspoon baking powder
5 to 6 medium fresh apricots (about 1 pound), halved and pitted	½ teaspoon salt
	¼ cup almond paste (not marzipan), crumbled
12 ounces fresh sweet cherries (such as Bing), stemmed, pitted, and halved	3 large eggs, separated
	¼ teaspoon pure vanilla extract
	½ teaspoon pure almond extract
¾ cup all-purpose flour	½ cup milk

Preheat the oven to 350°F. Butter an 8-by-3-inch round cake pan, and line bottom with parchment paper. In the bowl of an electric mixer fitted with the paddle attachment, beat 2 tablespoons butter with ¼ cup sugar on medium speed until light and fluffy, about 2 minutes. Spread evenly over bottom of prepared pan. Arrange apricot halves, cut sides down, in pan. Fit cherries into any gaps between apricots. Pack down the fruit slightly with your hands; set aside.

In a medium bowl, whisk together flour, cornmeal, baking powder, and salt; set aside. In the bowl of an electric mixer fitted with the paddle attachment, beat remaining 6 tablespoons butter until smooth, about 1 minute. Add almond paste and ¾ cup sugar, and beat until light and fluffy, about 2 minutes, scraping down the sides of the bowl as needed. Add the egg yolks, and beat until well combined. Beat in vanilla and almond extracts. Add the flour mixture in two parts, alternating with the milk and beginning and ending with the flour; beat until combined, and set aside.

In the clean bowl of an electric mixer fitted with the whisk attachment, beat egg whites on medium speed until foamy. Gradually sprinkle in the remaining ¼ cup sugar, and beat until soft peaks form. Fold a third of egg-white mixture into the batter with a spatula. Gently fold in remaining egg whites.

Spread batter over fruit, smoothing with an offset spatula. Bake, rotating pan halfway through, until a cake tester inserted in the center comes out clean, 1 hour to 1 hour 10 minutes. Transfer pan to a wire rack to cool slightly, about 15 minutes. Run a knife or small offset spatula around the edges to loosen, and invert cake onto a serving plate to cool completely. Cake can be kept at room temperature, loosely covered with foil, for up to 3 days.

APRICOT-CHERRY UPSIDE-DOWN CAKE HOW-TO
1. An offset spatula is used to evenly spread the creamed butter and sugar over the bottom of the pan. **2.** Apricot halves are arranged, cut sides down, atop the butter mixture, then halved cherries are tucked into the gaps.

PINEAPPLE-MANGO UPSIDE-DOWN CAKE

MAKES ONE 8-INCH CAKE *We like to serve this cake warm, topped with a scoop of vanilla ice cream. If you wish, you can make it a day in advance and keep it at room temperature loosely covered with foil. When ready to serve, warm the cake on a parchment-lined baking sheet in a 300°F oven for fifteen to twenty minutes.*

1¼ sticks (10 tablespoons) unsalted butter, room temperature, plus more for pan	1½ cups all-purpose flour
	½ teaspoon salt
1 medium ripe pineapple (about 3½ pounds), peeled and cut crosswise into ¼-inch-thick slices	¼ teaspoon baking soda
	¼ teaspoon baking powder
	1 cup granulated sugar
1 medium ripe mango (about ¾ pound), peeled	2 large eggs
	1 teaspoon pure vanilla extract
½ cup packed light-brown sugar	¼ cup sour cream

Preheat the oven to 350°F. Butter an 8-by-8-by-2-inch cake pan, line it with parchment paper, and butter parchment. Using a 3-inch cookie cutter, cut out rounds from centers of four of the pineapple slices. Using a 1½-inch cookie cutter, cut out the centers of each of the four rounds, and discard; set rings aside. Finely chop enough of the remaining pineapple to yield 1 cup (reserve remainder for another use). Place chopped fruit in a fine sieve set over a bowl to drain.

Cut the mango lengthwise into ¼-inch-thick slices. Using the 1½-inch cookie cutter, cut out four rounds from mango slices; set aside. Finely chop enough of the remaining mango to yield ½ cup; add to the pineapple in the sieve.

In the bowl of an electric mixer fitted with the paddle attachment, beat 2 tablespoons butter with the brown sugar until light and fluffy, 2 to 3 minutes. Using a small offset spatula, evenly spread butter mixture in the bottom of the prepared pan; set aside.

In a medium bowl, sift together the flour, salt, baking soda, and baking powder; set aside. Place a reserved pineapple ring in each corner of the prepared pan. Place a reserved mango round in the center of each ring.

In the bowl of a mixer fitted with the paddle attachment, beat remaining 1 stick butter with granulated sugar on medium speed until light and fluffy, 2 to 3 minutes. Add eggs, one at a time, beating well after each addition; scrape down the sides of the bowl as needed. Beat in the vanilla. With the mixer on lowest speed, add flour mixture in two parts, alternating with sour cream and beginning and ending with flour.

Transfer the chopped pineapple-mango mixture to cake pan; discard juice. Using a small offset spatula, carefully spread fruit in an even layer on top of cut-out fruit, making sure to fill all the empty spaces, including any gaps in the corners. Using the offset spatula, spread batter evenly over fruit.

Bake, rotating pan halfway through, until cake is golden brown and a cake tester inserted in the center comes out clean, about 50 minutes. Transfer pan to a wire rack to cool 30 minutes. Invert onto a cake plate; peel off the parchment paper. Serve cake slightly warm or at room temperature.

PINEAPPLE-MANGO UPSIDE-DOWN CAKE HOW-TO 1. Pineapple cores are removed with a round cookie cutter; the same cutter is used to make mango rounds that will fill in the holes in the pineapple rings. Some of the remaining fruit is finely chopped and drained. **2.** After pineapple rings and mango rounds are arranged on the bottom of the pan, the drained, chopped fruit is spread on top, before the cake batter.

BLACKBERRY ROULADE

MAKES ONE 17-INCH ROLLED CAKE *The combination of fresh fruit and whipped cream used to fill this cake, typically found in British desserts, is known as "fool." You can substitute raspberries or boysenberries for the blackberries in this recipe.*

BLACKBERRY ROULADE HOW-TO 1. While it's still warm, a sheet of freshly baked sponge cake is rolled in a clean kitchen towel that has been dusted with confectioners' sugar. **2.** Once it has cooled, the cake is unrolled and covered with a thick layer of blackberry fool before it is rolled and dusted once again.

3 tablespoons confectioners' sugar, plus more for dusting

1¼ cups cake flour (not self-rising)

1½ teaspoons baking powder

½ teaspoon salt

1 large whole egg, plus 2 large egg yolks and 3 large egg whites, all at room temperature

¼ cup vegetable oil

¼ cup honey

¼ cup plus 3 tablespoons granulated sugar

½ teaspoon pure vanilla extract

¼ cup warm water

1 pint fresh blackberries

1 cup heavy cream

Preheat the oven to 350°F. Line a 17-by-12-inch rimmed baking sheet with parchment paper. Dust a large, clean kitchen towel with confectioners' sugar; set aside. Into a medium bowl, sift together the flour, baking powder, and salt; set aside. Place the whole egg, egg yolks, vegetable oil, honey, ¼ cup granulated sugar, vanilla, and warm water in the bowl of an electric mixer fitted with the whisk attachment. Beat on medium speed until thick and pale (it should hold a ribbon-like trail on the surface when the whisk is raised), 6 to 7 minutes. Transfer to a large bowl; set aside.

With a clean bowl and whisk attachment, beat the egg whites on medium speed until soft peaks form, 1 to 2 minutes. Raise speed to medium-high; gradually add remaining 3 tablespoons granulated sugar, beating until stiff peaks form, 2 to 3 minutes. Using a rubber spatula, fold a third of the egg-white mixture into the egg-yolk mixture to lighten. Gently fold in remaining whites until just combined. Sift flour mixture over the top, and gently fold in until just combined. Pour batter onto prepared baking sheet; using an offset spatula, spread evenly.

Bake, rotating sheet halfway through, until the cake is golden and springs back when lightly touched in the center, about 10 minutes. Immediately invert cake onto prepared towel; carefully lift off pan and peel off parchment paper. Starting on a long side, roll towel and cake into a log, incorporating the towel as you go. Transfer cake (still in towel), seam side down, to a wire rack. Let cool completely.

In a medium bowl, crush the blackberries with a fork; set aside. In the bowl of an electric mixer fitted with the whisk attachment, beat cream with the confectioners' sugar on medium-high speed until stiff peaks form, about 2 minutes. Fold in crushed blackberries; set aside.

Unroll cake, leaving it on the kitchen towel. Using an offset spatula, spread blackberry mixture over top of cake, leaving a 1-inch border on both long sides. Gently roll cake again into a log (do not incorporate towel). Wrap with towel; refrigerate on a baking sheet until ready to serve, for at least 1 hour or up to 1 day. Remove towel, and generously dust cake with confectioners' sugar before serving; slice with a serrated knife.

MOCHA ROULADE

MAKES ONE 17-INCH ROLLED CAKE *This chocolate sponge cake should be baked the same day you plan to assemble the roulade, because it will be easier to fill and shape.*

¼ cup Dutch-process cocoa powder, sifted, plus more for dusting	6 large eggs, separated, room temperature
¼ cup all-purpose flour	¾ cup sugar
1 tablespoon instant espresso powder	Mocha Mousse (page 393)
1 tablespoon hot water	

Preheat the oven to 325°F. Line a 17-by-12-inch rimmed baking sheet with parchment paper; set aside. Dust a large, clean kitchen towel with cocoa; set aside. Into a medium bowl, sift together the cocoa and flour. In a small bowl, stir together the espresso powder and the hot water until dissolved; set aside.

In the bowl of an electric mixer fitted with the whisk attachment, beat the egg yolks on high speed until thick and pale (they should hold a ribbon-like trail on the surface when the whisk is raised), about 5 minutes. Transfer to a large bowl; set aside.

With a clean bowl and whisk attachment, whip the egg whites on low speed until foamy. Raise speed to medium-high, and add the sugar in a slow, steady stream, beating until stiff peaks form.

With a rubber spatula, fold a third of the egg-white mixture into the egg-yolk mixture to lighten. Gently fold in remaining egg whites until just combined. Fold in the espresso mixture, then gradually fold in the cocoa mixture until just combined. Do not overmix.

Pour batter onto prepared sheet; using an offset spatula, spread evenly and smooth the top. Bake, rotating pan halfway through, until the cake springs back when lightly touched, 10 to 12 minutes. Immediately invert cake onto prepared towel; carefully lift off pan and peel off parchment paper. Starting on a long side, roll towel and cake into a log, incorporating the towel as you go. Transfer cake (still in towel), seam side down, to a wire rack to cool completely.

Unroll cake, leaving it on the kitchen towel. Using an offset spatula, spread Mocha Mousse evenly over the cake. Gently roll cake again into a log (do not incorporate towel). Wrap with the towel; refrigerate on a baking sheet until filling is well chilled, for at least 2 hours or up to 1 day. When ready to serve, generously dust roulade with cocoa; slice with a serrated knife.

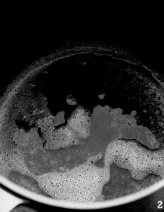

FINANCIERS HOW-TO
1. Whisking the butter as it cooks helps keep it from darkening too quickly. **2.** The butter is cooked until it turns golden brown and takes on a nutty aroma. **3.** The molds are coated with butter and flour and filled with the rich browned-butter batter.

miniature cakes

FINANCIERS

MAKES ABOUT 2 DOZEN *These traditional French cakes, usually baked in rectangular tartlet pans, are named for their resemblance to bankers' bars of gold.*

1¼ sticks (10 tablespoons) unsalted butter, plus more for pans	¾ cup all-purpose flour, plus more for pans
2 cups (6 ounces) sliced blanched almonds	½ teaspoon salt
2¼ cups confectioners' sugar	1 cup egg whites (about 8 large eggs), room temperature

In a medium saucepan, melt butter over medium-low heat, whisking frequently, until it is fragrant and golden brown (watch carefully to keep it from smoking), 6 to 7 minutes. Pour butter into a small bowl; set aside until slightly cooled. Place almonds and ¼ cup confectioners' sugar in a food processor, and pulse until nuts are finely chopped, about 1 minute. In a medium bowl, whisk together flour and salt; add nut mixture, and stir to combine.

In the bowl of an electric mixer fitted with the whisk attachment, beat egg whites and remaining 2 cups confectioners' sugar on medium-high speed until foamy. Reduce speed to medium-low, and add flour-nut mixture in three parts, alternating with the brown butter and beginning and ending with the flour; scrape down sides of bowl as needed. Cover with plastic wrap, and refrigerate for at least 2 hours or up to 4 days.

Preheat the oven to 400°F. Butter and flour twenty-four 3-inch round and oval individual tartlet pans, tapping out excess flour; place on a rimmed baking sheet. Fill each pan halfway full (about 2 tablespoons each). Bake cakes, rotating sheet halfway through, until the edges turn light golden brown, 10 to 12 minutes.

Transfer sheet to a wire rack to cool slightly. Using a small offset spatula, loosen cakes around the edges, and remove from tartlet pans. These are best served warm from the oven, or at least the same day they are baked.

PISTACHIO FINANCIERS VARIATION Follow instructions for Financiers, substituting 1¼ cups (6 ounces) unsalted pistachios for the almonds. To give the cakes a beautiful green hue, use the most brightly colored pistachios you can find.

CHOCOLATE FINANCIERS VARIATION Follow instructions for Financiers, whisking ¼ cup Dutch-process cocoa powder and 2 ounces finely ground semisweet chocolate into the flour and salt. Bake until edges have darkened slightly and begin to pull away from the sides of the pan, 12 to 15 minutes.

CHOCOLATE-GLAZED GINGERBREAD CAKES

MAKES 1 DOZEN *These lovely full-flavored cakes make a festive holiday dessert — but you can enjoy them any time of the year. The cakes can be baked a day in advance and kept in an airtight container at room temperature.*

- 5 tablespoons unsalted butter, room temperature, plus more for pan
- 1½ cups all-purpose flour, plus more for pan
- 1 teaspoon baking soda
- ⅔ cup boiling water
- 1 teaspoon baking powder
- 1 teaspoon ground ginger
- ¾ teaspoon ground cinnamon
- ¼ teaspoon ground cloves
- ¼ teaspoon ground nutmeg
- ¼ teaspoon salt
- ½ cup packed dark-brown sugar
- 1 large egg
- ⅔ cup unsulfured molasses
- 1½ teaspoons finely grated peeled fresh ginger
- ¼ recipe Chocolate Ganache (page 387)
- 2 pieces crystallized ginger, thinly sliced lengthwise, for garnish

CHOCOLATE-GLAZED GINGERBREAD CAKES HOW-TO
Rich chocolate ganache is spooned over the flat sides of miniature cakes, which are inverted after baking in muffin cups. Once glazed, the cakes are garnished with thin slivers of crystallized ginger.

Preheat the oven to 350°F. Generously butter and flour a standard 12-cup muffin pan, tapping out excess flour; set aside. In a small bowl, stir together the baking soda and boiling water; set aside. In a medium bowl, sift together the flour, baking powder, ground ginger, cinnamon, cloves, nutmeg, and salt; set aside.

In the bowl of an electric mixer fitted with the paddle attachment, beat the butter and brown sugar on medium speed until light and fluffy, 2 to 3 minutes. Add the egg, and beat until combined. Add molasses, fresh ginger, and reserved baking soda mixture; beat until combined. (The batter will look curdled but will come together once the flour is added.) Add the flour mixture, and beat until well combined.

Divide batter evenly among prepared muffin cups, filling each about halfway. Bake, rotating pan halfway through, until a cake tester inserted in the center of a cake comes out clean, about 20 minutes. Transfer pan to a wire rack to cool for 15 minutes. Invert cakes onto rack to cool completely.

Set rack over a parchment-lined rimmed baking sheet. Spoon about 1 tablespoon of Chocolate Ganache over each cake, letting some drip down the sides. Garnish with a couple of strips of crystallized ginger. Once glazed, cakes can be refrigerated, in airtight containers, for up to 3 days; bring to room temperature before serving.

PETITS FOURS

MAKES ABOUT 3 DOZEN *These moist almond cakes are glazed with a thin layer of white chocolate and then topped with crisp White Chocolate Cutouts. Feel free to use your imagination when it comes to shaping and decorating—customize your cakes with a favorite cookie cutter, or adjust the color of the glaze to suit your color scheme.*

1½ sticks (¾ cup) unsalted butter, room temperature, plus more for pan

2¼ cups all-purpose flour, plus more for pan

2 teaspoons baking powder

¾ teaspoon salt

1¾ cups sugar

½ cup almond paste (not marzipan)

6 large eggs, separated

1 teaspoon pure vanilla extract

1 cup milk

1½ pounds white chocolate, coarsely chopped

1¼ cups heavy cream

White Chocolate Cutouts (page 395)

Royal Icing, for decorating (page 389; optional)

Preheat the oven to 350°F. Butter a 17-by-12-inch rimmed baking sheet; line with parchment paper. Butter parchment and dust with flour, tapping out excess; set aside. Into a large bowl, sift together the flour, baking powder, and salt; set aside.

In the bowl of an electric mixer fitted with the paddle attachment, beat 1¼ cups sugar and the almond paste on medium-low speed until the mixture resembles coarse meal. Add the butter, and beat on medium-high speed until light and fluffy, about 2 minutes. Add the egg yolks and vanilla; mix to combine, scraping down the sides of the bowl as needed. Add flour mixture in three parts, alternating with the milk and beginning and ending with the flour; set aside.

In the bowl of an electric mixer fitted with the whisk attachment, whip egg whites until foamy. With the mixer running, gradually sprinkle in remaining ½ cup sugar, and beat until soft peaks form. Add a third of the egg-white mixture to the egg-yolk mixture, and fold with a whisk. Gently fold in remaining whites.

Spread batter evenly on prepared sheet, and bake, turning pan halfway through, until a cake tester inserted in the center comes out clean, about 20 minutes. Transfer pan to wire rack to cool completely. Cover tightly with plastic wrap, and refrigerate for at least 1 hour or up to 1 day.

Invert the cake onto a large work surface, and peel off parchment paper. Using assorted 2-inch cookie cutters, cut out cakes. Place cakes on wire racks set over rimmed baking sheets; set aside.

Place the white chocolate in a large heatproof bowl. In a small saucepan, bring the cream to a simmer over medium-high heat; pour over white chocolate, and let sit for 1 minute. Stir until mixture is smooth. Spoon melted chocolate over cakes, letting some run down the sides; spread with a small offset spatula to coat completely. Transfer glazed cakes to a parchment-lined baking sheet, and refrigerate at least 30 minutes. Place a White Chocolate Cutouts on top of each cake; decorate with Royal Icing, if desired. Cakes can be refrigerated, in an airtight container, for up to 3 days.

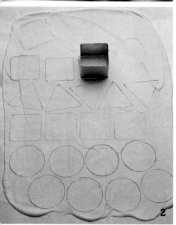

PETITS FOURS HOW-TO
1. A sheet of almond-flavored cake is cut into individual cakes with a set of 2-inch cookie cutters. **2.** Melted white chocolate, tinted in pastel shades, is spread over a sheet of parchment with an offset spatula; once set, the chocolate is cut with the same set of cutters into shapes that will top the glazed cakes.

PAVLOVAS WITH MIXED BERRIES

MAKES 6 *Meringues are baked on very low heat so they stay perfectly white. It's a good idea to check them periodically to make sure they don't take on color. To test if the meringues are done, try lifting one off the parchment—if it comes away easily, it is ready; if not, continue baking, checking every five minutes. Moisture will cause meringues to soften, so avoid making them on particularly humid days.*

2 large egg whites
¾ cup granulated sugar
  Pinch of salt
½ teaspoon pure vanilla extract
4½ tablespoons confectioners' sugar, plus more for dusting

1½ cups crème fraîche
2 cups assorted berries, such as golden raspberries and red currants

Preheat the oven to 200°F. Line a baking sheet with parchment paper; set aside. In the heatproof bowl of an electric mixer set over a pan of simmering water, combine egg whites, granulated sugar, and salt. Whisk constantly until the sugar has dissolved and the egg mixture is warm to the touch, about 2 minutes. Attach the bowl to the mixer fitted with the whisk attachment; beat on medium-high speed until stiff peaks form, 2 to 4 minutes. Beat in the vanilla.

Using a large spoon, scoop six fluffy mounds of meringue, each about 3½ inches in diameter, onto the prepared baking sheet. Using the back of the spoon, form a well in the center of each mound, being careful not to make meringue too thin in the center.

Dust mounds lightly with confectioners' sugar. Bake until just dry to the touch but still white in color, about 1½ hours. Transfer sheet to a wire rack and let meringues cool completely before carefully easing them off the parchment. Meringues can be kept in an airtight container at room temperature for up to 1 day.

When ready to serve, combine crème fraîche with 4½ tablespoons confectioners' sugar in a medium bowl. Whisk until soft peaks form. Divide crème-fraîche mixture among meringues, dolloping it in the wells. Garnish with fruit.

PAVLOVA HOW-TO **1.** Spoonfuls of the thick meringue are dropped onto a parchment-lined baking sheet; the same spoon is used to create a well in the center of each mound. **2.** A light dusting of confectioners' sugar will help them dry during baking.

Cannelés

Lemon Madeleines

CANNELÉS

MAKES 18 *The dark, crunchy crust of a cannelé gives way to a delicate, pudding-like center. Cannelés are baked in specially designed three-inch-deep molds made of copper, tin, ceramic, or silicone. If you do not have eighteen molds, bake the cakes in batches.*

CANNELÉ HOW-TO
The batter for these individual cakes is relatively thin and won't rise much during baking, so the molds are filled nearly to their tops.

4 cups milk	4 cups confectioners' sugar
7 tablespoons unsalted butter, cut into small pieces	2 tablespoons dark rum (optional)
1 vanilla bean, split lengthwise and seeds scraped	1½ cups all-purpose flour
4 large egg yolks	½ teaspoon salt
	Nonstick cooking spray

In a medium saucepan, bring 2 cups milk, the butter, and vanilla bean and seeds to a simmer over medium heat; cook, stirring occasionally, until butter has completely melted. Set aside to cool slightly; remove and discard bean.

In a large bowl, whisk together the egg yolks, sugar, rum (if using), and remaining 2 cups milk. Add the flour and salt; whisk to combine. Add the hot milk mixture to the egg-yolk mixture in a slow, steady stream, whisking constantly. Strain mixture through a fine sieve into a medium bowl. Cover with plastic wrap, and refrigerate for at least 1 day or up to 4 days.

Preheat the oven to 350°F. Place molds on a rimmed baking sheet, and coat with cooking spray; freeze for 20 minutes. Transfer molds to another baking sheet, 1½ inches apart. Remove batter from refrigerator and whisk vigorously (batter may have separated while chilling). Fill each mold to ⅛ inch from the top.

Bake, rotating sheet halfway through, until cannelés are dark brown and slip easily from their molds with a gentle tap, 1¼ to 2 hours. Check by removing a mold from the oven and gently turning out cake to see if it is brown enough. If not, slip cake back into mold and return to oven to continue baking. When done, transfer sheet to a wire rack to cool 15 minutes. Use a kitchen towel to grasp each mold and invert cannelés onto a rack to cool completely. (If necessary, use a small offset spatula to ease them out of their molds.) Cannelés should be served the same day they are baked.

LEMON MADELEINES

MAKES 2 DOZEN *In place of the almond flour, you can substitute two ounces (about ½ cup plus two tablespoons) blanched almonds, finely ground in a food processor. Feel free to vary the flavoring by replacing part or all of the lemon zest with orange zest, or omitting it altogether and adding one teaspoon of vanilla extract.*

- 1 stick (½ cup) unsalted butter, plus more for pans
- ¾ cup all-purpose flour, plus more for pans
- Scant ½ cup almond flour
- ½ cup plus 2 tablespoons sugar
- 2 tablespoons finely grated lemon zest
- ¼ teaspoon pure lemon extract
- 3 large eggs
- ½ teaspoon salt

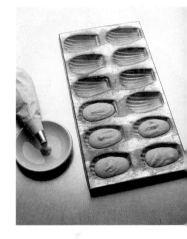

In a small saucepan, melt the butter over medium-low heat. Set aside to cool. In a large bowl, whisk together flours and sugar; set aside.

Add the lemon zest and extract to the cooled butter; stir to combine. In a large bowl, combine the eggs with the salt, and whisk until frothy. Whisk in reserved flour mixture to combine. With whisk, fold in butter mixture. Cover the bowl with plastic wrap, and refrigerate until chilled, at least 2 hours or overnight.

Preheat the oven to 350°F. Butter two 12-mold madeleine pans, and dust with flour, tapping out excess. Transfer batter to a pastry bag fitted with a ½-inch plain round tip (such as an Ateco #806). Pipe the batter into the prepared pans, filling each mold about halfway. Bake, rotating pan halfway through, until the edges of the cakes are golden brown, 12 to 14 minutes. Immediately invert madeleines onto a wire rack to cool. Madeleines should be served the same day they are baked.

LEMON MADELEINE HOW-TO
A pastry bag and plain round tip are used to pipe the thick batter into the shell-shaped molds; this helps keep the cakes uniform in shape, and ensures they bake evenly.

FRUITCAKES

MAKES TWO 8-INCH CAKES *Feel free to substitute 2½ pounds of your favorite dried fruits for the ones called for here. If you choose larger fruits, such as pears or apples, be sure to cut them into a ¼-inch dice before using. Cakes can be wrapped in plastic and kept at room temperature for up to three days or in the refrigerator for up to six months.*

2½ cups (15 ounces) raisins

2½ cups (15 ounces) golden raisins

2 cups (9 ounces) dried currants

2 cups (11 ounces) dried sour cherries

2½ cups (9 ounces) dried cranberries

1 cup (5 ounces) dried apricots, cut into ¼-inch dice

¾ cup honey

1 cup Cognac, Armagnac, or other brandy

3 sticks (1½ cups) unsalted butter, room temperature, plus more for pans

2¼ cups bread flour, plus more for pans

1 tablespoon coarse salt

1½ teaspoons ground ginger

1½ teaspoons ground cinnamon

1 teaspoon ground cloves

1½ cups (5 ounces) walnuts, coarsely chopped

1¼ cups sugar

7 large eggs

1½ cups apricot jam

Assorted nuts and dried fruits, for garnish (optional)

In a large nonreactive container (glass, ceramic, or plastic), combine the dried fruits, honey, and Cognac; set aside to macerate at room temperature for at least 24 hours, or up to 2 weeks, covered with plastic wrap.

Preheat the oven to 275°F. Generously butter and flour two 8-by-3-inch round cake pans; tap out any excess flour, and set aside. Sift the flour, salt, ginger, cinnamon, and cloves into a large bowl. Stir in the walnuts, and set aside.

In the bowl of an electric mixer fitted with the paddle attachment, beat the butter and sugar on medium speed until light and fluffy, 2 to 3 minutes. Add the eggs, one at a time, beating after each addition to incorporate, and scraping down the sides of the bowl as needed. Transfer to a large bowl. Using a rubber spatula, fold in the flour-nut mixture and the drained fruit mixture; stir to evenly distribute fruits and nuts.

Divide the batter between the prepared pans. Bake until a cake tester inserted in the centers comes out with only a few moist crumbs attached, 2 hours to 2 hours 15 minutes. Transfer pans to a wire rack to cool completely. Invert cakes onto rack to remove from pans. Reinvert, top sides up.

To decorate cakes, combine the apricot jam with ½ cup water in a small saucepan; stir until melted and combined. Strain through a fine sieve into a bowl; while jam is still hot, brush it liberally over cakes. Garnish cakes with additional dried fruits and nuts, if using, and top with a final coat of hot jam.

DOBOS TORTE

Tortes are common throughout central Europe, and Dobos is a popular one, named for the Hungarian chef who invented it in 1887.

- 3 sticks (1½ cups) unsalted butter, room temperature, plus more for pans
- 1½ cups all-purpose flour, plus more for pans
- 1½ cups cake flour (not self-rising)
- 1 tablespoon baking powder
- ½ teaspoon salt
- 2¼ cups sugar

- 8 large egg whites, plus 3 large egg yolks
- 1 cup milk
- ½ cup heavy cream
- Chocolate Swiss Meringue Buttercream (page 386)
- Caramel Sticks and Dots (recipe follows)

Preheat the oven to 350°F. Butter three 8-by-2-inch round cake pans, and line the bottoms with parchment paper. Butter parchment, and dust with flour, tapping out excess; set aside. Into a medium bowl, sift together the flours, baking powder, and salt.

In the bowl of an electric mixer fitted with the paddle attachment, beat butter and 2 cups sugar on medium-high speed until light and fluffy, 3 to 4 minutes; scrape down sides of bowl as needed. Add egg yolks, one at a time, and beat to combine. With mixer on low, add reserved flour mixture in three parts, alternating with the milk and beginning and ending with flour; scrape down the sides of the bowl as needed.

In the bowl of an electric mixer fitted with the whisk attachment, beat egg whites until foamy. Gradually sprinkle in the remaining ¼ cup sugar, and beat until soft peaks form. Add about a third of the egg-white mixture to the reserved batter, and gently fold in with a rubber spatula. Gently fold in the remaining egg whites.

Divide batter evenly among prepared pans; spread to smooth with an offset spatula. Bake, rotating pans halfway through, until cakes are golden and a cake tester inserted in the centers comes out clean, about 30 minutes. Transfer to a wire rack to cool for 20 minutes. Invert cakes onto rack; peel off parchment. Reinvert cakes; let them cool completely, top sides up. Meanwhile, in a clean bowl with a clean whisk attachment, whip cream until soft peaks form. Cover and refrigerate until ready to use.

Using a serrated knife, trim tops of cakes so surfaces are level, if necessary. Slice each cake horizontally into three equal layers. Place 2 cups Chocolate Swiss Meringue Buttercream in a medium bowl. (Set aside remaining buttercream.) Using a rubber spatula, fold in the whipped cream to lighten. Place one layer on a cake stand or serving plate; spread ⅓ cup of the lightened buttercream in an even layer. Repeat with remaining layers and lightened buttercream to make 9 layers.

Spread a thin layer of reserved Chocolate Swiss Meringue Buttercream over the top and sides of cake to seal in crumbs. Refrigerate until frosting is firm, about 30 minutes. Spread cake with the remaining buttercream, making smooth strokes with an offset spatula. Refrigerate until frosting is firm, at least 30 minutes or up to 2 days, covered with a cake dome. When ready to serve, arrange Caramel Dots around the sides of the cake in a decorative pattern. Arrange the Caramel Sticks on top of the cake.

CARAMEL STICKS AND DOTS

MAKES ENOUGH FOR ONE 8-INCH LAYER CAKE *Store shaped caramels in layers between sheets of parchment or waxed paper that have been lightly coated with nonstick cooking spray; keep in an airtight container at room temperature for up to one day. For the best results, avoid making these on a humid day.*

Nonstick cooking spray
2 cups sugar

¼ teaspoon freshly squeezed lemon juice

CARAMEL STICKS AND DOTS HOW-TO Hot caramel is drizzled onto an inverted baking sheet to make thin sticks that will decorate the top of the torte. Dots for the cake's sides are created by spooning caramel into rounds on a nonstick baking mat.

Lightly coat the underside of a rimmed baking sheet with cooking spray; place it, coated side up, on a work surface covered with parchment paper. Place a nonstick baking mat (such as Silpat) on the work surface.

In a medium heavy-bottom saucepan, combine sugar, ¼ cup water, and the lemon juice. Cook over high heat until sugar just begins to turn light golden around the edges, about 8 minutes. (The caramel will continue cooking in the pan, so watch the color carefully.) Immediately remove from heat, and swirl gently to color evenly. Let stand until caramel has thickened and cooled slightly, about 8 minutes.

To make sticks, use a metal spoon to drizzle caramel in strips across the inverted baking sheet, using quick zigzag movements. Let stand until firm, about 5 minutes. Using a knife or kitchen shears, trim the ends so they are straight.

To make dots, drop spoonfuls of caramel to form rounds, ranging in size from 1 to 1¼ inches, onto the baking mat; let stand until firm, about 5 minutes. Once firm, remove with a small offset spatula.

MARTHA'S BIRTHDAY CAKE

MAKES ONE DOMED 10-INCH LAYER CAKE *This spectacular cake, created for Martha's birthday several years ago, has since made memorable appearances at company events.*

4 sticks (1 pound) unsalted butter, room temperature, plus more for bowl

3 cups cake flour (not self-rising), plus more for bowl

4 teaspoons baking powder

¼ teaspoon salt, plus a pinch

2 cups plus 1 tablespoon sugar

2 vanilla beans, split lengthwise and seeds scraped

1 cup milk

8 large egg whites

Amaretto Simple Syrup (page 208)

Almond Buttercream (page 208)

½ cup apricot jam

Almond Swiss Meringue (recipe follows)

Preheat the oven to 350°F. Generously butter the inside of a 10-inch stainless steel bowl (4½ to 6 inches deep). Dust with flour, and tap out excess; set aside. Into a medium mixing bowl, sift together flour, baking powder, and ¼ teaspoon salt.

In the bowl of an electric mixer fitted with the paddle attachment, beat butter, 2 cups sugar, and vanilla seeds on medium speed until light and fluffy, about 3 minutes, scraping down the sides of the bowl as needed. With the mixer on low speed, add the flour mixture in four parts, alternating with the milk and beginning and ending with the flour; beat until just combined. Transfer mixture to a large, wide bowl; set aside.

With a clean bowl and whisk attachment, beat the egg whites and the pinch of salt on high speed until soft peaks form. Add the remaining tablespoon sugar, and continue to beat until medium-stiff peaks form, about 2 minutes. Whisk a third of the egg-white mixture into the butter-flour mixture to lighten, then use a rubber spatula to gently fold in remaining whites until just combined.

Pour the batter into the prepared bowl, and smooth the top with an offset spatula. Bake, rotating bowl halfway through, until the cake is golden brown and a cake tester inserted in the center comes out clean, about 1 hour 40 minutes. (If the cake begins to get too dark, cover loosely with aluminum foil.) Transfer bowl to a wire rack to cool for 30 minutes. Invert cake onto the rack and let cool completely.

Line a bowl slightly smaller than the cake with plastic wrap, leaving some overhang. Fit cake into bowl. Using a serrated knife, trim the bottom of the cake to make level. Invert cake onto a clean work surface or cake turntable. Using the serrated knife, cut cake horizontally into four layers of approximately the same height.

Place the bottom (largest) layer on a cardboard round or serving plate. Brush the top liberally with Amaretto Simple Syrup. Using an offset spatula, evenly spread about 1 cup Almond Buttercream over the top, about ¼ inch thick. Top with the next-largest layer, and brush with syrup. Spread apricot jam in an even layer over the top. Place the next-largest layer, and brush with syrup. Spread about ½ cup buttercream over the top. Place remaining (smallest) layer on top. Brush the surface of the entire cake with syrup. Spread about ½ cup buttercream over the entire cake in a thin layer. Cake can be made up to this point up to 1 day in advance; refrigerate, covered, until ready to proceed.

Fill a pastry bag fitted with a large star tip (such as an Ateco #5) with Almond Swiss Meringue. Pipe stars to cover the entire surface of the cake, pulling up as you pipe to form points. Using a small kitchen torch, lightly brown the meringue all over. Let cake stand at room temperature until ready to serve, up to 6 hours.

ALMOND SWISS MERINGUE
MAKES ENOUGH FOR ONE DOMED, 10-INCH LAYER CAKE (ABOUT 8 CUPS)

8 large egg whites	Pinch of salt
2 cups sugar	1 drop pure almond extract

In the heatproof bowl of an electric mixer, combine egg whites, sugar, salt, and almond extract. Set the bowl over a pan of gently simmering water. Whisk constantly until the sugar has dissolved and whites are hot to the touch, 3 to 5 minutes. Using a rubber spatula, scrape down the sides of the bowl.

Attach the bowl to the electric mixer fitted with the whisk attachment; mix on medium-high speed, about 2 minutes. Raise speed to high and beat until stiff, glossy peaks form, about 6 minutes. Use immediately.

MARTHA'S BIRTHDAY CAKE HOW-TO 1. The cake is baked in a stainless steel bowl, which gives the cake a dome shape when inverted. **2.** After splitting the dome into four layers, almond-flavored buttercream and apricot jam are used to flavor alternating layers. **3.** The filled cake is given a crumb coat of buttercream before its final layer of piped meringue.

Martha's Birthday Cake

AMARETTO SIMPLE SYRUP
MAKES ENOUGH FOR ONE DOMED, 10-INCH LAYER CAKE (ABOUT ¾ CUP)

½ cup sugar

3 tablespoons Amaretto liqueur

In a small saucepan, combine ½ cup water and the sugar over medium-high heat. Cook, stirring, until sugar has dissolved. Stop stirring, and bring to a boil; reduce to a simmer, and cook until mixture has thickened slightly, about 3 minutes. Remove from heat, and stir in Amaretto. Cool syrup to room temperature before using. The syrup can be refrigerated in an airtight container, up to 1 month.

ALMOND BUTTERCREAM
MAKES ENOUGH FOR ONE DOMED, 10-INCH LAYER CAKE (ABOUT 2½ CUPS)

3 large egg whites

⅔ cups sugar

2 sticks (1 cup) unsalted butter, cold, cut into tablespoons

½ teaspoon pure almond extract

In the heatproof bowl of an electric mixer set over a pan of simmering water, combine egg whites and sugar. Whisk constantly until the sugar has dissolved and mixture is very warm to the touch, 3 to 5 minutes.

Attach the bowl to the electric mixer fitted with the whisk attachment; beat, starting on low speed and gradually increasing to high, until stiff, glossy peaks form, about 5 minutes. Switch to the paddle attachment. With the mixer on medium-high speed, quickly add butter, a few tablespoons at a time, beating until mixture is smooth and has increased in volume. (If the frosting appears to separate after all the butter has been added, continue beating until smooth again.) Add almond extract, and continue beating until incorporated. Reduce speed to low, and continue beating for 2 minutes to eliminate any air bubbles.

MOCHA-PISTACHIO WEDDING CAKE

SERVES 75 *This cake, with its alternating white and pistachio-flavored layers, was originally created for the wedding of Fraser Lewis and Matthew Edwards. All components of the cake—the cake layers, pastry cream, and buttercream—can and probably should be made at least a day in advance. If you plan to transport the cake, assemble the individual tiers first, giving them their final coat of buttercream, then stack them. Place the bottom tier (still on its cardboard round) on a wooden cake board at least four inches wider than the tier. To keep the cake from slipping, line the wooden board with a rubberized nonslip mat, or secure the cardboard round to the board with hot glue. If possible, pipe the decorations once you have reached your location; wait to garnish the cake with the flowers until it is positioned on the serving table.*

	Unsalted butter, room temperature, for pans	2	recipes Mocha Buttercream (page 213)
4	recipes White Cupcake batter (page 169)		Mocha Pastry Cream (page 214)
¼	cup pure pistachio extract Simple Syrup (page 214)		Fresh garden roses, for garnish (choose organically grown blooms free of pesticides)
5	recipes Swiss Meringue Buttercream (page 386)		

Preheat the oven to 350°F, with racks in the upper and lower thirds. Generously butter two 6-by-3-inch round cake pans, two 10-by-3-inch round cake pans, and two 14-by-3-inch round cake pans; set aside.

Bake the white cakes: Divide about a third of the cake batter among one each of the 6-inch, 10-inch, and 14-inch pans, so that each is filled with about 1 inch of batter. (You will need about 2 cups batter for the 6-inch pan, 5 cups for the 10-inch, and 10 cups for the 14-inch.) Set aside remaining cake batter. Bake until the cakes are golden and a cake tester inserted in the centers comes out clean, 15 to 20 minutes for the 6-inch layer, 30 minutes for the 10-inch layer, and 40 minutes for the 14-inch layer. Transfer pans to a wire rack to cool completely. Cakes can be refrigerated in their pans, and wrapped in plastic, for up to 1 week.

Bake the pistachio cakes: Add the pistachio extract to the remaining two-thirds batter, and fold to combine. Distribute the pistachio cake batter among the remaining pans so that there is about 1½ inches of batter in each pan (about 3 cups batter for the 6-inch pan, 7½ cups for the 10-inch, and 15 cups for the 14-inch). Bake until the cakes are golden and a cake tester inserted in the centers comes out clean, about 25 minutes for the 6-inch layer, 35 minutes for the 10-inch layer, and 50 minutes for the 14-inch layer. Transfer pans to a wire rack to cool completely. Store cakes as above.

Prepare the cake layers: Working with one layer at a time, remove a cake from the refrigerator and place on a clean work surface. Trim the tops of the white cakes to make level; set aside. Trim the tops of the pistachio cakes to make level. To cut each pistachio cake into two layers, insert toothpicks at 2-inch intervals around the cake's circumference, halfway up the side. Holding the top of the cake steady with one hand, use the serrated knife to slice through the cake just above the toothpicks; carefully cut all the way through the cake with a gentle sawing motion. Set the two layers aside, and repeat with remaining cakes.

WEDDING CAKE HOW-TO
1. After the pistachio layers are trimmed and leveled, they are marked with toothpicks halfway up the sides, then cut in half. **2.** Each layer is lightly brushed with Simple Syrup to moisten the cake and add sweetness. **3.** A "dam" of buttercream is piped around the perimeter of the bottom layer to hold the filling in place.

4

5

6

4. Mocha Buttercream is spread over the bottom layer of the tier within the dam. **5.** The middle layer is placed on top and spread with Mocha Pastry Cream. **6.** Using an offset spatula, the vanilla frosting is spread over the assembled tier; it's best to start in the center and work out.

Assemble the tiers: Place the bottom layer of the 6-inch pistachio cake, cut side up, on a 6-inch cardboard round. Brush the layer with some of the Simple Syrup (about 2 tablespoons). Fit a pastry bag with a ½-inch plain round pastry tip (such as an Ateco #806), and fill halfway with Swiss Meringue Buttercream. Pipe buttercream in a circle around the top edge to create a dam. Remove the Mocha Buttercream and Mocha Pastry Cream from the refrigerator, and stir pastry cream until smooth. Using an offset or rubber spatula, spread a ½-inch-thick layer of Mocha Buttercream (about ¾ cup) over the top of the layer, inside the dam.

Place the 6-inch white cake layer, cut side up, on the bottom pistachio layer; brush the top with some syrup. Repeat the piping of the Swiss Meringue Buttercream to create a dam, and fill in with a ½-inch-thick layer of Mocha Pastry Cream. Place the top layer of the pistachio cake, trimmed side up, on the middle cake layer; brush with syrup.

Using a large offset spatula, spread a thin layer of Swiss Meringue Buttercream over the assembled tier, starting from the top center and working toward the edge, and then spreading over the sides. Cover all of the exposed cake; this will help to seal in crumbs and create a flawless finish. Use the spatula to smooth as much as possible, but don't worry about making it look perfect, as it will be covered by more buttercream. Refrigerate (uncovered) for at least 1 hour or overnight. Repeat to assemble remaining tiers, placing the 10-inch bottom layer on a 10-inch cardboard round and the 14-inch bottom layer on a 14-inch cardboard round. You will need about ¼ cup syrup for each 10-inch cake layer, and ½ cup syrup for each 14-inch layer. Allow about 2½ cups each buttercream and pastry cream for the 10-inch tier, and 5 cups for the 14-inch tier.

Assemble the cake: Remove the 14-inch tier from the refrigerator. Using the offset spatula, apply another (thicker) layer of Swiss Meringue Buttercream, starting at the top and then frosting the sides. Smooth the sides with a bench scraper, and the top with the spatula. For the cleanest surface and neatest edge, wipe off the spatula, dip it in a glass of hot water, and dry it with a clean kitchen cloth; use the warm spatula to smooth the top.

Insert a wooden dowel vertically through the center of the 14-inch tier; mark the dowel with a sharp knife at the point where it is level with the top of the cake, then remove the dowel. Using garden shears, cut the dowel at the marked point. Using this dowel as a guide, cut five more dowels to this length. With a toothpick, trace a 10-inch circle on top of the 14-inch tier (hold an empty cake pan or pot lid above the cake as a guide). Insert five dowels at regular intervals in a circle, just inside the traced circle; be sure to space the dowels evenly in order to fully support the upper tiers. Insert the final dowel in the hole in the center.

Remove the 10-inch tier from the refrigerator. Frost with a second layer of Swiss Meringue Buttercream, as described above. With a wide offset spatula, carefully lift the 10-inch cake from the cardboard round, and center it over the marked circle on the 14-inch tier; gently lower onto the tier, carefully removing the spatula once the cake has settled.

Remove the 6-inch tier from the refrigerator. Frost with a second layer of Swiss Meringue Buttercream, as described above. Trace a 6-inch circle on the top of the 10-

inch tier; lift the 6-inch tier off the cardboard round, center the cake over the marked circle on the 10-inch tier, and gently lower onto cake. Carefully remove the spatula.

Transfer Swiss Meringue Buttercream to a clean pastry bag. Using a medium-size leaf tip (such as an Ateco #69), pipe leaves of buttercream in two layers along the top edge of each tier. Switch to a medium plain round tip (such as an Ateco #10), and pipe a border of beads around the base of each tier. Switch to a small plain round tip (such as an Ateco #6), and pipe three small dots in a triangle formation above the beaded borders at ¾-inch intervals; pipe identical dot-clusters just below the bottom rows of leaves at the same interval. Decorate the finished cake with fresh garden roses, placing a few on each tier, as well as at the base of the cake.

MOCHA BUTTERCREAM
DOUBLE RECIPE FOR ONE TIERED WEDDING CAKE (ABOUT 6 CUPS TOTAL)

¼ cup instant espresso powder

¼ cup hot water

4 large egg whites

1¼ cups sugar

3 sticks (1½ cups) unsalted butter, cut into pieces, set out at room temperature for 20 minutes

8 ounces (½ pound) bittersweet chocolate, coarsely chopped, melted, and cooled

In a small bowl, combine the espresso powder with the hot water, and stir until dissolved; set aside. In a heatproof bowl set over a pan of simmering water, whisk together the egg whites and sugar until the sugar is dissolved, and the mixture is warm to the touch, 2 to 3 minutes.

In the bowl of an electric mixer fitted with the whisk attachment, beat the egg-white mixture on high speed until slightly cooled and stiff, and glossy (but not dry) peaks have formed, about 6 minutes.

Switch to the paddle attachment. With the mixer on medium-low speed, add the butter, several tablespoons at a time, beating well after each addition (the mixture will deflate slightly as butter is added). Continue beating until smooth and fluffy, 3 to 5 minutes. (If the frosting appears to separate after all the butter has been added, beat on medium-high speed until smooth again.) With the mixer on low speed, add the chocolate, then the espresso mixture; beat until smooth, about 1 minute. Beat on the lowest speed to eliminate any air bubbles, about 2 minutes. Cover with plastic wrap, and refrigerate until ready to use.

WEDDING CAKE HOW-TO
7. The frosting is smoothed with an offset spatula to make a crumb coat, then the cake is put in the refrigerator to set. **8.** Running a bench scraper around the sides of the cake creates a smooth and uniform surface. **9.** Wooden dowels inserted vertically into the bottom tier provide support for the top two tiers of the cake.

MOCHA PASTRY CREAM
MAKES ENOUGH FOR ONE TIERED WEDDING CAKE (ABOUT 8 CUPS)

3 tablespoons instant espresso powder

3 tablespoons hot water

6 large whole eggs, plus 6 large egg yolks

2 cups sugar

6 cups whole milk

1½ vanilla beans, split lengthwise and seeds scraped

1 cup plus 2 tablespoons cornstarch

¾ teaspoon salt

6 tablespoons unsalted butter, cut into small pieces

6 ounces bittersweet chocolate, coarsely chopped

Prepare an ice bath; set aside. In a small bowl, combine the espresso powder and hot water, and stir until dissolved; set aside. In a medium bowl, combine the whole eggs, egg yolks, and 1 cup sugar. Whisk to combine.

In a medium saucepan, combine the milk, vanilla seeds, cornstarch, salt, and remaining cup of sugar. Bring to a boil over medium-high heat, whisking constantly. Remove from the heat; slowly pour about a third of the hot milk mixture into the egg mixture, whisking constantly until combined. Pour egg mixture back into the remaining milk, whisking constantly. Return saucepan to medium-high heat. Bring to a boil, whisking constantly, until mixture is thick enough to hold a trail when you drag a wooden spoon through it, about 3 minutes.

Whisk in butter, one piece at a time. Whisk in chopped chocolate and espresso mixture; continue whisking until smooth and combined. Strain the mixture into a large, heat-proof bowl. Cover with plastic wrap, pressing it directly onto the surface to prevent a skin from forming. Place in the ice bath until completely chilled, stirring occasionally, about 30 minutes. Cover and refrigerate until ready to use, up to 3 days.

SIMPLE SYRUP

MAKES ENOUGH FOR ONE TIERED WEDDING CAKE (ABOUT 4 CUPS) *Syrup can be made up to one week in advance; refrigerate in an airtight container until ready to use.*

3 cups sugar

3 cups water

Prepare an ice bath; set aside. Combine sugar and water in a medium saucepan; bring to a boil over medium-high heat. Cook, stirring occasionally, until sugar has completely dissolved. Transfer to a medium bowl, and set in the ice bath; let stand until chilled, stirring occasionally, before using or storing.

PIES, TARTS, COBBLERS, AND CRISPS

The calendar has twelve months of the year; the kitchen has four seasons of pies and tarts. Autumn calls for the warm layers of an Apple Crumb Pie. The holidays summon the fragrant spices of a pumpkin filling. And spring beckons a long-awaited Rhubarb Tart.

HEN, OF COURSE, there's summer, the time of year when pies and tarts can flaunt nearly anything put forth by an orchard, a berry patch, or—in the case of our savory pies and tarts—a thriving vegetable garden.

Pie making almost always begins with the crust. If you haven't made your own crust before, don't be intimidated. Although the process requires precision, it's not difficult. And how satisfying it is to transform four humble ingredients—flour, butter, ice water, and salt—into the wonderfully versatile pâte brisée, the basic dough for many pies. Make it a few times, and you'll have tender, flaky crusts down pat. (And while you're learning, you'll no doubt discover that even pies that don't turn out perfectly are still devoured.) Regardless of your level of expertise when you begin, you'll soon be able to tackle any recipe in this chapter with aplomb.

For all the exactitude in making the dough, much of a pie's or tart's appeal lies in its homespun qualities: the free-form shape of a Cherry Galette, or the wine-dark syrup that bubbles up and over the sides of a Plum-Oat Crisp. And when it comes to filling pies, tarts, cobblers, and crisps, there is plenty of room for improvisation. You can add blueberries to an Apricot-Blackberry Galette, for example, or alternate piping lemon, lime, grapefruit, and passion fruit curds into multiple Fruit Curd Tartlets.

A crust or shell truly makes the perfect foundation, be it for a fanciful bouquet of fruit "roses" in a Nectarine Tart or an artful arrangement of nuts and pastry leaves on a Pecan Pie. Simply consider the bounty that the season offers, and take your pick.

When making pie dough, it is essential that the water (or other liquid) and butter (or shortening) **be chilled until very cold.** For best results, chill dry ingredients, such as flour and sugar, as well.

Pie dough must be made very quickly, before the ingredients have time to become warm. It's best to use a food processor for the job; the entire mixing process shouldn't take longer than 1 minute.

When **adding liquid to the dry ingredients** in a pie dough, pour it in a little at a time. Remember, too, that you might not need to add all of the liquid; stop when the dough starts to come together.

Handle the dough **as little as possible.**

Chilling dough will keep the butter from melting too quickly and help the pastry hold its shape as it bakes. If you are making a decorative crust, roll out the dough and chill it in the freezer for about 30 minutes before cutting it into shapes or strips. To help assembled pies hold their shape, chill them in the freezer for about 30 minutes before baking.

To **keep tart dough from shrinking in the oven,** use your fingers to press the dough up the side of the tart pan; make it a bit thicker on the edge of the shell, with some rising a bit above the rim. Chill the dough before you begin baking.

Prebaking, or **blind-baking,** means to bake a crust before filling it. The technique is often used with single-crust pies. Fit the dough into the pie plate or tart pan, prick it all over with a fork, and then cover the dough with pie weights (or dried beans bundled in cheesecloth) before baking.

Let blind-baked items cool completely before filling them; otherwise, you could end up cooking some of the filling, especially if it contains egg.

When **thickening fruit pies,** you can use an equal amount of instant tapioca in place of flour. The juices that run from the finished pie will be clearer, and the taste won't be affected at all.

Bake fruit pies on a rimmed baking sheet lined with parchment or a nonstick baking mat. The sheet will provide a constant heat source and encourage even browning. This also makes it easier to transport the pie and to rotate it halfway through the baking time. Your oven will also stay clean, since any juices will drop onto the sheet.

If a pie's top crust looks as though it's browning too quickly, **tent the pie with foil** to shield it from the heat until the rest of the pie has finished baking. If just the edges of the crust are browning too quickly, cover them with a ring of foil.

For most pies, the dough can be rolled out **up to a day ahead.** Refrigerate the pie shell (and sheet of dough for double-crust pies) wrapped in plastic.

To use up **leftover dough,** try cutting out decorative shapes and sprinkling them with cinnamon and sugar. Bake them in a 350-degree oven until golden brown, and serve them as treats.

1 Rolling pin
Look for a wooden pin that's slender and long—1½ by 18 inches is ideal—and without handles or tapered ends. Straight pins allow for the most control and let you "feel" the dough as you roll.

2 Glass pie plate
Heat disperses well in a tempered-glass pie plate, allowing for more even browning. The clear glass also lets you see the color of the bottom crust.

3 Pie weights in cheesecloth
Pie weights help prevent blind-baked crusts from shrinking and puffing up. Weights made of ceramic or metal are sold at baking-supply stores, but dried beans or rice—bundled in cheesecloth and secured with twine—also will do a fine job.

4 Decorative cutters
Pies with a top crust require vents or holes to let steam escape in the oven. These are usually cut with a sharp knife—but for a decorative touch, try using small cookie cutters of various shapes. An autumnal pie, for example, can have leaf cutouts. You can then use the dough cutouts to decorate the top crust. Or, in lieu of a crust, cover the entire surface of a pie filling with cutouts, overlapping them slightly and leaving some open areas for steam (see the Fourth of July Blueberry Pie, page 231). Cutouts can also be used to decorate edges of single-crust pies.

5 Metal pie tins
Although glass pie plates are preferable, metal ones certainly have old-fashioned appeal. We use them for our Tarte Tatin and for some individual tarts.

6 Pastry cutter
Use a pastry cutter to create lattice strips; one with a fluted edge adds decorative flair. A straight-edged pizza wheel can be used instead.

1 Fluted tart pan with removable bottom

Tarts owe much of their elegant appearance to the pans in which they're baked. Traditional pans have short, fluted sides and come in a variety of shapes and sizes. The delicate crust of a tart can be difficult to remove; a pan with a removable bottom allows you to easily unmold the tart.

2 Flan ring

If you prefer a tart with straight rather than fluted sides, bake it in a flan ring, which can come in various shapes. The thin molds don't have a base; they're meant to be placed on a parchment-lined cookie sheet and then filled with crust. The straight sides give tarts a clean, modern look, and the ring is easy to lift away once the pastry is baked.

3 Ceramic baking dish

These shallow ovenproof dishes are excellent for slow-cooked, individual desserts with crumbly tops and fruit-filled bottoms, such as cobblers and crisps. They're also beautiful enough to go straight from the oven to the table.

4 Cake rings (entremets)

Used for baking single-crust pies and tart shells, these rings—positioned on baking sheets—produce more dramatic-looking pies and tarts than those baked in traditional pie plates or tart pans.

5 Tartlet pans

These minitart pans are wonderful for baking an array of small treats. No removable bottoms are needed; the goods are tiny enough to flip right out.

6 Barquette molds

The name of this mold refers to its shape, which is thought to resemble a small ship called a bark (in French, *barquette*). It can be used to make tartlets.

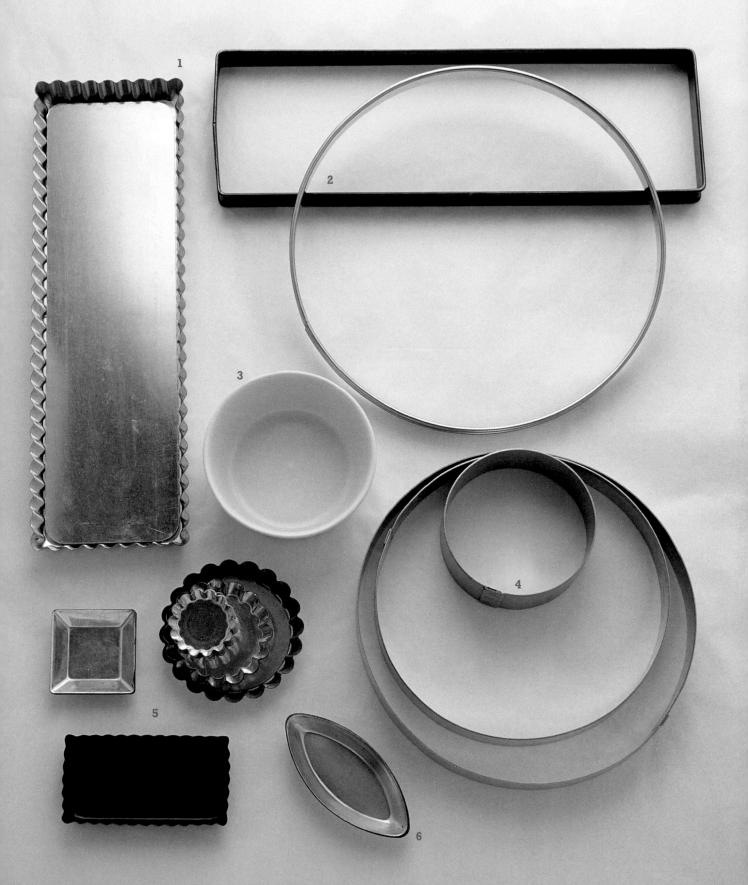

PÂTE BRISÉE

MAKES ENOUGH FOR ONE DOUBLE-CRUST OR TWO SINGLE-CRUST 9-INCH PIES *For the flakiest crust, make sure all ingredients (including the flour) are cold before you begin.*

2½ cups all-purpose flour

1 teaspoon salt

2 sticks (1 cup) unsalted butter, cold, cut into small pieces

¼ cup ice water, plus more if needed

In the bowl of a food processor, combine flour and salt; pulse to combine. Add the butter, and pulse until mixture resembles coarse crumbs with some larger pieces remaining, about 10 seconds. (To mix by hand, combine dry ingredients in a large mixing bowl, then cut in butter with a pastry blender.)

With the machine running, add the ice water through the feed tube in a slow, steady stream, just until the dough holds together without being wet or sticky. Do not process more than 30 seconds. Test by squeezing a small amount of the dough together; if it is still too crumbly, add a bit more water, 1 tablespoon at a time.

Turn out the dough onto a clean work surface. Divide in half, and place each half on a piece of plastic wrap. Shape into flattened disks. Wrap in plastic, and refrigerate at least 1 hour or overnight. The dough can be frozen for up to 1 month; thaw overnight in the refrigerator before using.

TART DOUGH

This dough yields enough to make any of the recipes in this chapter that call for it. The shape of your tart—round, square, or rectangular—should determine how you form the dough in the final step.

6 tablespoons unsalted butter, room temperature

½ cup confectioners' sugar

2 large egg yolks

1½ cups all-purpose flour

¼ teaspoon salt

2 teaspoons heavy cream

In the bowl of an electric mixer fitted with the paddle attachment, combine butter and confectioners' sugar. Mix on low speed until combined, about 2 minutes.

Add egg yolks, and mix until incorporated, about 1 minute, scraping down the sides of the bowl as necessary. Add ¾ cup flour, and mix on low speed just until the flour is incorporated, about 30 seconds. Add remaining ¾ cup flour along with the salt and cream, and mix just until flour is no longer visible, about 1 minute.

Turn out dough onto a piece of plastic wrap, and shape into a flattened disk. Wrap in plastic, and refrigerate for at least 2 hours or overnight. The dough can be frozen for up to 1 month; thaw overnight in the refrigerator before using.

MAKING PÂTE BRISÉE **1.** After the dry ingredients are pulsed together, the butter pieces are added all at once. The mixture is pulsed again until it has clumps ranging in size from coarse crumbs to $\frac{1}{2}$ inch. This usually requires only a few pulses; it's very important not to overprocess the dough. **2.** Ice water is added (with the machine running) until the texture of the dough is crumbly and just holds together; the dough should not be wet or sticky. **3.** The crumbly dough is transferred to a work surface and divided in half. Each portion is placed on a sheet of plastic wrap; the wrap is gathered around the dough and pulled toward the center to form a ball. The dough is then flattened into a disk and chilled.

FITTING PIE DOUGH The pie dough is rolled out to its proper dimension, and then rolled back up over the pin and gently draped over the pie plate. The dough is then fitted into it.

TRIMMING PIE DOUGH Once the dough is fit properly into the pie plate, kitchen shears are used to trim the dough, leaving an even overhang along the perimeter of the plate.

TRIMMING TART DOUGH Tart dough is draped into a fluted pan, then firmly pressed in place. A pin is rolled over the top edge of the pan, trimming the dough so it's flush with the pan.

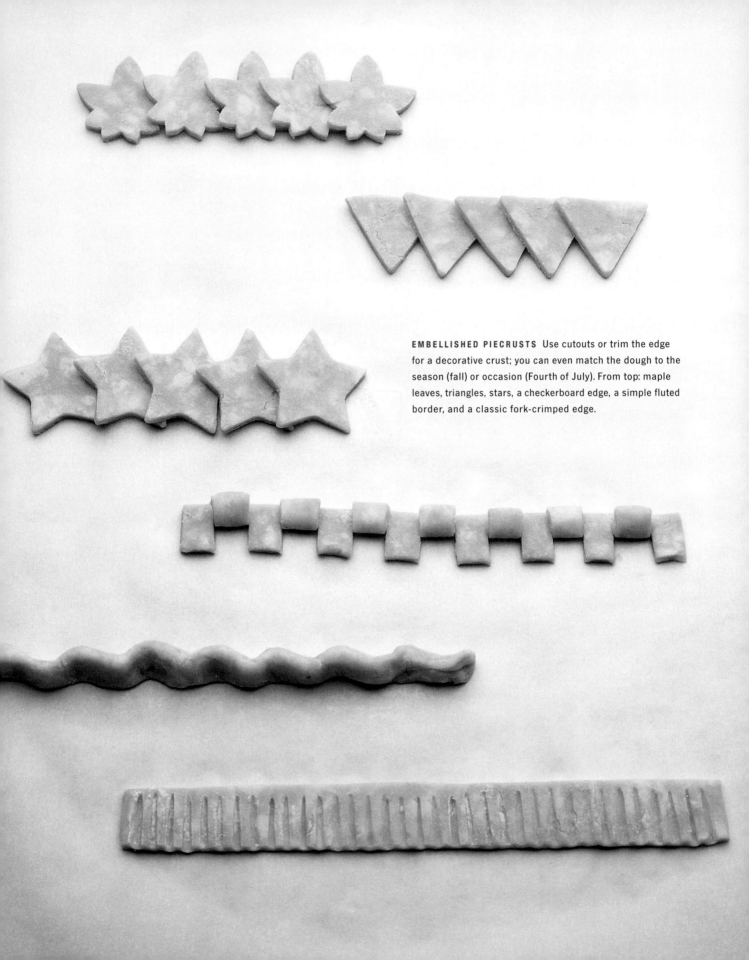

EMBELLISHED PIECRUSTS Use cutouts or trim the edge for a decorative crust; you can even match the dough to the season (fall) or occasion (Fourth of July). From top: maple leaves, triangles, stars, a checkerboard edge, a simple fluted border, and a classic fork-crimped edge.

MAKING A LATTICE TOP **1.** You can weave a lattice directly on the surface of your pie, but for beginners, it's easier to do it on a flat surface and then transfer the lattice to your pie: Lay strips of pastry dough vertically on a lightly floured, parchment-lined baking sheet. **2.** Starting at the middle, weave one horizontal strip at a time over and under the vertical strips (folding back every other vertical strip makes this easier). **3.** Continue weaving horizontal strips until lattice is complete. Chill on baking sheet until firm. Carefully place it on top of the pie; press ends onto edge of bottom crust to seal. Trim if necessary.

BLIND-BAKING SINGLE-CRUST PIES AND TARTS **1.** Before a shell is blind-baked (prebaked before the filling goes in), the bottom of the dough is pricked all over with the tines of a fork; this prevents the dough from puffing up as it bakes. **2.** The pie dough is then lined with parchment paper and topped with pie weights (the weights can be bundled in cheesecloth secured with kitchen twine). **3.** A foil ring can be used to shield the pie rim if it darkens too quickly. To make a ring, press foil onto an empty pie plate to shape; trim outer edge, and cut out center, making a ring that's about 2 inches wide.

fruit pies

CLASSIC APPLE PIE

MAKES ONE DOUBLE-CRUST 9-INCH PIE *A staff favorite, this pie was inspired by the large selection of apples available throughout the autumn months at the Union Square Greenmarket in New York City. Using many varieties produces the best flavor.*

3 tablespoons all-purpose flour, plus more for dusting	2 tablespoons fresh lemon juice
Pâte Brisée (page 224)	¼ cup granulated sugar
1 large egg yolk	1 teaspoon ground cinnamon
1 tablespoon heavy cream	¼ teaspoon freshly grated nutmeg
3 pounds assorted apples (such as Macoun, Granny Smith, Cortland, Jonagold, or Empire), peeled, cored, and cut into ¼-inch-thick slices	⅛ teaspoon salt
	1 tablespoon unsalted butter, cut into small pieces
	Sanding sugar (or granulated sugar), for sprinkling

On a lightly floured piece of parchment paper, roll out one disk of dough to a 12-inch round. With a dry pastry brush, sweep off the excess flour; fit dough into a 9-inch glass pie plate, pressing it into the edges. Trim to a ½-inch overhang all around. Roll out remaining disk of dough in the same manner; transfer dough (on parchment) to a baking sheet. Chill pie shell and dough until firm, about 30 minutes.

In a small bowl, whisk together the egg yolk and cream; set aside egg wash. In a large bowl, toss together the apples, lemon juice, granulated sugar, flour, cinnamon, nutmeg, and salt; arrange in the chilled pie shell. Dot with butter.

Brush the rim of the pie shell with egg wash. Place the second piece of dough on top, and gently press over the apples. Gently press the top and bottom pieces of dough together to seal. Using kitchen scissors, trim the top piece of dough to a 1-inch overhang all around. Tuck dough under, and crimp edge as desired. Brush the entire surface of the pie with egg wash, and sprinkle generously with sanding sugar. Cut three vents in the top to allow steam to escape. Freeze until firm, about 30 minutes. Meanwhile, preheat the oven to 400°F, with the rack in the lower third.

Place pie on a parchment-lined baking sheet. Bake until the crust begins to turn golden, about 20 minutes. Reduce oven temperature to 350°F. Continue baking, rotating sheet halfway through, until the crust is a deep golden brown and the juices are bubbling and have thickened, 40 to 50 minutes more. Transfer pie to a wire rack to cool completely. The pie is best eaten the day it is baked, but it can be kept at room temperature, loosely covered with plastic wrap, for up to 2 days.

FOURTH OF JULY BLUEBERRY PIE

MAKES ONE 9-INCH PIE *If you are fortunate enough to find wild blueberries while they are in season, by all means use them in this recipe; they are smaller than cultivated berries, so you may need an extra cup or two to make up the volume necessary for the pie.*

All-purpose flour, for dusting
Pâte Brisée (page 224)

8 cups (about 4 pints) fresh blueberries, picked over

½ cup sugar

¼ cup cornstarch

1 tablespoon freshly squeezed lemon juice

2 tablespoons unsalted butter, cut into small pieces

1 large egg yolk

1 tablespoon heavy cream

On a lightly floured piece of parchment paper, roll out one disk of dough to a 12-inch round. With a dry pastry brush, sweep off excess flour; fit dough into a 9-inch glass pie plate, pressing it into the edges. Trim dough to a ½-inch overhang all around. Fold edge of dough over or under, and crimp as desired. Roll out remaining dough in the same manner; transfer dough (on parchment) to a baking sheet. Chill pie shell and dough until firm, about 30 minutes.

Place blueberries in a large bowl; with your hands, crush about ½ cup of the berries, letting them fall into the bowl as you work. Add the sugar, cornstarch, and lemon juice; stir to combine. Spoon mixture into chilled pie shell, mounding berries slightly in the center. Dot with butter. Remove the dough from the refrigerator. Using a 2½-inch star cookie cutter, cut out about 25 stars; set aside.

In a small bowl, whisk together egg yolk and cream. Lightly brush rim of chilled pie shell with egg wash. Arrange the reserved stars in a circular pattern on top of the fruit (with the tips touching), gently pressing over the berries, until covered. Brush the entire surface of rim and stars with egg wash, being careful not to let it pool. Freeze or refrigerate pie until firm, about 30 minutes. Meanwhile, preheat the oven to 400°F, with the rack in the lower third.

Place pie on a parchment-lined baking sheet. Bake until the crust begins to turn golden, about 20 minutes. Reduce oven temperature to 350°F. Continue baking, rotating sheet halfway through, until the crust is deep golden brown and the juices are bubbling and have thickened, 40 to 50 minutes more. Transfer pie to a wire rack to cool completely. The pie is best eaten the day it is baked, but it can be kept at room temperature, loosely covered with plastic wrap, for up to 2 days.

BLUEBERRY PIE HOW-TO
1. Pâte brisée is chilled until firm, then cut into stars.
2. The stars are placed, slightly overlapping, atop the fruit filling, then brushed with egg wash before baking.

GOOSEBERRY PIE

MAKES ONE DOUBLE-CRUST 9-INCH DEEP-DISH PIE *Martha grows gooseberries, which inspired this pie, in her garden in Bedford, New York. Although their season is short (early summer), gooseberries are worth seeking out for their unique flavor. They can be very tart, so increase the sugar if you prefer your pie on the sweet side.*

	All-purpose flour, for dusting
	Tender Pie Dough (recipe follows)
6	cups fresh gooseberries, stemmed
1½	cups granulated sugar
2	tablespoons instant tapioca
1	teaspoon ground cinnamon
	Juice of ½ lemon (about 1 tablespoon)

¼	teaspoon salt
1½	tablespoons unsalted butter, cut into small pieces
1	large egg yolk
1	tablespoon heavy cream
	Sanding sugar (or granulated sugar), for sprinkling

On a piece of parchment generously dusted with flour, roll out one disk of dough to a 12-inch round. With a dry pastry brush, sweep off excess flour; fit dough into a 9-inch glass pie plate, pressing it into the edges. Trim dough to a ½-inch overhang all around. Roll out remaining disk of dough in the same manner; transfer (on parchment) to a baking sheet. Chill pie shell and dough until firm, about 30 minutes.

In a large bowl, toss together the gooseberries, granulated sugar, tapioca, cinnamon, lemon juice, and salt. Spoon into pie shell, mounding slightly in the center. Dot with butter. Lightly brush rim of pie shell with water. Center the remaining rolled dough on top of the fruit; gently press over the berries. Gently press the top and bottom pieces of dough together to seal. Using kitchen scissors, trim top piece of dough to a 1-inch overhang all around. Tuck dough under, and crimp edge as desired.

Using a 1-inch round cookie cutter, make cuts in the top crust to allow steam to escape (do not remove rounds of dough). In a small bowl, whisk together egg yolk and cream; brush egg wash over entire surface of pie, being careful not to let it pool. Sprinkle pie generously with sanding sugar. Freeze or refrigerate pie until firm, about 30 minutes. Meanwhile, preheat the oven to 400°F, with the rack in the lower third.

Place pie on a parchment-lined baking sheet. Bake until the crust begins to turn golden, about 20 minutes. Reduce oven temperature to 350°F. Continue baking, rotating sheet halfway through, until crust is deep golden brown and the juices are bubbling and have thickened, 40 to 50 minutes more. Transfer the pie to a wire rack to cool completely. The pie is best eaten the same day it is baked, but it can be kept at room temperature, loosely covered with plastic wrap, for up to 2 days.

TENDER PIE DOUGH

MAKES TWO 8- TO 10-INCH SINGLE-CRUST PIES OR ONE 8- TO 10-INCH DOUBLE-CRUST PIE *This dough gets its texture from a combination of butter and shortening.*

2½ cups all-purpose flour

1 teaspoon salt

½ teaspoon sugar

1 stick (½ cup) unsalted butter, cold, cut into small pieces

½ cup (4 ounces) vegetable shortening, cold, cut into small pieces

½ cup ice water, plus more if needed

Place the flour, salt, and sugar in the bowl of a food processor fitted with the metal blade. Add the butter and shortening, and process just until the mixture resembles coarse crumbs, about 10 seconds. (To mix by hand, combine the dry ingredients in a large bowl; use a pastry blender to cut in the butter and shortening.)

With the machine running, pour ice water through the feed tube in a steady stream until the dough just holds together without being too wet or sticky; do not process more than 30 seconds. Test the dough by squeezing a small amount together: If it is crumbly, add a bit more water.

Turn out the dough onto a work surface. Divide in half. Place each half on a sheet of plastic wrap; flatten into disks. Wrap in plastic, and refrigerate at least 1 hour or up to 2 days. Dough can be frozen, wrapped in plastic, up to 3 weeks; thaw in refrigerator.

Peach, Apricot, and Cherry Pie

PEACH, APRICOT, AND CHERRY PIE

MAKES ONE LATTICE-TOPPED 9-INCH PIE *We like this pie a little on the tart side; if you prefer a sweeter taste, increase the granulated sugar to ¾ cup. To keep the dough from getting soggy, fill the pie shell just before you're ready to cover with top crust.*

All-purpose flour, for dusting
Pâte Brisée (page 224)

1 pound fresh, ripe peaches, pitted and sliced into ¼-inch-thick wedges

1 pound fresh, ripe apricots, pitted and sliced into sixths

1 pound fresh sweet cherries (such as Bing), stemmed, pitted, and halved

⅔ cup granulated sugar

3 tablespoons cornstarch

¼ teaspoon coarse salt

Juice of 1 lemon (about 2 tablespoons)

2 tablespoons unsalted butter, cut into small pieces

1 large egg yolk

1 tablespoon heavy cream

Sanding sugar (or granulated sugar), for sprinkling

On a piece of parchment generously dusted with flour, roll out one disk of dough to a 12-inch round. With a dry pastry brush, sweep off excess flour; fit dough into a 9-inch glass pie plate, pressing it into the edges. Trim dough to a ½-inch overhang all around. Roll out remaining disk of dough in the same manner; transfer (on parchment) to a baking sheet. Chill pie shell and dough until firm, about 30 minutes.

In a large bowl, toss together peaches, apricots, and cherries. Add the granulated sugar, cornstarch, salt, and lemon juice; toss to combine. Remove baking sheet from the refrigerator; transfer dough to a clean work surface. Using a pastry cutter (preferably fluted) or sharp knife, cut dough into ¾- to 1-inch-wide strips.

Spoon the fruit mixture and any juices into the chilled pie shell, mounding fruit slightly in the center. Dot with butter. Brush the rim of the pie shell with water. Weave a tight lattice of dough strips on top of the fruit. Using kitchen scissors, trim dough strips to a ½-inch overhang; gently press top and bottom pieces together to seal. Fold edges over or under, and crimp edge as desired. In a small bowl, whisk together egg yolk and cream; brush on lattice and edge of pie shell, being careful not to let it pool. (If you have any scraps of dough, cut out some pretty shapes to place on top of lattice; adhere them with egg wash.) Generously sprinkle entire surface with sanding sugar. Freeze or refrigerate pie until firm, about 30 minutes. Meanwhile, preheat the oven to 400°F, with the rack in the lower third.

Place pie on a parchment-lined baking sheet. Bake until the crust begins to turn golden, about 20 minutes. Reduce oven temperature to 350°F. Continue baking, rotating sheet halfway through, until the crust is deep golden brown and the juices are bubbling and have thickened, 40 to 50 minutes more. Transfer to a wire rack to cool completely. The pie is best eaten the same day it is baked, but it can be kept at room temperature, loosely covered with plastic wrap, for up to 2 days.

APPLE CRUMB PIE

MAKES ONE 9-INCH PIE *The almond crumb crust is mixed by hand and doesn't require any rolling, which makes this a great pie for beginning bakers.*

Almond Crumb Crust (recipe follows)

3½ pounds assorted apples (such as Macoun, Cortland, Jonagold, Empire, or Rome), peeled, cored, and cut into ¼-inch-thick slices

Juice of 1 lemon (about 2 tablespoons)

⅓ cup sugar

¾ teaspoon ground cinnamon

¼ teaspoon freshly grated nutmeg

¼ teaspoon salt

2 tablespoons unsalted butter, cut into small pieces

Preheat the oven to 350°F. Evenly and firmly press a little more than half of the crumbs (about 2½ cups) into the bottom, up the sides, and onto the rim of a 9-inch glass pie plate. Press firmly into the edges. Freeze pie shell until firm, about 15 minutes.

In a large bowl, toss together apples, lemon juice, sugar, cinnamon, nutmeg, and salt. Pour mixture into the chilled pie shell, mounding apples slightly in the center. Dot with butter. Sprinkle the remaining crumbs in clumps over the apples to cover completely.

Bake, rotating halfway through, until the crust turns golden and the juices begin to bubble, about 1 hour. Transfer to a wire rack to cool completely. The pie can be kept at room temperature, loosely covered with plastic wrap, for up to 2 days.

ALMOND CRUMB CRUST

MAKES ENOUGH FOR ONE 9-INCH PIE *We use a very similar crumb mixture to make the Torta Sbrisolona (page 99) and the Jam Crumb Bars (page 122).*

1½ cups all-purpose flour	¼ teaspoon salt
1 cup plus 2 tablespoons blanched almonds, finely ground	1½ sticks (¾ cup) unsalted butter, room temperature, cut into small pieces
½ cup plus 2 tablespoons sugar	

In a large bowl, whisk together the flour, almonds, sugar, and salt. Using a pastry blender, cut in the butter until the mixture resembles coarse crumbs with a few larger clumps remaining. Using your fingers, squeeze the mixture together to create pea-size to ¾-inch pieces. If not using right away, cover and chill until ready to proceed.

SLAB PIE

MAKES ONE 15-BY-10-INCH PIE *This pie can be made with any berry or stone fruit, although we prefer sour cherries, peaches, or blueberries. If you can't find fresh sour cherries, use two pounds of frozen pitted cherries instead; defrost and drain well before using.*

All-purpose flour, for dusting	1¼ cups granulated sugar
Slab Pie Pâte Brisée (page 394)	¼ cup cornstarch
2½ pounds (about 6 cups) fresh sour cherries, stemmed and pitted; or 2¼ pounds (about 6 cups) fresh blueberries; or 7 medium peaches (2¾ pounds), cut into ½-inch pieces (about 8 cups)	Juice of ½ lemon (about 1 tablespoon)
	¼ teaspoon salt
	2 tablespoons heavy cream
	¼ cup sanding sugar (or granulated sugar)

Preheat the oven to 375°F. On a lightly floured surface, roll out the larger piece of dough to an 18-by-13-inch rectangle. Fit into a 15-by-10-inch rimmed baking sheet, pressing into corners (pastry will hang over sides). Chill while assembling the filling.

In a large bowl, combine the fruit, granulated sugar, cornstarch, lemon juice, and salt. Stir to combine. Spread mixture over the chilled pie shell.

On a lightly floured surface, roll out remaining piece of dough to a 16-by-11-inch rectangle; drape over filling. Fold edge of bottom dough over top dough. Pinch edges to seal. Prick the top dough all over with a fork. Brush the entire surface of the pie with the cream, and sprinkle with the sanding sugar.

Bake until the crust is golden brown and the filling is bubbling, 40 to 55 minutes. Transfer to a wire rack, and let the pie cool until it is just warm to the touch, about 45 minutes. Serve warm or at room temperature, cut into 12 pieces. Slab pie is best eaten the same day it is baked, but it can be kept at room temperature, loosely covered with plastic wrap, for up to 2 days.

COCONUT CREAM PIE

MAKES ONE 9-INCH PIE *This pie can be made ahead and kept in the refrigerator, loosely covered with plastic wrap, for up to three days. Applying a thin coating of melted chocolate to the baked pie shell before filling seals the crust and helps it stay crisp.*

All-purpose flour, for dusting
½ recipe Pâte Brisée (page 224)
1 large whole egg, lightly beaten, plus 4 large egg yolks
Fresh Coconut Curls (page 395)
3 cups canned unsweetened coconut milk

⅔ cup granulated sugar
5 tablespoons cornstarch
¼ teaspoon salt
2 ounces semisweet chocolate
1 cup heavy cream
¼ cup confectioners' sugar
Chocolate Curls (page 395)

**COCONUT CREAM PIE
HOW-TO** The cooled crust
is brushed with a thin layer
of melted semisweet chocolate to keep it crisp once
the filling is added.

Preheat the oven to 375°F. On a lightly floured work surface, roll out the dough to a 12-inch round, a bit less than ¼ inch thick. Fit dough into a 9-inch glass pie plate. Using kitchen shears or a sharp knife, trim the crust to a ½-inch overhang all around. Fold under overhang so it extends slightly beyond the edge of the pie plate. Crimp edge as desired. Prick the dough all over with a fork. Brush the rim of the dough with the beaten egg. Chill pie shell until firm, about 30 minutes.

Line chilled pie shell with a round of parchment paper, leaving a 1-inch overhang. Fill with pie weights or dried beans. Bake until the edges of the crust are just beginning to turn golden, 15 to 20 minutes. Remove parchment and pie weights. Return crust to oven, and continue baking until golden all over, 15 to 20 minutes more. Place pie shell on a wire rack to cool completely. Reduce oven temperature to 325°F.

Place Coconut Curls on a rimmed baking sheet and bake, tossing occasionally, until fragrant and lightly golden, about 10 minutes. Set aside.

Prepare an ice bath; set aside. In a bowl, lightly whisk the egg yolks; set aside. In a saucepan, whisk together coconut milk, granulated sugar, cornstarch, and salt. Bring to a simmer (do not boil), and cook, whisking constantly, 3 to 4 minutes.

Whisk a quarter of the hot milk mixture into the egg yolks; whisk in remaining milk mixture. Strain into a clean saucepan, and cook over medium-high heat, whisking constantly, until custard is thick and bubbles appear in the center, 2 to 3 minutes. Transfer to a medium bowl, and cover with plastic wrap, pressing it directly onto the surface to prevent a skin from forming. Set in the ice bath until completely chilled, 30 to 35 minutes. (Filling can be kept in the refrigerator, covered with plastic wrap, up to 1 day.)

Melt the chocolate in the top of a double boiler or a heatproof bowl set over a pan of simmering water (do not let the bowl touch the water), or in the microwave. Stir until smooth, and set aside until cool to the touch, stirring occasionally.

Using a pastry brush, coat the inside of the cooled crust with melted chocolate. Place in the refrigerator or freezer until firm to the touch, about 10 minutes.

**CHOCOLATE CREAM PIE
HOW-TO** Using a pastry bag
and a decorative leaf tip,
whipped cream is piped on
top of the chocolate filling,
then covered with a sprinkling
of Chocolate Curls.

**BANANA CREAM PIE
HOW-TO** A layer of sliced
bananas is arranged
directly on the baked and
cooled crust; custard,
whipped cream, and more
banana slices follow.

Fill crust with coconut custard, spreading evenly with an offset spatula. In the bowl of an electric mixer fitted with the whisk attachment, combine cream and confectioners' sugar; beat until soft peaks form. Using a small offset spatula, spread the whipped cream on top of the custard. Refrigerate pie at least 3 hours before serving. Garnish with toasted Coconut Curls and Chocolate Curls just before serving.

CHOCOLATE CREAM PIE VARIATION Follow instructions for Coconut Cream Pie. Prepare filling as described, using 3 cups whole milk in place of coconut milk, reducing granulated sugar to ½ cup, increasing cornstarch to 6 tablespoons, and adding ¼ cup Dutch-process cocoa powder. Omit Coconut Curls.

Immediately after whisking hot-milk mixture into egg yolks, add 4 ounces finely chopped semisweet chocolate; whisk until chocolate has melted completely. Strain filling into a medium bowl and cover with plastic wrap, pressing it directly onto the surface to prevent a skin from forming. Set bowl in the ice bath until filling is completely chilled, 30 to 35 minutes. (Filling can be kept in the refrigerator, covered with plastic wrap, up to 1 day.)

Fill coated crust with the custard. Refrigerate pie, loosely covered with plastic wrap, for at least 2 hours and up to 2 days. Whip the cream as instructed in the Coconut Cream Pie recipe, reducing confectioners' sugar to 2 tablespoons. Using a pastry bag fitted with a leaf tip (such as an Ateco #113), pipe whipped cream decoratively on top of filling. Garnish pie with Chocolate Curls. You can refrigerate the pie, with the whipped cream and Chocolate Curls, up to 2 hours before serving.

BANANA CREAM PIE VARIATION Follow instructions for Coconut Cream Pie, allowing crust to cool completely (do not brush with chocolate). Prepare the filling as described, using 3 cups whole milk in place of the coconut milk.

Cut 3 or 4 medium ripe bananas into ¼-inch slices, slightly on the bias. Beginning at the edge of the piecrust, arrange the slices in slightly overlapping rows. Cover with the custard, using an offset spatula to smooth it into an even layer. Whip cream as instructed, reducing confectioners' sugar to 2 tablespoons. Using a small offset spatula, spread whipped cream over custard. Refrigerate pie, loosely covered with plastic wrap, for at least 1 hour or up to 2 days. Just before serving, cut 4 medium ripe bananas in half crosswise, then thinly slice lengthwise. Arrange the banana slices in three slightly overlapping rows on top of the whipped cream. Omit the Fresh Coconut Curls and the Chocolate Curls.

Banana Cream Pie

TORTA DELLA NONNA

MAKES ONE 9-INCH DOUBLE-CRUST PIE *Almost every region in Italy has a variation of "grandmother's cake," but this one was created after tasting a version at an Italian restaurant in New York City. Durum wheat, included here, is most commonly used to make semolina for pasta. This pie is best eaten the same day it is baked.*

4 large egg yolks	½ teaspoon salt
1 cup granulated sugar	4 tablespoons unsalted butter, cut into small pieces
2 cups milk	All-purpose flour, for dusting
½ vanilla bean, split lengthwise, seeds scraped	Pasta Frolla (recipe follows)
½ cup durum wheat	Confectioners' sugar, for dusting

Prepare an ice bath; set aside. In a medium bowl, whisk together the egg yolks and ½ cup granulated sugar until thick and lightened; set aside.

In a saucepan, combine milk, vanilla bean and seeds, remaining ½ cup granulated sugar, durum wheat, and salt. Cook over medium-high heat, stirring constantly, until slightly thickened, about 3 minutes. Remove from heat; slowly pour about a third of the milk mixture into the egg-yolk mixture, whisking constantly until combined. Pour mixture back into the remaining milk, whisking constantly to combine.

Return pan to medium-high heat. Bring mixture to a boil, whisking constantly, until custard is thick enough to hold a clear trail when the whisk is lifted, 2 to 4 minutes.

Transfer the custard to a large heatproof bowl. Whisk in the butter until combined. Set bowl in the ice bath, and stir frequently until completely cool, 30 to 35 minutes. Cover with plastic wrap, pressing it directly onto the surface of the custard to prevent a skin from forming. Use the custard immediately or keep in the refrigerator, covered with plastic wrap, until ready to use, up to 3 days.

Preheat the oven to 350°F. On a lightly floured work surface, roll out the larger disk of Pasta Frolla to an 11-inch round, about ⅛ inch thick. Fit into a 9-inch tart pan with a removable bottom, pressing into edges. Using a sharp paring knife, trim dough to within ¼ inch of the top of the pan. Roll out the smaller disk to slightly less than 9 inches in diameter so that it will fit atop the filling.

Using a small offset spatula, spread the custard evenly in the tart shell, then lay the smaller round of dough on top. Brush the rim of the bottom crust with water, and gently press the excess dough over the top crust to seal.

Bake, rotating the tart halfway through, until golden brown, about 45 minutes. Transfer to a wire rack to cool for 20 minutes. Remove from the tart pan, and let tart cool completely. Just before serving, generously dust with confectioners' sugar.

PASTA FROLLA

MAKES ENOUGH FOR ONE 9-INCH DOUBLE-CRUST PIE *Pasta frolla is commonly used in Italian pies and tarts. It can be frozen for up to one month; thaw before using.*

2⅓ cups all-purpose flour	½ cup sugar
1 teaspoon baking powder	Freshly grated zest of ½ orange
Pinch of salt	1 large whole egg, plus
1 stick (½ cup) unsalted butter, room temperature	1 large egg yolk

In a medium bowl, whisk together the flour, baking powder, and salt; set aside.

In the bowl of an electric mixer fitted with the paddle attachment, beat butter and sugar on medium speed until light and fluffy, about 2 minutes. Beat in the orange zest. Add whole egg and egg yolk, beating until incorporated. Reduce speed to low, and beat in reserved flour mixture. Divide dough into two pieces, one slightly larger than the other. Flatten into disks, and wrap each in plastic. Refrigerate 1 hour or overnight. Before using, let dough sit at room temperature until pliable enough to roll.

RUM-RAISIN PIE

MAKES ONE 9-INCH SINGLE-CRUST PIE *This was inspired by a favorite ice cream, rum raisin. For the deepest flavor, use a dark rum, such as Myer's; light rum just won't taste the same.*

All-purpose flour, for dusting

½ recipe Pâte Brisée (page 224)

3 cups heavy cream, plus
⅔ cup for serving

⅔ cup granulated sugar

4 large whole eggs, plus 2 large egg yolks

¼ teaspoon salt

¼ cup dark rum

¼ cup golden raisins

¼ cup confectioners' sugar

On a lightly floured work surface, roll out the dough to a 12-inch round, a bit less than ¼ inch thick. Fit into a 9-inch glass pie plate, pressing into the edges. For the checkerboard edging, trim the dough to the outer edge of the pie plate, then make ½-inch cuts at ¾-inch intervals all around. Bend every other tab of crust forward. Chill pie shell until firm, about 30 minutes. Meanwhile, preheat the oven to 400°F.

Line chilled pie shell with a round of parchment paper, leaving a 1-inch overhang. Fill with pie weights or dried beans. Bake until the edges of the crust are just beginning to turn golden, about 15 minutes. Remove parchment and weights. Reduce oven temperature to 375°F. Return crust to the oven; continue baking until light golden all over, 15 to 20 minutes more. Cool completely on a wire rack.

Pour 3 cups cream into a medium saucepan, and place over medium-high heat; cook until just beginning to boil. Remove from heat. Meanwhile, whisk together granulated sugar, whole eggs, egg yolks, and salt in a medium bowl. Whisking constantly, slowly pour in hot cream until combined; pour back into saucepan. Cook over medium-low heat, stirring constantly with a wooden spoon, until mixture is thick enough to coat the back of the spoon and hold a line when you drag a finger through it, 10 to 12 minutes. Stir in the rum. Remove from heat; set aside.

Sort through the raisins, separating any that are stuck together. Arrange the raisins in an even layer on the bottom of the cooled crust. Carefully pour in the hot custard; bake, rotating the pie halfway through, until filling is set in the middle, 25 to 30 minutes. Transfer pie to a wire rack to cool completely.

Just before serving, combine the remaining ⅔ cup cream and the confectioners' sugar in the bowl of an electric mixer fitted with the whisk attachment; beat until soft peaks form. Serve slices of pie with a dollop of whipped cream on each. Pie can be kept, chilled and loosely covered with plastic wrap, for up to 3 days.

PUMPKIN PIE

MAKES ONE 9-INCH SINGLE-CRUST PIE *To use fresh pumpkin, halve and place a 1¾-pound sugar pumpkin, cut sides down, in a baking pan. Roast in a 400°F oven until very soft, fifty to sixty minutes. Scoop out flesh and purée in a food processor until very smooth.*

All-purpose flour, for dusting	¾ teaspoon ground cinnamon
Pâte Brisée (page 224)	¾ teaspoon ground ginger
3 large whole eggs, plus	½ teaspoon salt
1 large egg yolk	⅛ teaspoon freshly grated nutmeg
1½ cups canned or fresh pumpkin purée	1½ cups canned evaporated milk
¾ cup packed light-brown sugar	

On a lightly floured work surface, roll out one disk of dough to a 12-inch round. With a dry pastry brush, sweep off excess flour; fit dough into a 9-inch glass pie plate, pressing into the edges. Trim dough to meet the edge of the pie plate. Prick the bottom of the dough all over with a fork. On a lightly floured piece of parchment, roll out the other disk of dough. Transfer dough (on parchment) to a baking sheet. Chill pie shell and dough until firm, about 30 minutes.

Using a triangle-shaped cutter or a sharp knife, cut out about 40 triangles (each side about 1 inch long) from the sheet of dough. In a small bowl, whisk together the egg yolk and 1 tablespoon water; lightly brush the bottoms of the triangles with egg wash, and gently press, slightly overlapping, to adhere to the dough, until the entire rim is covered. Lightly brush the decorated edge with egg wash; don't let it pool. Chill pie shell until firm, about 30 minutes. Meanwhile, preheat the oven to 375°F.

Line shell with parchment paper, leaving a 1-inch overhang. Fill with pie weights or dried beans. Bake until the edges are just beginning to turn golden, 15 to 20 minutes. Remove parchment and weights. Return crust to the oven; continue baking until light golden all over, 15 to 20 minutes more. Cool completely on a wire rack.

Reduce oven temperature to 350°F. In a large bowl, whisk together pumpkin, sugar, cinnamon, ginger, salt, nutmeg, whole eggs, and evaporated milk until combined. Pour mixture into the cooled crust, and bake until the filling is set around the edges but still slightly soft in the center, 40 to 45 minutes. (Check crust periodically; if it gets too dark, cover the edges with foil.) The filling will be just slightly loose in the center, but will firm up as it cools. Transfer to a wire rack to cool completely. Pie can be kept at room temperature, loosely covered with aluminum foil, for up to 2 days.

PECAN PIE

MAKES ONE 9-INCH PIE *If you don't have a cake ring, you can use a nine-inch springform pan instead; make sure the dough comes up 1½ inches from the bottom of the pan.*

All-purpose flour, for dusting	⅓ cup unsulfured molasses
Pâte Brisée (page 224)	1 tablespoon bourbon or dark rum
6 large eggs	1 teaspoon pure vanilla extract
1 tablespoon heavy cream	¼ teaspoon salt
1¼ cups packed light-brown sugar	1⅔ cups pecans, coarsely chopped, plus ⅓ cup whole pecan halves
6 tablespoons unsalted butter, melted	
⅓ cup light corn syrup	

PECAN PIE HOW-TO
Leaf-shaped cutouts of pie dough are placed among whole pecans in a decorative pattern over the filling before the pie is baked.

Set a 9-inch cake ring (with 1½-inch sides) on a baking sheet lined with parchment paper; set aside. On a lightly floured work surface, roll out one disk of dough to a 13-inch round. With a dry pastry brush, sweep off the excess flour; fit dough into cake ring, gently pressing into the edges and up the sides. Freeze until firm, about 15 minutes. Using a sharp paring knife, trim dough flush with the top edge of ring. Chill pie shell until firm, about 30 minutes. Meanwhile, preheat the oven to 375°F.

Line another baking sheet with parchment paper; set aside. On a lightly floured surface, roll out the remaining dough to an ⅛-inch thickness. Using leaf-shaped cutters, cut out 12 leaves (we made seven larger ones for the outside edge and five smaller ones for the middle); transfer to the prepared sheet. In a small bowl, whisk together 1 egg and the heavy cream; brush over leaf cutouts, and transfer to the refrigerator.

Line chilled pie shell with parchment paper, leaving a 1-inch overhang. Fill with pie weights or dried beans. Bake until the edges begin to turn golden, about 20 minutes. Remove parchment and weights; transfer to a wire rack to cool completely.

In a medium bowl, whisk together the remaining 5 eggs, the brown sugar, butter, corn syrup, molasses, bourbon, vanilla, and salt. Stir in the chopped pecans. Pour filling into the cooled pie shell; arrange reserved leaves and whole pecans on top of pie.

Reduce oven temperature to 350°F. Bake until a knife tip inserted into the center of the pie comes out clean, 40 to 45 minutes. Transfer the pie (still on the baking sheet) to a wire rack to cool completely before unmolding. Pie can be kept at room temperature, loosely covered with aluminum foil, for up to 4 days.

Pumpkin Pie and Pecan Pie

RHUBARB TART

MAKES ONE 9-INCH TART *Look for rhubarb stalks of the same width to ensure even cooking. If necessary, you can cut differently sized stalks lengthwise to match. The crust, filling, and poached rhubarb can be made one day ahead. The baked crust can be kept, loosely covered, at room temperature; refrigerate the filling and the rhubarb (in the poaching liquid) separately. Strain the rhubarb and reduce liquid several hours before serving.*

All-purpose flour, for dusting
Cream-Cheese Tart Dough
(recipe follows)

1½ cups plus 2 tablespoons sugar

1 vanilla bean, split lengthwise,
seeds scraped

1 small red beet, well scrubbed,
cut into wedges (optional)

1½ pounds rhubarb, leaves trimmed
and stalks sliced diagonally
into 2-inch pieces

4 ounces cream cheese, room
temperature
Freshly grated zest of 1 lemon

¼ cup sour cream

On a lightly floured piece of parchment paper, roll out the dough to a 12-inch square, about ⅛ inch thick. With a dry pastry brush, sweep off excess flour; fit dough into a 9-inch square fluted tart pan with a removable bottom, pressing into corners. Using a sharp knife or a rolling pin, trim dough flush with pan. Prick the bottom of the dough all over with a fork. Chill tart shell until firm, about 30 minutes.

Preheat the oven to 350°F. Line chilled shell with parchment, leaving at least a 1-inch overhang. Fill with pie weights or dried beans. Bake until edges are just beginning to turn golden, 20 to 25 minutes. Remove parchment and weights; continue baking until crust is deep golden brown all over, 10 to 15 minutes. Cool completely on a rack.

Stir together 1½ cups water, 1½ cups sugar, vanilla bean and seeds, and beet (if using) in a large skillet. Cook over medium-high heat, stirring occasionally, until the sugar is completely dissolved and the mixture comes to a boil. Add rhubarb; turn off heat. Cover, and let stand until the rhubarb is tender and gives only slight resistance when pierced with the tip of a sharp paring knife, about 20 minutes.

Carefully remove the rhubarb from the skillet with a slotted spoon, and spread it in a single layer in a baking pan lined with several layers of paper towels. Strain 1 cup of poaching liquid into a medium skillet. Cook over high heat until the syrup has thickened to a glaze, about 10 minutes; set aside until cool.

Combine cream cheese, remaining 2 tablespoons sugar, and lemon zest in the bowl of an electric mixer fitted with the paddle attachment; beat until smooth. Add sour cream, and beat until mixture is very smooth.

Using an offset spatula, spread cream-cheese mixture evenly over the bottom of the cooled crust. Carefully arrange the poached rhubarb on top of the cream-cheese mixture, and drizzle with the reserved cooled syrup. Chill tart in the refrigerator, loosely covered with plastic wrap, until ready to serve, up to 4 hours.

RHUBARB TART HOW-TO
Adding a sliced beet to the
poaching liquid helps the
rhubarb take on a rosier hue;
the vanilla bean adds
an extra note of flavor.

CREAM-CHEESE TART DOUGH
MAKES ENOUGH FOR ONE 9-INCH TART

1 cup all-purpose flour

1 tablespoon sugar

½ teaspoon baking powder

¼ teaspoon salt

6 tablespoons unsalted butter, cold, cut into small pieces

3 ounces cream cheese, cold

Place flour, sugar, baking powder, and salt in the bowl of a food processor, and pulse several times to combine. Add the butter, and pulse until pieces are the size of peas. Add the cream cheese, and pulse until mixture resembles coarse crumbs.

Turn out the dough onto a piece of plastic wrap; use the plastic to help bring the dough together into a ball. Flatten to form a square, and wrap well with plastic. Chill the dough for at least 1 hour and up to 1 day before using.

SUMMER FRUIT TART WITH LAVENDER SYRUP

MAKES ONE 14-BY-4-INCH TART *If fresh lavender is not available, you can use another fresh herb, such as rosemary or thyme. Half of a vanilla bean also works well.*

All-purpose flour, for dusting

Tart Dough (page 224)

½ cup sugar

⅓ cup loosely packed fresh lavender leaves (or dried organic lavender)

1 teaspoon freshly squeezed lemon juice

¼ cup heavy cream

Pastry Cream (page 392)

½ small ripe Charentais melon, peeled and thinly sliced

10 small fresh strawberries, halved

½ pint fresh blackberries

½ pint fresh blueberries

On a well-floured surface, roll out dough to a 16-by-6-inch rectangle, about ¼ inch thick. With a dry pastry brush, sweep off excess flour; fit dough into a 14-by-4-inch rectangular tart pan with a removable bottom, pressing into corners. Using a rolling pin or a sharp paring knife, trim dough flush with top edge of pan. Prick the bottom of the dough all over with a fork. Chill tart shell until firm, about 30 minutes.

Preheat the oven to 375°F. Line the chilled tart shell with parchment paper, leaving a 1-inch overhang. Fill with pie weights or dried beans. Bake until edges are golden, 15 to 17 minutes. Remove parchment and weights. Return to oven; continue baking until golden brown all over, about 20 minutes more. Cool completely on a wire rack.

In a small saucepan, combine sugar with ¼ cup water, lavender, and lemon juice. Bring mixture to a boil, then turn off heat. Set aside to steep, covered, for 20 minutes. Strain syrup into a bowl and set aside to cool.

In an electric mixer fitted with the whisk attachment, beat the heavy cream until stiff peaks form. Using a rubber spatula, fold whipped cream into 1½ cups of Pastry Cream until combined; pour into the tart shell. Arrange fruit on top of cream. Using a pastry brush, gently brush lavender syrup over fruit. Serve immediately.

PISTACHIO TARTLETS WITH
CRÈME FRAÎCHE AND BERRIES

MAKES EIGHT 4-INCH TARTLETS *You can also make this recipe in a fourteen-by-four-inch rectangular tart pan with a removable bottom. Roll out the dough to a sixteen-by-six-inch rectangle before fitting it into the pan; bake with parchment and weights for fifteen minutes, then remove parchment and weights and bake for eight to nine minutes more.*

All-purpose flour, for dusting	3 tablespoons confectioners' sugar
Pistachio Tart Dough (recipe follows)	8 ounces fresh strawberries, hulled
¾ cup (about 7 ounces) crème fraîche	6 ounces fresh raspberries
½ cup heavy cream	¼ cup unsalted shelled pistachios

On a lightly floured work surface, roll out dough to ¼-inch thickness. With a dry pastry brush, sweep off excess flour. With a 6-inch dessert plate as a guide, use a sharp knife to cut out eight rounds, rerolling scraps as necessary. Fit dough rounds into eight 4-inch flan rings, pressing into the edges. Chill for 10 minutes. Using a sharp paring knife, trim dough flush with the top edge of each ring. Refrigerate the tartlet shells until well chilled, about 30 minutes.

Preheat the oven to 375°F. Line shells with parchment, leaving a 1-inch overhang. Fill with pie weights. Bake until edges are just beginning to turn light golden, about 15 minutes. Remove parchment and weights; continue baking until surface is light golden all over, about 6 minutes. Transfer to a wire rack to cool completely.

After 10 minutes, remove tartlets from the rings. In the bowl of an electric mixer fitted with the whisk attachment, combine crème fraîche, cream, and sugar. Whisk until soft peaks form. Using an offset spatula, spread mixture into cooled tartlet shells. Arrange berries and pistachios on top. Serve immediately.

PISTACHIO TARTLET HOW-TO
Rounds of nut-studded tart dough are draped into 4-inch flan rings, then trimmed with a sharp paring knife before being blind-baked.

PISTACHIO TART DOUGH
MAKES ENOUGH FOR EIGHT 4-INCH TARTLETS OR ONE 14-BY-4-INCH TART

1½ sticks (¾ cup) unsalted butter, room temperature	½ cup unsalted shelled pistachios, finely ground
½ cup confectioners' sugar	¼ teaspoon salt
2 large egg yolks	2 teaspoons heavy cream
1¼ cups all-purpose flour	

In the bowl of an electric mixer fitted with the paddle attachment, mix butter and confectioners' sugar on low speed until combined, about 2 minutes.

Add egg yolks, and mix until incorporated, about 1 minute, scraping down the sides of the bowl as needed. Add 1 cup flour, and mix on low speed until just incorporated, about 30 seconds. Add remaining ¼ cup flour, pistachios, salt, and cream; mix just until flour is no longer visible, about 1 minute. Turn out dough onto a piece of plastic wrap, and flatten to form a disk. Wrap tightly, and refrigerate for 1 hour or overnight.

NECTARINE TART

MAKES ONE 9-INCH TART *This artfully composed tart looks like an elegant tapestry, with carefully placed fruit "roses" in a prebaked tart shell. While it is easy to make, it's essential to use a very sharp knife in order to cut the nectarine slices precisely. You can make the tart shell one day ahead; keep at room temperature, loosely covered.*

1½ tablespoons all-purpose flour, plus more for dusting	2 teaspoons freshly squeezed lemon juice
Tart Dough (page 224)	1 tablespoon Chambord or brandy
3 tablespoons unsalted butter, room temperature	¼ teaspoon salt
1 large egg	8 ripe but firm nectarines (about 2½ pounds)
¼ cup sugar	

On a lightly floured work surface, roll out dough to a 12-inch round, about ¼ inch thick. With a dry pastry brush, sweep off excess flour; fit dough into a 9-inch round fluted tart pan with a removable bottom, pressing into edges. Using a sharp paring knife, trim dough flush with the pan. Chill tart shell until firm, about 30 minutes.

Preheat the oven to 375°F. Prick bottom of dough all over with a fork. Line with parchment paper, leaving at least a 1-inch overhang. Fill with pie weights or dried beans. Bake until the edges are just beginning to turn golden, 20 to 25 minutes. Remove parchment paper and weights; continue baking until lightly golden all over, 20 to 25 minutes more. Cool tart shell completely on a wire rack.

In a small saucepan, melt butter over medium heat; cook, whisking occasionally, until butter solids begin to brown, about 5 minutes. Remove from heat, and set aside.

In a medium bowl, whisk together egg, sugar, lemon juice, Chambord, and salt until light in color and doubled in volume, about 2 minutes. Add flour and reserved brown butter, and whisk until well combined. Set filling aside.

Using a sharp knife, cut as far as you can into one nectarine on either side, then trim the opposite ends. You will have four nectarine pieces. Place these pieces cut side down on the cutting board, and slice each into ⅛-inch-thick pieces; set the ends aside. Repeat with remaining nectarines. Starting with the thinnest slices, curl the nectarine around itself with the skin side up. Wrap another slice of nectarine around the first, making sure to keep the end of one slice at about the center point of the previous slice. Continue this circular pattern until the "rose" is about 1½ inches in diameter. Using an offset spatula, carefully transfer to cooled tart shell. Make and transfer enough additional roses to tightly fill the shell. Using the remaining nectarine slices, fill in any gaps between roses.

Whisk the reserved filling briefly, then pour it evenly over the fruit. Use a spoon to fill any empty spaces. Bake, rotating tart halfway through, until crust is golden brown and filling has slightly puffed, about 40 minutes. Cool completely on a wire rack.

FRUIT CURD TARTLETS

MAKES EIGHTEEN 3-INCH TARTLETS OR EIGHT 4-INCH TARTLETS *We love to serve a variety of shapes and sizes of tartlet shells filled with different flavors of fruit curd; feel free to mix and match flavors to your liking. Similarly, you may choose to top some with meringue while leaving others unadorned. The ones pictured at right are filled with Lemon and Passion Fruit curds. Grapefruit Curd and Lime Curd work equally well. These tartlets are especially appropriate for garden parties or bridal showers.*

All-purpose flour, for dusting	½ cup egg whites (about 4 large eggs)
Tart Dough (page 224)	¾ cup sugar
Lemon Curd (page 390), Grapefruit Curd (page 391), Lime Curd (page 390), or Passion Fruit Curd (page 390)	Pinch of salt

On a lightly floured surface, roll out dough to an ⅛-inch thickness. With a sharp paring knife, cut out rounds of dough using a tartlet pan as a guide, leaving a ½-inch border around the edge. Fit the dough into tartlet pans, and lightly prick the bottom of the dough in each pan all over with a fork. Place the tartlet shells on a rimmed baking sheet, and refrigerate until chilled, about 30 minutes. Meanwhile, preheat the oven to 350°F.

Bake tartlet shells until light golden brown, about 10 to 12 minutes for 3-inch tartlets, or 12 to 14 minutes for 4-inch ones. Cool completely on a wire rack. Remove the shells from the pans and set aside.

When ready to serve, place desired curd in a pastry bag fitted with a ½-inch plain tip (such as an Ateco #806), and pipe into the cooled tartlet shells to fill. (Use about 1 tablespoon for 3-inch tartlets, about 2 tablespoons for 4-inch ones. You may have some curd left over; reserve it for another use.)

In the heatproof bowl of an electric mixer, combine the egg whites, sugar, and salt. Set the bowl over a saucepan of simmering water (do not let bowl touch water); whisk until the mixture registers 140°F on an instant-read thermometer and sugar is completely dissolved. Transfer to the mixer, and beat on medium-high speed with the whisk attachment until stiff, glossy peaks form, about 7 minutes. Transfer the meringue to a pastry bag fitted with a clean ½-inch plain tip. Pipe the meringue around the edge of the 4-inch tartlets, forming mounded peaks. (Alternatively, spoon the meringue over the curd, and swirl with a small offset spatula, or leave meringue off some tartlets altogether.)

Using a kitchen torch, lightly brown the meringue. (You can also briefly run the tarts under the broiler.) The tartlet shells can be baked a day in advance and kept in an airtight container at room temperature. Once filled with curd, tartlets can be kept in an airtight container in the refrigerator for up to 2 days. Prepare the meringue and finish the tartlets just before serving.

KEY LIME TART

MAKES ONE 9-INCH TART *We've reinvented the classic Key lime pie as a tart made with a homemade graham cracker crust. Key limes are smaller, rounder, and have a yellower cast than regular limes; look for them in gourmet shops and some supermarkets. Otherwise, substitute regular limes; six limes should yield ½ cup juice.*

All-purpose flour, for dusting

Graham Cracker dough
(page 90)

4 large egg yolks

1 can (14 ounces) sweetened
condensed milk

2 teaspoons grated Key lime zest

½ cup freshly squeezed Key lime
juice (about 12 Key limes)

Pinch of salt

1 cup heavy cream

2 tablespoons confectioners' sugar

Candied Key Lime Slices
(recipe follows)

On a lightly floured work surface, roll out dough to a 12-inch round. With a dry pastry brush, sweep off excess flour; fit dough into a 9-inch flan ring (set on a parchment-lined baking sheet) or tart pan with a removable bottom, pressing into the edges. Using a sharp paring knife, trim dough flush with the rim. Prick the bottom of the dough all over with a fork. Chill the tart shell until firm, about 30 minutes.

Preheat the oven to 350°F. Line tart shell with parchment, leaving a 1-inch overhang. Fill with pie weights. Bake until the crust is just beginning to turn golden, 12 to 15 minutes. Remove parchment and weights. Return to oven; continue baking until crust is golden brown, 12 to 15 minutes more. Transfer to a wire rack to cool completely.

In the bowl of an electric mixer fitted with the whisk attachment, beat yolks on medium-high speed until pale and fluffy, 2 to 3 minutes. Add condensed milk, lime zest, lime juice, and salt, and beat to combine, about 1 minute, scraping down the sides of the bowl as needed.

Pour filling into cooled crust; bake until set, about 10 minutes. Transfer tart (still on parchment if using a flan ring) to a wire rack to cool. Once completely cool, loosely cover with plastic wrap; refrigerate until chilled, at least 1 hour or up to 1 day.

When ready to serve, combine cream and confectioners' sugar in the bowl of an electric mixer fitted with the whisk attachment; beat until soft peaks form. Garnish tart with Candied Key Lime Slices, and serve with whipped cream on the side.

CANDIED KEY LIME SLICES
MAKES ENOUGH TO GARNISH ONE 9-INCH TART

1 cup sugar

2 Key limes (about 1 ounce each),
very thinly sliced into rounds

In a 10-inch sauté pan, bring sugar and 1 cup water to a boil, stirring constantly until sugar dissolves. Reduce heat to a gentle simmer. Add lime slices in a single layer, arranging them so they do not overlap. Cook until white pith is translucent, 30 to 40 minutes, turning slices two or three times during cooking. Using a slotted spatula, carefully transfer slices to a wire rack to cool completely before using.

CHERRY-FRANGIPANE GALETTE

MAKES ONE 14-INCH GALETTE *This tart can be made with store-bought or homemade puff pastry. If using store-bought, you will need one 17¼-ounce package, which includes two sheets; divide the filling and the cherries in half, and bake two galettes instead of one.*

⅔ cup sliced blanched almonds	All-purpose flour, for dusting
½ cup plus 1 tablespoon sugar	18 ounces Puff Pastry (page 359)
¼ teaspoon salt	1 tablespoon heavy cream
3 tablespoons unsalted butter, cold, cut into ½-inch pieces	2 pounds fresh sweet cherries, stemmed and pitted
1 large whole egg, plus 1 large egg yolk	

Preheat the oven to 375°F. Spread almonds in a single layer on a parchment-lined baking sheet. Toast until golden and fragrant, 7 to 9 minutes. Set aside to cool completely.

Raise oven temperature to 425°F. In a food processor, pulse nuts, ½ cup sugar, and salt until nuts are finely ground. With the machine running, add butter and the whole egg; continue processing until mixture is smooth.

On a lightly floured piece of parchment, roll out Puff Pastry to a 16-inch rough oval shape, about ⅛ inch thick. In a small bowl, whisk together the egg yolk and the heavy cream; brush over the surface of the pastry. Fold up the edges to create a 1-inch crimped edge. Prick dough all over with a fork. Transfer parchment and pastry to a large baking sheet; freeze until firm, about 15 minutes.

Using an offset spatula, spread the almond mixture in an even layer (about ⅛ inch thick) over the bottom of the chilled crust; freeze 15 minutes more. Arrange the cherries in a single layer over the almond mixture.

Bake the tart for 15 minutes. Sprinkle the remaining tablespoon of sugar over the tart, and continue baking until edges are deep golden brown, 5 to 10 minutes. Transfer parchment and tart to a wire rack to cool. Serve warm or at room temperature.

TARTE TATIN

MAKES ONE 9-INCH TART *This traditional French apple tart is really more of an upside-down single-crust pie. Our method is unique because the apples are not cooked on the stovetop before baking; instead, they cook entirely in the oven.*

4 tablespoons unsalted butter, cut into small pieces, plus more for pan	Dash of lemon juice
All-purpose flour, for dusting	2½ medium baking apples, such as Rome or Cortland (about 1¼ pounds), peeled, cored, and cut into quarters
½ recipe Pâte Brisée (page 224), chilled	
1 cup sugar	Crème fraîche, for serving (optional)

TARTE TATIN HOW-TO
Apple pieces are arranged in a single layer atop the caramel, then covered with pastry and baked until golden.

Preheat the oven to 425°F. Generously butter a 9-inch metal pie plate; set aside. Line a baking sheet with parchment paper, and set aside. On a lightly floured work surface, roll out the dough to a 9-inch round, about ¼ inch thick. Place dough on the prepared baking sheet, and chill until firm, about 30 minutes.

Meanwhile, in a small saucepan, mix together the sugar, 2 tablespoons cold water, and the lemon juice to form a thick syrup. Bring to a boil over high heat, swirling pan; cook until the mixture turns medium amber, about 3 minutes. Remove the pan from heat, and pour the mixture onto the bottom of the prepared pie plate. Immediately add the butter, distributing evenly.

Arrange the apples, rounded sides down, around the bottom of the pan in a circular pattern, starting from the outside and working in, fitting them as close together as possible (the apples will be the top of the tart when served). Drape the chilled dough round over the apples to cover the mixture completely.

Bake until golden, about 25 minutes. Meanwhile, line a rimmed baking sheet with a clean nonstick baking mat, such as a Silpat. Remove the tart from the oven, and immediately invert it onto the mat, working quickly but carefully to avoid contact with the hot caramel. Using tongs, carefully lift the pie plate off of the tart. Transfer the sheet to a wire rack to cool. Serve warm with crème fraîche, if using.

APRICOT-BLACKBERRY GALETTE

MAKES ONE 10-INCH GALETTE *This dessert works with a variety of fresh summer fruits; experiment with different combinations of stone fruits and berries, using the same proportions but adjusting the sugar accordingly.*

All-purpose flour, for dusting	Juice of ½ lemon (about 1 tablespoon)
½ recipe Cornmeal Pâte Brisée (recipe follows)	2 tablespoons cornstarch
12 fresh apricots (1½ pounds), pitted and cut into sixths	Pinch of salt
2 cups fresh blackberries	1 large egg, lightly beaten
½ cup granulated sugar	Sanding sugar (or granulated sugar), for sprinkling (optional)

On a lightly floured work surface, roll out dough to a 14-inch round, about ⅛ inch thick. Transfer dough to a large parchment-lined baking sheet. Refrigerate until ready to use, up to 1 hour. Meanwhile, preheat the oven to 375°F.

In a large bowl, gently toss together apricots, blackberries, granulated sugar, lemon juice, cornstarch, and salt. Arrange fruit mixture on top of dough, leaving a 2-inch border all the way around. Fold border over the fruit mixture, overlapping where necessary and pressing gently to adhere the folds.

Brush edges of dough with egg, and sprinkle with sanding sugar, if using. Bake until crust is golden brown and the juices are bubbling, about 1 hour. Transfer the baking sheet to a wire rack to cool the galette. Serve warm or at room temperature.

APRICOT-BLACKBERRY GALETTE HOW-TO 1. Dough is rolled into a round, then filling is mounded in the center, leaving a 2-inch border. 2. The border is folded up to partially cover fruit, then overlapped and pressed to adhere.

CORNMEAL PÂTE BRISÉE

MAKES ENOUGH FOR TWO 9-INCH SINGLE-CRUST PIES OR ONE 9-INCH DOUBLE-CRUST PIE
The dough can be frozen, wrapped well in plastic, for up to three weeks before using.

2 cups all-purpose flour	2 sticks (1 cup) unsalted butter, cold, cut into small pieces
½ cup cornmeal	¼ to ½ cup ice water
1 teaspoon salt	
1 teaspoon sugar	

Place the flour, cornmeal, salt, and sugar in the bowl of a food processor, and pulse several times to combine. Add the butter, and process until the mixture resembles coarse meal, about 10 seconds. With the machine running, pour the ice water through the feed tube in a slow, steady stream, until the dough just holds together (do not process for more than 30 seconds).

Turn out the dough onto a clean work surface. Divide in half, and place each half on a piece of plastic wrap. Flatten each to form a disk. Wrap, and refrigerate at least 1 hour or up to 1 day before using.

INDIVIDUAL POTATO AND ONION TARTES TATIN

MAKES SIX 5-INCH TARTLETS *These tartlets can be assembled and refrigerated, covered with plastic wrap, three to four hours in advance; bake just before serving.*

POTATO TARTE TATIN

HOW-TO Thinly sliced layers of onions and potatoes are topped with rounds of puff pastry before baking.

4 tablespoons unsalted butter, cold, cut into small pieces, plus more for pans	4 medium yellow onions, peeled, cut into ¼-inch-thick rounds
All-purpose flour, for dusting	5 small new potatoes, peeled
1 pound Puff Pastry (page 359) or 1 standard package (17¼ ounces) store-bought puff pastry	Coarse salt and freshly ground pepper
	¼ cup balsamic vinegar
	Pinch of sugar

Very generously butter six 5-inch round metal pie plates; set aside. On a lightly floured work surface, roll out Puff Pastry to a scant ¼-inch thickness. Using a cutter or a small plate as a guide, cut dough into 4½-inch rounds. Prick rounds all over with a fork. Transfer to a parchment-lined baking sheet, and chill until firm, about 30 minutes. Meanwhile, preheat the oven to 425°F.

Lay two or three onion rounds on the bottom of each pie pan. Using a mandoline or sharp knife, slice the potatoes into thin rounds, about a scant ¼ inch thick. Place the potato slices, slightly overlapping, over the onion in two layers of concentric circles (they should completely cover the onion). Sprinkle potatoes generously with salt and pepper. Place chilled Puff Pastry rounds on top of the potatoes in each pie plate. Bake until golden brown, about 20 minutes.

Immediately invert the tartlets onto a platter. In a small saucepan, combine the balsamic vinegar and sugar. Bring to a simmer and cook until the mixture reduces to a syrup, about 4 minutes. Whisk in the butter, a piece at a time, until incorporated. Season with salt and pepper. Glaze the tartlets with the balsamic syrup and serve warm.

TOMATO TART

MAKES ONE 10-INCH TART *This tart can be made a day ahead and kept at room temperature, loosely covered with plastic wrap. Reheat in a 300°F oven until warmed through.*

1 head garlic	1½ pounds ripe but firm tomatoes (about 4 medium), sliced ¼ inch thick
3 tablespoons extra-virgin olive oil	
All-purpose flour, for dusting	Coarse salt and freshly ground pepper
½ recipe Pâte Brisée (page 224)	
¾ cup grated Italian Fontina cheese (about 3 ounces)	12 fresh basil leaves

Preheat the oven to 350°F. Place the garlic on a piece of aluminum foil; drizzle with 1 tablespoon olive oil. Fold foil to encase the garlic, sealing edges well, and place on a small baking sheet. Roast in oven until golden brown and the tip of a sharp paring knife easily pierces the flesh, about 45 minutes. Remove from oven; set aside.

Tomato Tart

Raise oven temperature to 450°F. When garlic is cool enough to handle, use your fingers or the handle of a knife to squeeze the cloves out of their skins and into a small bowl; mash with a fork, and set aside. Discard the papery skins.

On a lightly floured work surface, roll out the dough to a 13-inch round, about ⅛ inch thick. With a dry pastry brush, remove excess flour. Fit the dough into a 10-inch fluted tart pan with a removable bottom, pressing into the edges. Using a rolling pin or a sharp paring knife, trim dough flush with the top edge of the tart pan; chill tart shell until firm, about 30 minutes.

Spread roasted garlic evenly on the bottom of the chilled shell. Sprinkle with ¼ cup cheese. Arrange the tomato slices in an overlapping circular pattern on top of the cheese, working from the outer edge toward the center. Season with salt and pepper. Sprinkle with remaining ½ cup cheese, and drizzle with remaining 2 tablespoons oil.

Reduce oven temperature to 425°F. Bake tart until crust is golden and tomatoes are soft but still retain their shape, 45 to 55 minutes. Cool on a wire rack for 20 minutes. Thinly slice basil leaves lengthwise. Sprinkle tart with basil, and serve warm.

TOMATO TART HOW-TO
A layer of mashed roasted garlic adds an intense flavor to this savory pastry.

SAUSAGE AND FETA HAND PIES

MAKES 1 DOZEN *If you prefer less spice, omit the red pepper flakes. When you make the dough for this recipe, instead of shaping the pieces into disks, pat them into rectangles; this will make the dough easier to roll out and cut into squares.*

¼ cup extra-virgin olive oil	6 plum tomatoes, quartered lengthwise, seeded, and cut into ½-inch dice
1 pound sweet Italian sausage, casings removed	8 ounces feta cheese, crumbled
1 large onion, thinly sliced	½ cup fresh flat-leaf parsley leaves, coarsely chopped
1 small head fennel (about 1 pound), trimmed, cored, and thinly sliced	All-purpose flour, for dusting
½ teaspoon crushed red pepper flakes (optional)	Pâte Brisée (page 224)
Coarse salt and freshly ground black pepper	1 large egg, lightly beaten
	3 tablespoons fennel seeds

Heat 2 tablespoons oil in a large skillet over medium heat. Crumble sausage into pan; cook, stirring occasionally, until browned, about 4 minutes. Using a slotted spoon, transfer the sausage to a paper towel–lined plate; set aside.

Add remaining 2 tablespoons oil to skillet along with the onion; cook, stirring occasionally, for 2 minutes. Add sliced fennel and red pepper flakes; season with salt and pepper. Continue cooking, stirring occasionally, until vegetables are tender, about 8 minutes. Add tomatoes and cook, stirring, until they release their juices, 3 to 4 minutes. Add the reserved sausage, and stir to combine. Remove from heat, and let cool completely. Stir in feta cheese and parsley; set filling aside.

Preheat the oven to 425°F, with racks in the upper and lower thirds. Line two baking sheets with parchment paper, and set aside.

HAND PIE HOW-TO
The corners of these squares of pastry dough are folded toward the center to cover, but not enclose, a savory filling of sausage, fennel, and feta cheese.

Sausage and Feta Hand Pies

On a lightly floured piece of parchment paper, roll out one piece of dough to a 16-by-11-inch rectangle. Trim to 15 by 10 inches. Cut into six 5-inch squares. With a dry pastry brush, sweep off excess flour. Place ½ cup filling in the center of each square. Fold up all four corners around the filling, so that the points meet in the center but do not touch (leave about ¼ inch of space between them). Repeat with remaining piece of dough and filling. Transfer to prepared baking sheets.

Brush tops of dough with the beaten egg, and sprinkle with fennel seeds. Bake, rotating sheets halfway through, until pies are golden brown and filling is set, about 40 minutes. Cool slightly on a wire rack. Serve warm.

CORN AND SHIITAKE TART

MAKES ONE 10-INCH TART *If fresh corn is not in season, you can use frozen corn instead; be sure to thaw and drain the kernels well before using.*

All-purpose flour, for dusting	2 cups fresh corn kernels (about 4 ears)
½ recipe Cornmeal Pâte Brisée (page 266)	¼ cup chopped fresh chives (cut into 1-inch pieces), plus more for garnish
3 tablespoons extra-virgin olive oil	Coarse salt and freshly ground pepper
6 ounces (about 6 cups) shiitake mushrooms, stemmed and sliced into ¼-inch-thick pieces	½ cup milk
	½ cup heavy cream
1 medium onion, finely diced	3 large eggs

On a lightly floured surface, roll out dough to a 13-inch round, about ¼ inch thick. With a dry pastry brush, sweep off excess flour; fit dough into a 10-inch round flan ring or a tart pan with a removable bottom, pressing into the edges. Using a rolling pin or a sharp paring knife, trim the dough flush with the edge of the pan. Chill shell until firm, about 30 minutes. Meanwhile, preheat the oven to 375°F.

Line chilled shell with parchment paper, leaving a 1-inch overhang. Fill with pie weights or dried beans. Bake 30 to 40 minutes. Remove weights and parchment; continue baking until tart shell is golden brown all over, 10 to 15 minutes more. Cool completely on a wire rack.

Heat olive oil in a large nonstick skillet over medium heat. Add mushrooms, and cook until they start to give off moisture, 2 to 3 minutes. Add the onion and cook, stirring occasionally, until softened and translucent, 2 to 3 minutes. Stir in the corn and the chives and cook, 1 to 2 minutes more. Remove filling from heat and season with salt and pepper; stir to combine. Set filling aside.

In a bowl, whisk together milk, cream, and eggs; season with salt and pepper. Pour mushroom filling into cooled tart shell. Place tart on a rimmed baking sheet; pour in milk mixture. Bake, rotating the sheet halfway through, until custard is set in the center, 20 to 25 minutes. Cool slightly on a wire rack. Garnish with chives, and serve warm or at room temperature.

Corn and Shiitake Tart

Easter Pie

EASTER PIE

MAKES ONE 9-INCH SQUARE PIE *This savory Italian pastry is traditionally served on Easter Sunday, but it is delicious any time of year. If you want to drain the ricotta, place it in a sieve lined with cheesecloth for about an hour; discard the liquid before proceeding.*

All-purpose flour, for dusting
Easter Pie Dough (recipe follows)
1 tablespoon extra-virgin olive oil
1½ pounds fresh spinach, trimmed
3¼ cups whole-milk ricotta cheese
½ cup grated Parmesan cheese (1½ ounces)

½ cup grated mozzarella cheese (1½ ounces)
½ pound thinly sliced prosciutto, chopped
1 large whole egg, plus 2 large egg yolks
¼ teaspoon salt
⅛ teaspoon freshly grated nutmeg
1 tablespoon heavy cream

Line a 9-inch square cake pan with parchment paper, leaving a 1-inch overhang on two sides. On a lightly floured piece of parchment paper, roll out one piece of dough to a 12-inch square, about ⅛ inch thick. With a dry pastry brush, sweep off excess flour; fit dough into the prepared pan, pressing into corners. Prick the bottom of the dough all over with a fork. Roll out the remaining dough in the same manner and, using a pastry wheel, cut into ½-inch-wide strips. Transfer dough strips (on parchment) to a baking sheet. Chill pie shell and dough strips until firm, about 30 minutes. Meanwhile, preheat the oven to 350°F.

Line the chilled pie shell with parchment paper, leaving a 1-inch overhang; fill with pie weights or dried beans. Bake until the edges just begin to turn golden, about 15 minutes; remove parchment and weights. Return to oven; continue baking until the edges turn light golden brown, 15 to 20 minutes. Cool completely on a wire rack.

In a medium skillet, heat oil over medium heat; add spinach, and cook until just wilted. Drain spinach on paper towels, then finely chop (for about 4 cups).

In a medium bowl, combine spinach, ricotta, Parmesan, mozzarella, prosciutto, the whole egg, 1 egg yolk, salt, and nutmeg. Spread evenly into cooled pie shell. Weave dough strips on top to form a lattice. Using kitchen shears, trim dough flush with the top of the pan. In a small bowl, whisk together the remaining egg yolk and the cream; brush egg wash over the lattice top and the edge of the pie shell.

Bake, rotating pan halfway through, until crust is golden brown, about 45 minutes. (If edges or top of crust browns too quickly, loosely cover with aluminum foil.) Cool slightly on a wire rack. Using parchment paper overhang, gently lift pie out of pan. Serve warm or at room temperature. The pie is best eaten the same day it is baked, but it can be kept, covered, in the refrigerator for up to 2 days.

EASTER PIE DOUGH

MAKES ENOUGH FOR ONE 9-INCH LATTICE-TOPPED SQUARE PIE *The addition of grated Parmesan cheese makes this savory piecrust even more rich.*

4½ cups all-purpose flour, plus more for dusting

½ cup finely grated Parmesan cheese (1½ ounces)

1 teaspoon coarse salt

¾ teaspoon freshly ground pepper

1½ sticks (¾ cup) unsalted butter, cold, cut into pieces

¾ cup vegetable shortening, cold, cut into small pieces

½ to ¾ cup ice water

Put flour, cheese, salt, and pepper in the bowl of a food processor; pulse several times to combine. Add butter and shortening; process until the mixture resembles coarse crumbs, about 10 seconds. With the machine running, pour the ice water through the feed tube in a slow, steady stream until the dough just holds together.

Turn out the dough onto a lightly floured work surface. Divide the dough in half, and form each piece into a flattened square. Wrap each piece of dough in plastic, and chill at least 1 hour or overnight before using.

DRIED PEACH AND GOAT CHEESE GALETTE

MAKES ONE 13-BY-6-INCH GALETTE *Small squares of this tart make excellent hors d'oeuvres. Save the extra peach purée to blend with sparkling white wine for a refreshing cocktail.*

All-purpose flour, for dusting

½ recipe Pâte Brisée (page 224)

1½ cups dry white wine

½ cup sugar

5 ounces dried peach slices

1 large egg

¼ cup plus 1 tablespoon heavy cream

½ cup fresh goat cheese, room temperature

1 teaspoon honey

1 teaspoon freshly grated lemon zest

1 teaspoon fresh thyme leaves, plus more for garnish

⅛ teaspoon salt

On a large piece of lightly floured parchment paper, roll out dough to a 17-by-10-inch rectangle, about ⅛ inch thick. Trim dough to a 15-by-8-inch rectangle. Transfer to a baking sheet, and fold dough onto itself to make a 1-inch border, keeping corners square. Chill dough until firm, about 30 minutes.

In a saucepan, combine wine, 1½ cups water, and the sugar. Bring to a simmer, and remove from heat. Add peaches to the hot liquid; cover, and let stand until liquid cools to room temperature, 45 minutes. Meanwhile, preheat the oven to 350°F.

Beat the egg with 1 tablespoon heavy cream. Brush border of chilled shell with egg wash. Prick the bottom of the dough all over with a fork. Bake, rotating the sheet halfway through, until the crust is golden brown around the edges, about 20 minutes. Cool completely on a wire rack. The tart shell can be made 1 day in advance and kept, wrapped in plastic, at room temperature.

Drain peaches, reserving soaking liquid. Cut the peaches diagonally into paper-thin strips. Purée the ends with ¼ cup reserved soaking liquid in a food processor until

smooth. Transfer 3 tablespoons to a medium bowl, and add goat cheese, remaining ¼ cup cream, honey, lemon zest, thyme, and salt. Stir to combine, and spread evenly over the cooled tart shell. Arrange peach strips in a single layer on top of the goat cheese. Lightly brush the peaches with the reserved soaking liquid.

Bake, rotating halfway through, until peaches just begin to lose their sheen, 10 minutes. Cool on a wire rack. Galette can be kept in the refrigerator, covered with plastic wrap, for up to 1 day. Garnish with thyme leaves just before serving.

SOUR-CHERRY LATTICE COBBLER

SERVES 6 TO 8 *Adjust the amount of granulated sugar you use in the filling according to how sweet you want the cobbler to be. If you cannot find fresh sour cherries, substitute 2¼ pounds pitted frozen sour cherries; thaw and drain before using. We baked ours in a fluted eighteen-by-twelve-inch dish, but any 1½-quart baking dish will do—just adjust the length of the lattice strips to fit the dish.*

3¼ pounds fresh sour cherries, stemmed and pitted

1 to 1¼ cups granulated sugar

2½ tablespoons cornstarch

1½ tablespoons balsamic vinegar

Pinch of salt

All-purpose flour, for dusting

Pâte Brisée (page 224; leave dough in one piece)

1 large egg yolk

1 tablespoon heavy cream

Sanding sugar (or granulated sugar), for sprinkling

Vanilla ice cream or whipped cream, for serving (optional)

Line a baking sheet with parchment; set aside. In a bowl, combine cherries, granulated sugar, cornstarch, vinegar, and salt. Pour into a 1½-quart baking dish; set aside.

On a lightly floured work surface, roll out the dough to an 18-by-13-inch rectangle at least ⅛ inch thick. Trim to 17 by 12 inches. Cut lengthwise into ¾-inch-wide strips. Trim five strips to 13 inches in length. Cut the remaining strips in half crosswise to form 8½-inch strips. Lay the five long strips lengthwise over tops of cherries. Use the 8½-inch strips to weave a lattice. (Alternatively, weave the lattice on the back of a baking sheet, transfer to freezer for 5 minutes, then slide off the baking sheet over the fruit.) Press ends of dough strips into the filling. Freeze until firm, about 30 minutes. Meanwhile, preheat the oven to 400°F, with the rack in the center.

Remove cobbler from freezer and transfer baking dish to the prepared baking sheet. In a small bowl, whisk together egg yolk and cream; brush lattice with egg wash, and sprinkle with sanding sugar. Bake until crust is golden brown and the juices are bubbling, 50 minutes to 1 hour. Cool on a wire rack. Serve warm or at room temperature, with vanilla ice cream or whipped cream, if using.

Sour-Cherry Lattice Cobbler

PLUM-OAT CRISP

SERVES 8 TO 10 *This easy dessert can also be made in eight six-ounce ramekins—simply divide the filling and topping evenly among the dishes. The baking time will be the same.*

- 2 sticks (1 cup) unsalted butter, cold, cut into small pieces, plus more for baking dish
- 2¼ cups all-purpose flour
- ¾ cup packed light-brown sugar
- ⅓ cup plus ½ cup granulated sugar
- ½ teaspoon ground cinnamon
- ½ teaspoon salt
- ½ cup old-fashioned rolled oats

- 2½ pounds red or black plums, halved, pitted, and cut into eighths
- Juice of ½ lemon (about 1 tablespoon)
- 2 tablespoons cornstarch
- ¼ teaspoon ground cardamom
- Vanilla ice cream or whipped cream, for serving (optional)

PLUM-OAT CRISP HOW-TO The topping for a crisp should contain crumbs that vary in size. Oats make the texture especially appealing.

Preheat the oven to 375°F, with the rack in the lower third. Butter a 3-quart baking dish, and place on a parchment-lined baking sheet; set aside.

In a large bowl, whisk together flour, brown sugar, ⅓ cup granulated sugar, cinnamon, and ¼ teaspoon salt. Using a pastry blender, cut in butter until large clumps form. Using a rubber spatula, mix in oats. Set aside.

In a large bowl, toss together plums, lemon juice, the remaining ½ cup granulated sugar, cornstarch, cardamom, and remaining ¼ teaspoon salt to combine. Pour the plum mixture into the prepared baking dish; sprinkle with reserved oat mixture, covering fruit evenly. Bake until the juices are bubbling and the topping is evenly browned, about 50 minutes. Cool slightly on a wire rack. Serve crisp warm, topped with vanilla ice cream or whipped cream, if using.

PEAR-OAT CRISP VARIATION Follow instructions for Plum-Oat Crisp, replacing the plums with 2½ pounds of ripe pears (preferably Anjou), peeled, cored, and cut into 1-inch-thick wedges. Substitute ¼ teaspoon allspice for the cardamom and proceed.

RASPBERRY-RHUBARB BISCUIT COBBLERS

MAKES 6 TO 8 *This versatile cobbler can be baked in ramekins, for single servings, or prepared in a larger dish to feed a wide range of appetites.*

- 2 pints (about 12 ounces) fresh raspberries
- 1½ pounds rhubarb, trimmed and cut diagonally into ¾-inch pieces
- 1½ cups sugar
- ⅓ cup instant tapioca
- Juice and zest of ½ lemon
- ½ teaspoon plus a pinch of salt

- 1 cup all-purpose flour
- ⅓ cup cake flour (not self-rising)
- 2 teaspoons baking powder
- ½ teaspoon baking soda
- 6 tablespoons unsalted butter, cold, cut into small pieces
- ¾ cup plain whole-milk yogurt
- 2 to 3 tablespoons heavy cream

COBBLER HOW-TO This easy, biscuit-style topping is dropped by heaping tablespoons onto the fruit filling before baking.

Preheat the oven to 400°F, with racks in the center and lower third. Line a rimmed baking sheet with parchment paper; set aside. In a large bowl, toss together the raspberries, rhubarb, 1¼ cups sugar, tapioca, lemon juice, and pinch of salt; stir to com-

bine. Let stand 15 minutes, stirring once or twice. Divide the filling among six to eight 10-ounce baking dishes, or pour into a 2½-quart baking dish.

In a medium bowl, whisk together both flours, remaining ¼ cup sugar, baking powder, baking soda, lemon zest, and remaining ½ teaspoon salt. Using a pastry blender, cut in butter until the mixture resembles coarse crumbs. Add the yogurt, and stir with a fork to form a moist dough with the consistency of thick cake batter. Using a large spoon, top filling with dollops of dough, leaving a 1-inch border.

Brush dough with cream. Transfer baking dishes to prepared baking sheet; bake, rotating sheet halfway through, until biscuits are golden brown and juices are bubbling, 50 to 60 minutes. (If the biscuits are browning too quickly, cover loosely with aluminum foil during the last 15 minutes of baking.) Cool on a wire rack, at least 1 hour. Serve warm or at room temperature.

chapter five

YEASTED
BAKED GOODS

recipes

Making bread is deeply satisfying. There's the tactile thrill of putting your hands into whisper-weight flour, the invigorating exercise of kneading a mixture until it's smooth, and the enjoyable charge that comes with punching down a pillow of dough.

AMAZINGLY, SUCH EMOTIONAL rewards are brought about by cool calculations and science. In that regard, the following recipes are really formulas—but ones that result in tasty Croissants, Olive-Oil Bread, Chocolate Babkas, and more.

The closer you stick to the formula, the better the result. Doughs for yeasted baked goods rely heavily on accurate measurements. This is why flour should be weighed on a kitchen scale, not scooped into cups, which can result in heavier amounts. Vigilance is also needed with temperatures. You'll want to monitor not only the oven, but also the warmth of the water used to make the dough and even the heat of the kitchen. The environment needs to be just right for the most vital ingredient: yeast.

Yeast is a hard worker—it feasts on sugar, water, and oxygen; rapidly multiplies; and, given time, triggers the chemical reaction that transforms flour and other ingredients into a lush cushion of dough. In doing so, yeast also adds texture, structure, and flavor. It is what elevates flour and water to such gratifying sustenance.

So get to know yeast, its properties and reactions. As you do, you'll appreciate what distinguishes Challah from Focaccia, or Brioche from Cheese Danish. Your fluency will improve with each loaf of Honey Whole-Wheat Bread or batch of pecan-laced Sticky Buns. Which brings us back to that satisfaction—the happy realization that what at first seemed a mystery is actually simple to understand.

Our recipes call for **fresh or dry yeast.** To substitute one for the other: One cake compressed fresh yeast (0.6 ounces) equals one envelope (¼ ounce or 2½ teaspoons) active dry or instant yeast.

Start with warm liquids to achieve a final dough temperature of 75 to 80 degrees. When adding liquids to yeast, keep them at or less than 110 degrees; yeast dies at about 140 degrees.

Salt kills yeast when in direct contact, so when adding salt to a dough, do so as the bulk of the flour is added, then immediately mix well to disperse. Never add salt to a "starter" (the mixture of warm liquid, yeast, and other dry ingredients that forms the base of the dough).

The most **accurate way to measure flour** is by weight, not volume, using a kitchen scale.

It's a good idea to **store specialty flours in the freezer** to prevent rancidity. This includes nut, wheat, rye, and graham flours. They will keep in the freezer for 6 to 8 months. Smell flour before using it; rancid flour will not harm you, but it will impart a bitter flavor to your bread.

If adding whole grains such as wheat, oats, or rye to a bread dough, soak them in water first. This will prevent the grains from absorbing additional moisture from the dough, which could make the bread dry and heavy. Add equal amounts of water and grains to a bowl and soak them overnight. If the water has not been absorbed completely, drain the grains before adding them to the dough.

Never add all of the flour in a recipe to the dough until you are sure it is needed. It's usually better for the dough to be slightly wet and sticky, which encourages fermentation better than if the dough were too dry.

Always **cover bread dough** while it is rising; otherwise a skin will develop on the dough and it will be tough once the bread is baked. You can use either plastic wrap (lightly oiled in case the dough touches it) or a slightly damp cloth.

Don't try to rush rising times. Flavor develops during the fermentation process, so slower and longer is always the best way to proceed.

It is important to let the dough rest, covered, before **shaping bagels.** This gives it a chance to relax and makes shaping easier.

Creating steam in the oven will give bread a crisp crust. The humidity will keep the crust from setting and thus prevent the bread from expanding too quickly. To do this in a home oven, use a spray bottle filled with cold water to spritz the inside of the oven several times during the first few minutes of baking. Make sure to do this quickly, spraying the floor and walls of the oven, but avoid the bread itself and the oven light. Or you can place a heavy-duty metal pan in the bottom portion of the oven as it preheats. A couple of minutes after you have put in the bread, pour cold water or a half-dozen ice cubes into the pan to create steam.

Checking the **internal temperature of bread** is a foolproof way to tell if it is fully baked. Insert an instant-read thermometer through the side of the loaf (so you don't puncture the top), straight into the center. The temperature should be 190 degrees.

1 Pullman loaf pan (pain de mie)

When dough hits the top of the tight-fitting lid on this pan, it flattens, creating a loaf of bread with a level top—ideal for sandwiches. Look for a standard 12-by-4-inch model in tinned steel.

2 Baking stone

Making bread and pizza on a baking stone is a great way to create a crisp crust. Place the stone directly on the oven floor, if possible. Always put a cold stone into a cold oven and heat the two together; placing a stone in a preheated oven could cause it to crack. Get the biggest stone that will fit in your oven (more mass means more heat is retained). You can't put a stone on the floor of an electric oven, however—you must use a rack.

3 Instant-read thermometer

This kitchen basic is indispensable for monitoring the temperature of breads to see if they're done, and for checking the warmth of water (water that is too hot can kill yeast). Look for one that's calibrated and has easy-to-read numbers; it can take 20 to 30 seconds for the temperature to register.

4 Lame

This device, with a razorlike blade attached to a handle, is used to make slits in the tops of loaves. The marks allow for the controlled expansion of the bread; hard-crusted breads, such as baguettes, often get slashed. Lames are available at specialty baking-supply stores; if you can't find one, you can use a single-edged razor blade instead.

5 Panettone mold

This star-shape mold is generally used to bake its namesake bread during the Christmas season. Heavy metal pans will promote even browning.

6 Baba molds

These molds, used for preparing baba au rhum, should have smooth sides and seams, since any marks will show in the finished cakes. As with panettone molds, look for those made of heavy metal to encourage proper browning.

7 Brioche molds

These baking pans come in a variety of sizes for making individual or larger brioche. The pans are available in black and tinned steel. Their slightly flared tops create a wider surface area (crust) than those baked in slim, straight-sided molds.

8 Wooden peel

Use this handled tool for getting loaves of bread and pizza in and out of a hot oven. A peel cut from a single piece of wood makes for easy sliding; a flat handle provides more stability than a round one.

9 English muffin cutter and ring

When shaping the dough for English muffins, cutters work best; they yield clean results. Rings help the dough keep its shape as it rises: The cut dough is placed inside a ring, then set aside to proof before it is fried and, finally, baked.

WORKING WITH YEAST 1. Once the dry yeast is dissolved in warm water, the mixture is left to stand until foamy, usually about 5 minutes; this is known as the starter. **2.** After the remaining ingredients are combined with the starter, the dough is placed in a lightly oiled bowl that can accommodate it as it expands. The bowl is covered with plastic wrap, which is also oiled to prevent it from sticking to the dough. **3.** The best indicator of whether the dough is ready for the oven is its size—the dough should have approximately doubled its original bulk. It's important to be patient during the rising process (also known as proofing), but setting the bowl in a warm place accelerates the process.

FORMING A LOG 1. The dough is patted into a rectangle on a lightly floured surface, and the long sides are folded in slightly. The dough is rolled from the top, and pressed gently into a tight log. **2.** Once the log is shaped, the final seam is sealed with the heel of your hand. The loaf is then rolled gently back and forth to smooth, and is set in a warm place to rise again before baking.

TESTING FRESH YEAST Fresh yeast, also known as compressed yeast, should be smooth, relatively dry (not soggy), and free of any mold. A good test of freshness is to press a piece of the yeast between your fingers—it should flake and crumble easily. If there is any hint of gumminess or moisture, the yeast is probably past its prime. Both fresh and dry yeasts should be stored in the refrigerator to maintain their potency.

OLIVE-OIL BREAD

MAKES ONE 12-INCH ROUND LOAF *This rustic loaf is a perfect platform for making Italian sandwiches and is a natural accompaniment to antipasti. The bread can be wrapped in plastic and kept at room temperature for up to four days.*

2 cups water, room temperature	¾ cup extra-virgin olive oil, plus more for bowl and plastic wrap
1½ pounds (about 4½ cups) bread flour, plus more for dusting	1 tablespoon coarse salt
1 ounce fresh yeast	Cornmeal, for dusting

In the bowl of an electric mixer, combine the water, flour, yeast, and olive oil; stir with a wooden spoon until all ingredients are incorporated. Cover with plastic wrap, and let rise in a warm place until doubled in bulk, 1 hour to 1 hour 15 minutes.

Attach the bowl to the mixer fitted with the dough hook. Add the salt, and mix to combine on low speed. Raise the speed to medium, and beat until the dough pulls away from the sides of the bowl but is still sticky, about 3 minutes.

Turn out the dough onto a lightly floured work surface. Knead it for 1 minute, then transfer to a large, lightly oiled bowl. Cover with lightly oiled plastic wrap. Let rise in a warm place until doubled in bulk, about 1 hour.

Return the dough to a lightly floured work surface. Fold in the following fashion: Fold the bottom third of the dough up, the top third down, and the right and left sides over, tapping the dough after each fold to release excess flour, and pressing down to seal. Flip the dough seam side down on the work surface, and cover with oiled plastic wrap; let rest for about 15 minutes.

Dust a large wooden peel with cornmeal; set aside. Transfer dough to a clean work surface. (If the dough is overly sticky, you can lightly flour the surface.) To shape the dough, cup it between your rounded palms; roll it in a circular motion, pulling down on the surface of the dough to form a tight, smooth round. (The bottom of the dough should "catch" or drag a bit on the table as you roll; this will help it take shape.) Transfer the round of dough to the prepared peel, and drape with a piece of oiled plastic wrap. Let the dough rest on the peel until slightly puffed, about 30 minutes. Meanwhile, place a baking stone on the floor of the oven. Preheat the oven to 450°F.

With a lame or a razor blade, make four slashes on top of the loaf to form a square. Slide the loaf onto the stone, and bake until the crust is dark golden brown, about 35 minutes. Place bread on a wire rack to cool before slicing.

OLIVE-OIL ROLLS VARIATION Follow instructions for Olive-Oil Bread, dividing the dough into 16 pieces (2½ ounces each) with a bench scraper. Shape the dough balls as directed above, and transfer to a baking sheet lined with oiled parchment paper. Let rise, then bake until rolls are golden brown, about 20 minutes. Makes 16.

OLIVE-OIL BREAD HOW-TO
Once the loaf is shaped, a square is slashed into the risen dough. The slashes help ensure that the bread will expand evenly as it bakes.

HONEY WHOLE-WHEAT BREAD
MAKES TWO 9-INCH LOAVES

3½ cups warm water (about 110°F)

3 tablespoons honey

2 envelopes (¼ ounce each) active dry yeast

1½ pounds (about 4½ cups) bread flour, plus more for dusting

1½ pounds (about 4½ cups) whole-wheat flour

5 ounces (about 1 cup) wheat germ

2 tablespoons coarse salt

Vegetable oil, for bowl, pans, and plastic wrap

1 large egg yolk

1 tablespoon heavy cream

Combine the warm water, honey, and yeast in a large liquid measuring cup, stirring until the yeast dissolves. Let stand until foamy, about 5 minutes.

In a large bowl, whisk 1 pound 5 ounces (about 4 cups) bread flour with the whole-wheat flour, wheat germ, and salt. Make a well in the center. Pour in the yeast mixture, and stir with a wooden spoon, gradually drawing in the dry ingredients until combined.

Turn out the dough onto a lightly floured work surface. Gently knead in the remaining 3 ounces (about ½ cup) bread flour a little at a time until dough is smooth and elastic, 10 to 15 minutes. Place in a lightly oiled bowl; cover with lightly oiled plastic wrap. Let rise in a warm place until doubled in bulk, 1 to 1½ hours.

Preheat the oven to 400°F, with the rack in the center. Brush two 9-by-5-inch loaf pans with oil. Punch down the dough with your fist, then turn it out onto a lightly floured work surface. Divide dough in half. Flatten one half into an oval approximately the length of the pan, and roll up lengthwise, gently pressing as you go to form a tight log. Place the log, seam side down, into a prepared pan. Repeat with remaining dough. Cover loaf pans with oiled plastic wrap. Let rise in a warm place until doubled in bulk, 30 to 45 minutes.

Using a lame or a razor blade, slash the loaves down the center in one quick, even motion. In a small bowl, beat the egg yolk with the heavy cream, and brush over the tops of the loaves.

Bake, rotating pans halfway through, until bread is deep golden brown, 50 to 60 minutes. (If the tops are browning too quickly during the last 30 minutes of baking, tent with aluminum foil.) Transfer pans to a wire rack, and let cool 5 minutes. Turn out the loaves onto the rack to cool completely before serving.

PULLMAN BREAD

MAKES ONE 12-INCH LOAF *If you a prefer a loaf with a rounded top, you can bake the dough without the lid in place; the baking time should be the same.*

- 1½ pounds (about 4½ cups) bread flour, plus more for dusting
- 3½ teaspoons instant yeast
- 1½ tablespoons coarse salt
- 1½ tablespoons sugar
- ⅓ cup nonfat dry milk
- 2 tablespoons unsalted butter, room temperature
- 1¾ cups warm water (about 110°F)
- Vegetable oil, for bowl and pan

In the bowl of an electric mixer fitted with the dough hook, combine the flour, yeast, salt, sugar, dry milk, and butter. Add the warm water, and beat on low speed until the dough is smooth, elastic, and uniform in color, about 5 minutes.

Turn out the dough onto a lightly floured work surface and finish kneading it by hand, about five times, making sure that all ingredients are fully incorporated and the dough forms a smooth ball. Place the dough in a lightly oiled bowl, cover with plastic wrap, and let rise in a warm place until doubled in bulk, about 1 hour.

Punch down the dough. Pull the sides into the center. Invert the dough in the bowl, so that it rests smooth side up. Cover with plastic wrap, and let rise again until doubled in bulk, about 1 hour more.

Generously brush a 12-inch Pullman loaf pan with vegetable oil, making sure to coat the underside of the lid, as well as the bottom and sides of the pan. Set aside. Turn out the dough onto a lightly floured surface. Roll out the dough to a 12-by-8-inch rectangle, with a long side facing you. Starting at the top, roll the dough toward you, gently pressing as you go to form a tight log. Pat in the ends to make even. Gently roll the log back and forth to seal the final seam. Place the loaf, seam side down, in the prepared pan, and slide the lid three-quarters of the way closed. Let rise in a warm place until the dough is almost touching the lid, 45 to 60 minutes. Meanwhile, preheat the oven to 425°F.

Close the lid completely and bake, rotating pan halfway through, until loaf is light golden brown, about 45 minutes. Reduce the oven temperature to 350°F, close the lid, and continue baking another 30 minutes.

Transfer pan to a wire rack to cool for 10 minutes. (The bread should have a hollow sound when tapped on the bottom. If not, continue baking, covered, checking at 5-minute intervals, until the crust is deep golden brown.) Remove bread from pan, and let cool completely before slicing. The bread can be wrapped in plastic and kept at room temperature for up to 4 days.

PULLMAN BREAD HOW-TO
The shaped loaf is placed in a lidded pan and left to rise until the dough almost touches the lid. Coating the lid with oil prevents any dough that might touch it from sticking.

CRANBERRY-PECAN RYE BREAD

MAKES ONE 18-INCH LOAF *This free-form dough can be shaped into two longer loaves or one big round; you may need to adjust the baking time.*

1	cup (4 ounces) pecan pieces	
	Vegetable oil, for bowl and baking sheet	
1¼	cups warm water (about 110°F), plus more if needed	
1	envelope (¼ ounce) active dry yeast	
10	ounces (about 2 cups) bread flour	
5½	ounces (about 1 cup) rye flour	

2½	teaspoons table salt
1	tablespoon sugar
1½	tablespoons caraway seeds
¾	cup dried cranberries, coarsely chopped
1	large egg
	Sea salt, such as Maldon (or other coarse salt), for sprinkling

Preheat the oven to 350°F. Spread pecans in a single layer on a rimmed baking sheet. Toast until fragrant, about 10 minutes. Set aside to cool completely. Meanwhile, line a baking sheet with parchment paper, and brush with oil; set aside.

In the bowl of an electric mixer fitted with the paddle attachment, stir yeast into the warm water to dissolve. Let stand until foamy, about 5 minutes. Add the flours, table salt, sugar, and caraway seeds, and mix on medium-low speed until dough just comes together. If the dough is too dry, add more warm water, 1 tablespoon at a time, and continue beating. Switch to the dough hook, and beat on medium speed until dough is smooth, elastic, and slightly tacky, 4 to 5 minutes. With mixer on low speed, mix in cranberries and reserved pecans. The dough will feel stiff; push in any loose cranberries and pecans with your fingers. Transfer dough to a lightly oiled bowl, cover with oiled plastic wrap, and let rise in a warm place until doubled in bulk, about 1 hour.

In a small bowl, beat the egg with 1 tablespoon water. Turn out the dough onto a lightly floured work surface. Roll out dough to a rectangle, about 13 by 10 inches and ½ inch thick, with a short side facing you. Fold ½-inch flaps inward on the shorter sides of the rectangle: Starting at the top, roll the dough toward you, gently pressing as you go to form a tight log. Gently roll the log back and forth to seal the seam. (If the seam doesn't stay sealed, brush it with beaten egg, and press down again to seal.) Transfer loaf to the prepared baking sheet, seam side down; cover loosely with plastic wrap, and let rise in a warm place until dough is puffed and holds an impression from your fingertip, about 45 minutes.

Brush the loaf generously with the egg wash, and sprinkle with sea salt. Bake, rotating sheet halfway through, until the crust is deep golden brown, and an instant-read thermometer inserted in the center of the bread registers 190°F, 35 to 40 minutes. Transfer bread to a wire rack to cool completely before slicing. Bread can be kept, wrapped tightly in plastic, at room temperature for up to 3 days.

CINNAMON-RAISIN BREAD
MAKES TWO 9-BY-5-INCH LOAVES

For the dough:

- 1 envelope (¼ ounce) active dry yeast
- 2 cups warm milk (about 110°F)
- 2 pounds 2 ounces (about 6½ cups) all-purpose flour, plus more for dusting
- 1 stick (½ cup) unsalted butter, room temperature, cut into pieces, plus more for pans
- ½ cup sugar
- 2 large eggs, plus 1 large egg, lightly beaten
- 2½ teaspoons coarse salt
- 1 cup raisins
- 1 tablespoon ground cinnamon
- Vegetable oil, for bowl and plastic wrap

For the filling:

- 1½ cups sugar
- 2 tablespoons ground cinnamon

Make the dough: In the bowl of an electric mixer, sprinkle the yeast over the warm milk; whisk to combine. Add the flour, butter, sugar, 2 eggs, and salt. Attach bowl to mixer fitted with the dough hook. Mix on low speed until all the ingredients are well combined, about 3 minutes. Raise the speed to medium-low, and continue to mix until the dough is uniformly smooth and pulls away from the sides of the bowl, about 3 minutes more.

Turn out dough onto a lightly floured work surface. Pat out dough into a 9-inch round, about 1¼ inches thick. Sprinkle with raisins and cinnamon, and knead until they are just incorporated. Place the dough in a lightly oiled bowl, and cover with oiled plastic wrap; let rise in a warm place until doubled in bulk, about 1 hour.

Return the dough to a lightly floured work surface, and pat into a round. Fold in the following manner: Fold the bottom third of the dough up, the top third down, and the right and left sides over, tapping the dough after each fold to release excess flour, and pressing down to seal. Return the dough to the bowl, seam side down, and let rise again until doubled in bulk, about 40 minutes.

Make the filling: Combine sugar and cinnamon with 2 tablespoons water in a small bowl. Return the dough to a lightly floured work surface, and divide in half. Roll out one half to a 12-by-10-inch rectangle; brush with beaten egg, and sprinkle with half the filling. Repeat with the remaining dough and filling.

Generously butter two 9-by-5-inch loaf pans; set aside. With a short end of the rectangle facing you, fold in both long sides of the dough, about 1 inch. Then roll the dough toward you, gently pressing as you go to form a tight log. Gently roll the log back and forth to seal the seam. Place the loaf in a prepared pan, seam side down. Repeat with remaining rectangle. Cover pans loosely with oiled plastic wrap, and let rest in a warm place until dough rises just above the rim of the pan, about 30 minutes. Meanwhile, preheat the oven to 425°F.

Brush the tops of the loaves with beaten egg, and transfer pans to a parchment-lined rimmed baking sheet. Bake, rotating pans halfway through, until loaves are golden brown, about 45 minutes. (If the tops begin to brown too quickly, tent with aluminum foil.) Turn out the bread onto a wire rack to cool completely before slicing. The bread can be kept, wrapped in plastic, at room temperature up to 4 days.

CINNAMON-RAISIN BREAD HOW-TO 1. Ground cinnamon and raisins are sprinkled over and then kneaded into the dough. 2. The dough is proofed in a lightly oiled bowl until it has doubled in bulk. 3. The dough is rolled out into a rectangle, sprinkled with filling, and then rolled into a log.

BRIOCHE

MAKES 20 PETITES BRIOCHES, TWO 7-INCH LOAVES, OR TWO 9-BY-5-INCH LOAVES *Because brioche is made with a large amount of butter, it is important to use the best quality you can find. Remember: The butter and eggs must be cold, or you may end up with something that resembles cake batter, rather than bread dough. If this happens, chill the dough until it becomes workable. Never add more flour, which toughens the dough.*

<table>
<tr><td>1/3</td><td>cup warm water (about 110°F)</td><td>4</td><td>large eggs, cold, plus 1 large egg, lightly beaten</td></tr>
<tr><td>1</td><td>tablespoon active dry yeast</td><td></td><td></td></tr>
<tr><td>9</td><td>ounces (about 1½ cups) bread flour, plus more for dusting</td><td>3</td><td>tablespoons sugar</td></tr>
<tr><td></td><td></td><td>2</td><td>tablespoons plus 1 teaspoon nonfat dry milk</td></tr>
<tr><td>5</td><td>ounces (about ¾ cup) pastry flour</td><td></td><td></td></tr>
<tr><td>1¼</td><td>sticks (10 tablespoons) unsalted butter, cold, cut into pieces, plus more for pans</td><td>1</td><td>teaspoon salt</td></tr>
<tr><td></td><td></td><td></td><td>Canola oil, for plastic wrap</td></tr>
</table>

PETITE BRIOCHE HOW-TO
The dough is weighed and divided into 20 equal pieces, which are then split in two, so that one is twice the size of the other. The larger piece is rolled into a smooth ball, and a deep hole is pressed into the center. The smaller piece is rolled into a teardrop, then fit, tip-first, into the hole. The assembled brioches are placed in buttered molds and left to proof before baking.

Make the dough: In a medium bowl, sprinkle yeast over the warm water; stir with a fork until dissolved. Let stand until foamy, about 5 minutes. Add 2 ounces bread flour; stir until well combined. Cover with a clean kitchen towel; let rise in a warm spot until doubled in bulk and bubbles appear on the surface, about 1 hour.

Place remaining 7 ounces bread flour and the pastry flour in the bowl of an electric mixer fitted with the dough hook. Add the butter, eggs, sugar, and dry milk, and beat on low speed until well combined, about 5 minutes. Add the yeast mixture; beat on low speed for 5 minutes. Sprinkle in salt; beat on medium speed until dough is smooth, shiny, and elastic, about 5 minutes more.

Cover the bowl with plastic wrap; immediately place in freezer for 30 minutes (this will keep the dough from rising too quickly). Remove from freezer; punch down dough in bowl. Fold sides into the center, and invert, so dough is smooth side up. Cover with plastic wrap, and refrigerate, at least 10 hours or overnight.

To make Petites Brioches: Butter 20 small brioche molds; set aside. Divide the dough into 20 equal pieces (1½ ounces each). Working with a few pieces at a time (return the rest of the dough to the refrigerator), divide each piece in two, making one twice as big as the other.

On a lightly floured surface, roll the larger piece into a round ball using the cupped palm of your hand. Press your thumb into the center of the ball to form a deep well. Then rotate your thumb to widen the hole. Shape the smaller piece into a teardrop. With lightly floured fingers, press the tip of the teardrop gently into the bottom of the hole. Place in a prepared mold. Repeat with remaining dough.

Drape the dough pieces with a well-oiled piece of plastic wrap. Set aside in a warm, nondrafty place until fully doubled in bulk. This could take anywhere from 1 to 3 hours. Meanwhile, preheat the oven to 375°F.

Just before baking, brush dough gently but generously with beaten egg. Place molds on two rimmed baking sheets, and bake until deep golden brown, 8 to 12 minutes. Immediately remove Brioches from molds, and cool on a wire rack.

To make 7-inch round loaves: Butter two 7-inch molds. Divide the dough into 10 equal pieces (3 ounces each). Return five pieces to the refrigerator. On a lightly floured surface, roll five pieces of dough into smooth balls. Add as little extra flour as possible. Shape each ball into a teardrop. With the tips pointed toward the center, arrange four teardrops around the edge of a prepared pan, leaving a hole in the center. Pinch the tips together and then press onto the bottom of the pan, leaving only a little pan showing; this will help the pieces stay together during baking. Press your thumb lightly in the center of each piece to nudge the dough together.

Gently press the tip of the last teardrop into the center of the pan; it should sit above the others. Repeat with remaining five pieces. Cover each pan with a bowl or a container large enough to give the dough ample room to double in bulk. (The bowls should not touch the rising loaves.) Set aside in a warm, nondrafty place until more than doubled in bulk, 1 to 3 hours. Meanwhile, preheat the oven to 375°F. Just before baking, lightly brush the surface of the dough with beaten egg. Bake loaves until they sound hollow when the bottom is tapped, about 45 minutes. Immediately remove from pan and cool on a wire rack.

To make 9-by-5-inch loaves: Butter two 9-by-5-inch loaf pans. Divide the dough into 16 equal pieces (2 ounces each), and roll pieces into balls. Place eight balls in each prepared pan. Cover loosely with oiled plastic wrap, and let rise until doubled in bulk, 1 to 3 hours. Meanwhile, preheat the oven to 375°F. Just before baking, brush dough gently but generously with beaten egg. Bake loaves until they sound hollow when the bottoms are tapped, about 40 minutes. Immediately remove from pans and cool on a wire rack.

RECTANGULAR LOAF HOW-TO The balls of dough are placed side by side in a buttered 9-by-5-inch loaf pan, so they are just touching. After doubling in bulk, they are brushed with egg before baking.

CHALLAH

MAKES ONE 18-INCH LOAF *Challah is sometimes garnished with poppy seeds before being baked; sprinkle 1½ teaspoons poppy seeds over the bread after brushing with egg wash.*

1½ pounds bread flour
(about 4½ cups),
plus more for dusting

¾ ounce fresh yeast

¼ cup sugar

3 tablespoons honey

1 tablespoon coarse salt

¼ cup vegetable oil, plus more
for bowl, plastic wrap, and
baking sheet

8 large egg yolks,
plus 1 large whole egg

In the bowl of an electric mixer fitted with the dough hook, combine the flour, yeast, sugar, honey, salt, vegetable oil, egg yolks, and 1 cup water. Mix on low speed until the dough is smooth and stiff with a slight sheen, 8 to 10 minutes.

Turn out the dough onto a lightly floured work surface, and knead to make sure any loose bits are incorporated. Fold in the following manner: Fold the bottom third of the dough up, the top third down, and the right and left sides over, tapping the dough after each fold to release excess flour, and pressing down to seal. Gently gather the dough and flip it over, seam side down. Place the dough in a lightly oiled bowl, cover with oiled plastic wrap, and let rise in a warm place until doubled in bulk, about 1 hour. Brush an unrimmed baking sheet with vegetable oil or line with parchment paper. Set aside.

Return the dough to a lightly floured work surface, and divide into three equal pieces. Roll each piece into an 18-inch log, and place the logs parallel to one another; pinch the ends together at the top. Weave the three strands into a tight braid, tugging gently as you go. Press the ends together to seal. Place loaf on the prepared sheet. Loosely cover with oiled plastic wrap, and let rise until doubled in bulk, about 1 hour.

Meanwhile, preheat the oven to 375°F. Lightly beat the remaining whole egg and brush gently but thoroughly over loaf, making sure to cover any seams and crevices. Bake until the crust is dark brown, 50 to 60 minutes. The bread should reach an internal temperature of 190°F on an instant-read thermometer, and should have a hollow sound when tapped on the bottom. Transfer the bread to a wire rack to cool completely before slicing. Bread can be wrapped in plastic and kept at room temperature for up to 3 days.

CHALLAH HOW-TO 1. The dough is divided into three strands and pinched together at the top. An outer strand is folded over the center one to begin the braid. **2.** To eliminate slack and ensure a tight braid, each strand is given a gentle tug as it is folded over. **3.** The braid is completed by pinching the ends together.

PANETTONES

MAKES 2 LOAVES *Our version of this traditional Christmas bread calls for an assortment of dried fruits; feel free to include candied citrus peel, whose distinctive, slightly bitter flavor is more characteristic of Italian panettone. If substituting larger fruits, such as apricots, pears, or cherries, chop them finely before using.*

PANETTONE HOW-TO
The fruit-studded dough is placed in the mold to rise. When it has risen just barely above the edge of the pan, it has proofed sufficiently and is ready to bake.

⅓ cup warm water (about 110°F)	1½ sticks (¾ cup) unsalted butter, cold, cut into pieces, plus melted butter for bowl, plastic wrap, and molds
2 envelopes (¼ ounce each) active dry yeast	
1 pound 5 ounces (about 4 cups) all-purpose flour, plus more for dusting	1¼ teaspoons salt
½ cup warm milk (about 110°F)	2 cups mixed dried fruit, such as currants, raisins, and cranberries
⅔ cup sugar	Finely grated zest of 1 lemon
4 large whole eggs, plus 3 large egg yolks	Finely grated zest of 1 orange
1 teaspoon pure vanilla extract	1 tablespoon heavy cream

In a medium bowl, sprinkle 1 envelope yeast over the warm water. Stir with a fork until yeast has dissolved, and let stand until foamy, 5 to 10 minutes. Stir in ½ cup flour, and cover the bowl with plastic wrap. Let rise in a warm place until doubled in bulk, about 30 minutes.

Pour warm milk into a small bowl, and sprinkle with remaining envelope yeast. Stir with a fork until yeast has dissolved, and let stand until foamy, 5 to 10 minutes. Meanwhile, in a medium bowl, whisk together sugar, whole eggs, 2 egg yolks, and vanilla. Whisk in milk-yeast mixture.

In the bowl of an electric mixer fitted with the paddle attachment, beat the butter, salt, and remaining 3½ cups flour on low speed until mixture is crumbly. With mixer on low speed, slowly add egg mixture, and beat on medium speed until smooth. Add the water-yeast mixture; beat on high speed until dough is sticky and elastic, and forms long strands when stretched, about 9 minutes. Beat in dried fruits and zests. Transfer dough to a buttered bowl, and cover with buttered plastic wrap. Let rise in a warm place until doubled in bulk, about 2 hours.

Generously butter two panettone molds; set aside. Turn out dough onto a lightly floured surface; knead a few times, turning each time, until smooth. Divide dough in half, and knead into balls. Drop balls into prepared molds. Place on a rimmed baking sheet; cover loosely with buttered plastic wrap. Let rise in a warm place until dough reaches just above the top of the mold, 45 to 60 minutes. Meanwhile, preheat the oven to 400°F, with a rack in the lower third.

In a small bowl, whisk together remaining yolk and the cream. Brush tops of dough with egg wash. Using kitchen scissors, cut an X in the top of each ball of dough. Bake 15 minutes. Reduce oven temperature to 350°F; continue baking, rotating sheet halfway through, until panettones are deep golden brown and an instant-read thermometer inserted in the centers registers 190°F, about 45 minutes. (If the tops brown too quickly, tent with aluminum foil.) Transfer baking sheet to a wire rack to cool 15 to 20 minutes. Turn out loaves onto rack to cool completely. Loaves can be wrapped in plastic and kept at room temperature for up to 3 days.

Baguettes

Fougasse

BAGUETTE HOW-TO

1. After being shaped into an oval on a floured surface, the top third of the dough is folded toward the center. **2.** The bottom third is then folded up and over the first fold, and sealed with the heel of the hand at 1-inch increments. **3.** The log is rolled out by hand into a long, thin loaf of uniform thickness.

BAGUETTES

MAKES TWO 16-INCH LOAVES *Instead of making two large loaves, divide the dough into four equal pieces for demi-baguettes.*

For the starter:

7 ounces (about 1½ scant cups) bread flour

¾ cup plus 2 tablespoons warm water (about 110°F)

1 envelope (¼ ounce) active dry yeast

For the dough:

7½ ounces (about 1½ cups) bread flour, plus more for dusting

1½ tablespoons coarse salt

Vegetable oil, for bowl and plastic wrap

Fine cornmeal, for dusting

Make the starter: In the bowl of an electric mixer fitted with the paddle attachment, combine the flour, warm water, and yeast; mix to form a thin batter. Cover with plastic wrap, and let stand at room temperature for 12 to 16 hours; it should have tripled in size and then deflated (look for residue around the top of the bowl), and have a ripe, yeasty smell.

Make the dough: Add the flour, ⅓ cup plus 2 tablespoons room-temperature water, and salt to the starter. Attach the bowl to the mixer fitted with the dough hook, and mix on low speed for 2 to 3 minutes. Raise the speed to medium, and beat until the dough is smooth and elastic, 2 to 3 minutes more.

Using a plastic bowl scraper, turn out the dough onto a lightly floured work surface. Knead gently for 1 minute to thoroughly incorporate all ingredients. Place the dough in a large, lightly oiled bowl; cover with plastic wrap, and let rise in a warm place until doubled in bulk, about 1 hour.

Return the dough to a lightly floured work surface, and pat into a rough oval. Fold in the following manner: Fold the bottom third of the dough up, the top third down, and the right and left sides over, tapping the dough after each fold to release excess flour, and pressing down to seal. Using the outer edges of your palms, gather the dough and flip it over, seam side down; pat to dislodge excess flour. Return the dough (still seam side down) to the mixing bowl. Cover with oiled plastic wrap, and let rise in a warm place until doubled in bulk, about 1 hour.

Using the bowl scraper, return the dough to a lightly floured work surface. Pat into a round, and divide into two equal pieces. With lightly floured hands, gently shape each piece into a rough oval, handling the dough carefully to avoid deflating the air pockets. Cover with plastic wrap, and let rest, undisturbed, for 15 to 20 minutes. (This will relax the dough so it is easier to stretch.)

Sprinkle a large wooden peel (or the flat side of a heavy baking sheet) with cornmeal. Set one piece of the dough on a floured work surface. With your palm, press to flatten. With a long side facing you, fold the top third of the dough toward the center; press gently to seal. Fold the bottom third up, overlapping the first seam. Press down firmly with the heel of your hand at 1-inch increments along the seam. Starting at the middle and working toward the ends, roll the log until it is about 16 inches long. Place the loaf, seam side down, on the prepared peel. Repeat with the other piece of dough.

Cover loaves loosely with plastic wrap, and let rise until puffed, about 30 minutes. Meanwhile, place a baking stone on the floor of the oven. Preheat the oven to 450°F.

Using a lame or a razor blade, make three or four shallow slashes diagonally down the length of each loaf. Slide the formed loaves onto the stone, taking care to maintain their shape as much as possible. Bake until golden brown, 30 to 35 minutes. Transfer the baguettes immediately to a wire rack to cool completely. This bread is best eaten the day it is baked, but it can be kept wrapped in plastic at room temperature for up to 1 day or frozen, wrapped in plastic and aluminum foil, for up to 3 weeks.

FOUGASSE

MAKES ONE 14-INCH LOAF *This classic French loaf is traditionally formed into a leaf. You can scatter the dough with fresh herbs, such as thyme or rosemary, before baking.*

Baguettes dough (recipe above)

Fine cornmeal, for dusting

All-purpose flour, for dusting

Extra-virgin olive oil, for brushing

Sea salt, such as Maldon (or other coarse salt), for sprinkling

Prepare the Baguettes dough, following the recipe through the second 1-hour rise. Sprinkle a large wooden peel with cornmeal. On a lightly floured work surface, roll out the dough to an oval, about 12 to 14 inches long and ½ to ¾ inch thick. Transfer to the prepared peel, and cover loosely with plastic wrap. Let the dough rest in a warm place for 10 to 15 minutes. (This will relax the dough so it is easier to stretch.)

Place a baking stone on the floor of the oven. Preheat the oven to 400°F. Using a lame or a razor blade, make five slits as illustrated, cutting all the way through the dough, and gently stretching slits to widen openings. Cover dough loosely with plastic wrap, and let rest for about 15 minutes.

Brush the dough generously with olive oil, and sprinkle with salt. Slide the loaf onto the stone, taking care to maintain the shape as much as possible. (Quickly reshape the loaf with your hands, if necessary.) Bake until golden brown, 25 to 27 minutes. Transfer loaf to a wire rack to cool completely. This bread is best eaten the day it is baked, but it can be kept wrapped in plastic at room temperature for up to 1 day, or frozen, wrapped in plastic and aluminum foil, for up to 3 weeks.

FOUGASSE HOW-TO
1. The dough is left to relax on the prepared peel, making it easier to stretch.
2. A lame or a razor blade is used to make five slits in the dough to form a leaf pattern.

ENGLISH MUFFINS

MAKES 8 *Placing the dough in English muffin rings will allow it to rise and bake taller, but you can still make the muffins without them—simply let the rounds rise on their own, then fry and bake them as directed. They will taste just as delicious.*

- 11 ounces (about 2¼ cups) all-purpose flour, plus more for dusting
- 1 teaspoon instant yeast
- 1 cup warm water (about 110°F)
- 1 tablespoon honey
- 2 tablespoons nonfat dry milk
- 3 tablespoons unsalted butter, room temperature, plus more for skillet

- 1¼ teaspoons coarse salt, plus more for sprinkling (optional)
- Vegetable oil, for bowl, plastic wrap, parchment, and rings
- Semolina flour, for pan
- Anise seeds, for sprinkling (optional)
- Unhulled sesame seeds, for sprinkling (optional)

In a medium bowl, combine 5 ounces (1 cup) all-purpose flour, ½ teaspoon yeast, the warm water, and the honey; whisk vigorously until mixture is thick and slightly foamy, about 1 minute.

In another medium bowl, whisk together the remaining 6 ounces (1¼ cups) all-purpose flour, the remaining ½ teaspoon yeast, and the dry milk. Sprinkle over the wet flour mixture, cover tightly with plastic wrap, and let rise in a warm place until doubled in bulk, about 2 hours. Refrigerate until chilled, about 1 hour.

Transfer to the bowl of an electric mixer fitted with the dough hook. Mix on medium-low speed until all dry ingredients have been incorporated into the dough, about 2 minutes. Add the butter and salt, and continue to mix on medium speed until combined (the dough should be smooth but slightly tacky), about 5 minutes. If the dough is too dry, add a little room-temperature water, 1 teaspoon at a time; if the dough is too wet, add more flour, 1 teaspoon at a time.

Transfer dough to a lightly oiled large bowl. Cover bowl with oiled plastic wrap, and let rise in a warm place until the dough has doubled in bulk, about 1½ hours.

With lightly oiled hands, gently knead dough in the bowl, covering all sides with oil. Turn out dough onto a piece of plastic wrap. Form dough into a flattened rectangle; wrap in plastic, and refrigerate until well chilled, at least 1 hour or overnight.

Line a baking sheet with parchment, brush with oil, and lightly dust with semolina flour. Lightly oil eight English muffin rings, and place on prepared sheet. Transfer dough to a lightly floured work surface, and roll out to ¾ inch thick. Using a floured 3-inch biscuit cutter, cut out eight rounds; place each round in one of the oiled rings. (Dough can be rerolled in order to cut all eight muffins.) Set aside in a warm place until rounds have risen slightly, about 30 minutes. Meanwhile, preheat the oven to 350°F.

Sprinkle rounds with seeds or salt, as desired (about 1 teaspoon per muffin). In a large skillet over medium heat, melt enough additional butter to coat the bottom of the pan. When the butter is bubbling, carefully transfer rounds to the skillet with a wide spatula, leaving muffin rings in place. Do not crowd the pan; rounds should fit comfortably without touching. Cook muffins until golden brown, about 4 minutes. Flip them over, and cook until golden, about 4 minutes more. Return muffins to the

ENGLISH MUFFIN HOW-TO
1. The rounds of dough are fitted into oiled rings, and set aside to rise slightly before cooking. **2.** The dough rounds, still in their rings, are transferred to a skillet and cooked in butter until well-browned on both sides. They are finished in the oven.

baking sheet, and remove muffin rings. Bake until muffins are cooked through, 7 to 10 minutes. (They should reach an internal temperature of 190°F.) Transfer to a wire rack to cool. Muffins can be eaten warm, or allowed to cool and then split open with a fork and toasted. The muffins can be wrapped in plastic and kept at room temperature for up to 3 days.

WHOLE-WHEAT ENGLISH MUFFINS VARIATION After combining the first yeast mixture, substitute 3 ounces (about ½ cup plus 2 tablespoons) whole-wheat flour for 3 ounces (½ cup plus 2 tablespoons) of all-purpose flour. Mix with yeast and dry milk. Proceed with English Muffins recipe.

BAGELS

MAKES 10 *In keeping with traditional methods, we boil our bagels briefly before baking. This ensures that they will have a chewy interior, as well as a crisp outer crust.*

¾ teaspoon active dry yeast	1½ tablespoons table salt
1⅔ cups warm water (about 110°F)	Vegetable oil, for bowl, plastic wrap, and parchment
3 tablespoons sugar	
3 tablespoons barley malt syrup	Fennel seeds, poppy seeds, and sesame seeds, for topping (optional)
1 pound 6 ounces (about 4¼ cups) bread flour	Coarse salt, for topping (optional)

In the bowl of an electric mixer, whisk together yeast and water. Let stand until foamy, about 5 minutes. Attach bowl to mixer fitted with the dough hook. With the mixer on a low speed, add sugar, 1 tablespoon malt syrup, flour, and salt. Knead until a dough forms, about 1 minute. The dough should be slightly tacky but not sticky (if necessary, add more flour or water, 1 tablespoon at a time). Continue to knead dough for 5 more minutes. Transfer the dough to a lightly oiled bowl; cover with oiled plastic wrap. Let rise in a warm place until doubled in bulk, about 2 hours.

Divide dough into 10 equal pieces. Cover with a damp, clean kitchen towel, and let rest for about 20 minutes. (This will relax the dough and make it easier to shape.)

Line two unrimmed baking sheets with parchment paper, and lightly brush with oil; set aside. With lightly oiled hands, roll each piece of dough into a 6-inch rope. Holding one end of rope between your thumb and forefinger, wrap dough around your hand to form a circle with overlapping ends (they should overlap by a few inches). Still holding the dough, press the overlapping ends on the work surface, rolling back and forth to seal with the palm of your hand.

Place the bagels 2 inches apart on the prepared baking sheets. Cover with a piece of oiled plastic wrap, and let rest until slightly puffed, about 20 minutes.

Preheat the oven to 500°F, with racks in the upper and lower thirds. Fill a large stockpot (the wider, the better) with about 5 quarts of water, and bring to a boil. Add remaining 2 tablespoons malt syrup. Gently drop bagels into the water. (Add as many bagels as will comfortably fit without touching each other.) After 30 seconds, use a slotted spoon or skimmer to flip bagels over; simmer for 30 seconds more. Using

BAGELS HOW-TO
The dough is rolled into a log and then formed into a doughnut shape; the ends should overlap. With the dough wrapped around your hand, the seam is smoothed by gently rolling it against the work surface.

the slotted spoon, return bagels to parchment-lined sheets. Top with seeds or coarse salt, as desired, while bagels are still wet.

Immediately place sheets in the oven. Bake for 5 minutes, then rotate sheets and reduce oven temperature to 350°F. Continue to bake until the tops of the bagels begin to turn golden brown, about 10 minutes. Using a spatula, flip bagels over, and continue to bake until other sides turn golden brown, about 5 minutes more. Transfer bagels to a wire rack to cool completely. Bagels can be kept in an airtight container at room temperature for up to 1 day, or frozen, tightly wrapped in plastic or stored in resealable bags, for up to 3 weeks. Preslice bagels before freezing for easy toasting.

crackers and rolls

PARMESAN-ROSEMARY CRACKERS
MAKES 16

**PARMESAN-ROSEMARY
CRACKERS HOW-TO**
After being rolled out into
thin sheets, the dough is
brushed with egg wash
then sprinkled with grated
Parmigiano-Reggiano,
ground black pepper, salt,
and fresh rosemary.

 1 cup warm water (about 110°F)

 1 teaspoon active dry yeast

 3 tablespoons extra-virgin olive oil,
plus more for bowl and plastic wrap

15 ounces (about 3 cups) all-purpose
flour, plus more for dusting

 2 teaspoons coarse salt,
plus more for sprinkling

 2 teaspoons honey

¼ cup freshly grated Parmigiano-
Reggiano, plus more for sprinkling

 1 large egg, lightly beaten
Freshly ground pepper

 3 tablespoons fresh
rosemary leaves

In the bowl of an electric mixer, stir together ¼ cup warm water with the yeast. Let stand until foamy, about 5 minutes. Add olive oil, flour, salt, honey, and remaining ¾ cup warm water. Attach to a mixer fitted with the paddle attachment, and mix on low speed for 1 minute. Switch to the dough hook, and mix on medium-low speed until dough is soft but not tacky, 2 minutes. Add cheese and mix for 1 minute more.

Transfer dough to a lightly floured work surface; knead four or five times, forming into a ball. Cover with lightly oiled plastic wrap; let rest for 10 minutes. Place dough in a lightly oiled bowl and cover with plastic wrap. Refrigerate until well chilled, at least 1 hour or overnight. Meanwhile, line two baking sheets with parchment.

Turn out dough onto a lightly floured work surface. Divide dough into 16 equal pieces. Using a pasta machine, pass dough through the second-thinnest setting, dusting generously with flour. Each piece should be about 8 by 5 inches. (Alternatively, you can roll out the dough with a rolling pin.) Transfer pieces of dough to prepared baking sheets. In a small bowl, whisk the egg with 1 tablespoon water; brush over dough. Sprinkle with salt, pepper, and additional cheese, and top with rosemary.

Preheat the oven to 350°F. Bake, rotating sheets halfway through, until crisp and golden, 15 to 20 minutes. Cool on a wire rack. Repeat with remaining dough. Crackers can be kept in an airtight container at room temperature for up to 3 days.

PARKER HOUSE ROLLS
MAKES 30

1¾ sticks (14 tablespoons) unsalted
butter, cut into small pieces,
plus more for bowl and pan

1¼ cups warm milk (110°F)

 2 envelopes (¼ ounce each)
active dry yeast

 3 tablespoons sugar

1¼ teaspoons salt

 1 pound 14 ounces (about
5½ cups) all-purpose flour,
plus more for dusting

 3 large eggs, lightly beaten

Butter a 12-by-9-inch rimmed baking sheet. Place ½ cup warm milk in a small bowl, and sprinkle with yeast; stir to dissolve yeast. Let stand until foamy, about 5 minutes.

In a medium saucepan over medium-high heat, bring remaining ¾ cup milk just to a simmer. Remove from heat; add 6 tablespoons butter, along with the sugar and salt, stirring until butter has completely melted. Set aside.

Place 4½ cups flour in the bowl of an electric mixer. Make a well in the center with your hands, and pour in the yeast mixture, butter mixture, and eggs. Attach bowl to mixer fitted with the dough hook, and beat on low speed until dough just starts to come together, about 2 minutes. Turn out dough onto a lightly floured surface, and knead until smooth and no longer sticky, 5 minutes, adding remaining cup flour as needed. Butter a large bowl; place dough in bowl, turning to coat evenly with butter. Cover with a clean kitchen towel. Let rise in a warm place until doubled in bulk, about 1½ hours. Punch down dough, and let rest 10 minutes.

Melt remaining stick of butter. Divide dough into two equal pieces. On a lightly floured surface, roll out one piece into a 12-by-10-inch rectangle, keeping the second piece covered with the towel. Refrigerate dough until well chilled, about 30 minutes. Repeat with remaining dough. Meanwhile, preheat the oven to 400°F.

Cut one piece of chilled dough lengthwise into five 2-inch-wide strips. Cut each strip into three 4-inch-long rectangles. With a short side facing you, brush the top half of one rectangle with some melted butter, and fold over, about one-third of the way. Transfer to prepared pan, folded side down. Repeat with remaining rectangles, arranging in pan so they overlap slightly. Repeat with remaining dough. Cover with a clean kitchen towel. Let rolls rise in a warm place until doubled in bulk, about 30 minutes. Brush melted butter over top of each roll. Bake until golden brown, 15 to 20 minutes. Brush with remaining melted butter; serve hot or at room temperature.

PARKER HOUSE ROLLS
HOW-TO The folded dough rectangles should be placed in rows on the prepared baking sheet, folded sides down, so that they slightly overlap one another.

MULTIGRAIN ROLLS

MAKES 2 DOZEN *These rolls can be stored in an airtight container for up to two days.*

½ cup oat bran

¼ cup flaxseeds

½ cup boiling water

1 cup warm milk (about 110°F)

1 envelope (¼ ounce) active dry yeast

¼ cup honey

2 large whole eggs, lightly beaten, plus 1 large egg yolk

⅔ cup old-fashioned rolled oats (not instant)

7 ounces (about 1¼ cups) whole-wheat flour

1 teaspoon freshly ground black pepper

1 tablespoon table salt

15 ounces (about 3 cups) all-purpose flour

Extra-virgin olive oil, for bowl, plastic wrap, and pans

3 tablespoons mixed seeds, such as poppy, sesame, and fennel, for sprinkling

1 tablespoon sea salt, such as Maldon (or other coarse salt), for sprinkling

Combine the oat bran and flaxseeds in a medium bowl, and cover with the boiling water. Let sit until water is absorbed, about 5 minutes. Set aside to cool completely.

In the bowl of an electric mixer, whisk together the warm milk, yeast, and honey. Let stand until foamy, 5 minutes. Attach bowl to a mixer fitted with the dough hook. With mixer on low speed, add whole eggs, oats, whole-wheat flour, pepper, salt, and reserved oat-bran mixture. Slowly add enough all-purpose flour, ½ cup at a time, to make a soft, slightly sticky dough. Knead on medium-low speed until it is springy to the touch, about 3 minutes. Place dough in a lightly oiled bowl; cover with oiled plastic wrap. Let rise in a warm place until dough has doubled in bulk, 1½ to 2 hours.

Generously brush three 8-inch round cake pans with olive oil. Divide the dough into 24 equal pieces (2 ounces each). Roll each piece into a ball. Place eight balls of dough in each prepared pan. Cover with plastic wrap, and let rise until doubled in bulk, 20 to 25 minutes. Meanwhile, preheat the oven to 375°F.

In a small bowl, whisk together the egg yolk and 1 tablespoon water. Brush rolls with egg wash, and sprinkle with seeds and coarse salt. Bake until dark golden brown on top, 20 to 22 minutes. Transfer pans to a rack to cool for 10 to 15 minutes before unmolding.

flatbreads and pizza

FOCACCIA

MAKES ONE 17-BY-12-INCH BREAD *Focaccia is best eaten the same day it is made, although it will keep for up to one day at room temperature; wrap well with plastic. It tastes great when warmed in a 250-degree oven until heated through, about 15 minutes.*

2¼ pounds (about 7 cups) bread flour, plus more for dusting	2 tablespoons coarse salt
3½ cups warm water (about 110°F)	¾ cup extra-virgin olive oil
1 teaspoon active dry yeast	Sea salt, such as Maldon (or other coarse salt), for sprinkling

In the bowl of an electric mixer, whisk together the flour, water, and yeast. Cover the bowl with plastic wrap, and let rise in a warm place until the mixture is tripled in bulk and full of spongelike bubbles, about 2 hours.

Add the salt. Attach the bowl to a mixer fitted with the dough hook. Mix on low speed for 3 to 5 minutes, scraping down the sides of the bowl as needed. When the dough begins to cling to and almost climb the sides of the bowl, raise the speed to medium and beat for about 15 seconds. The dough will be wet, slack, and very sticky.

Using a plastic bowl scraper, turn out the dough onto a well-floured work surface. (The dough will be hard to handle, but resist the urge to add flour to the top—instead, keep your hands and tools well dusted.) Fold the dough in the following manner: With the bowl scraper (and, to a lesser degree, your fingertips), gather and fold the bottom edge of the dough about one-third of the way toward the center. Pat down lightly to deflate slightly and dislodge any extra flour. Fold the top edge down one-third of the way toward the center; the two folds should overlap slightly. Repeat with left and right sides, until all edges meet and overlap in the center. Tap off excess flour as you go. Gently scoop up the dough and flip it over, seam side down. Place the dough in a lightly floured bowl, smooth side up. Cover the bowl with plastic wrap, and let rise in a warm place until doubled in bulk, about 1 hour.

Return dough to a well-floured work surface. Repeat the folding process, making sure to brush off excess flour. Lightly flour the mixing bowl, and return dough to the bowl, smooth side up. Cover with plastic wrap, and let rise in a warm place until it has doubled in bulk again, about 1 hour. Meanwhile, preheat the oven to 450°F, with a rack in the lower third. Pour ½ cup of the olive oil onto a 17-by-12-inch rimmed baking sheet, coating the bottom completely; set aside.

Return dough to a well-floured surface; it should be very soft and springy. Place the dough on the prepared sheet. With your hands, flip dough over and thoroughly coat both sides with oil. With your fingertips, push the dough out toward the edges of the sheet. Cover with plastic wrap, and let rest for 10 minutes (this will relax the dough). With the plastic wrap still on top, continue to press out the dough to fill the pan. Remove the plastic; the dough should be very bubbly and supple. Drizzle the remaining ¼ cup oil over the top of the dough. Sprinkle liberally with sea salt.

Focaccia and
Dried-Fruit
Focaccia

FOCACCIA HOW-TO

1. Olive oil is poured onto a rimmed baking sheet, then topped with focaccia dough. **2.** The dough is carefully flipped in the pan, so that both sides are completely coated with oil. **3.** Gradually, the dough is pressed and patted out toward the edges of the pan. It should be dimpled and full of bubbles.

Bake, rotating sheet halfway through, until focaccia is evenly browned on top and bottom, 25 to 30 minutes. Immediately slide the focaccia onto a wire rack set over another rimmed baking sheet; pour any olive oil in the pan over it. Serve warm or at room temperature. Slice with a serrated knife or pizza wheel.

FENNEL, ONION, AND OLIVE FOCACCIA VARIATION Heat 3 tablespoons extra-virgin olive oil in a medium skillet over medium heat. Add a small onion and ½ fennel bulb, both thinly sliced; sauté until soft, about 4 minutes. Remove from heat, and season with coarse salt and freshly ground pepper. Follow instructions for Focaccia dough. After drizzling dough with oil, scatter fennel and onion mixture on top, and sprinkle with ¼ cup Kalamata olives (pitted and halved) and some salt. Bake as instructed. While focaccia is still warm, sprinkle with chopped fresh flat-leaf parsley.

DRIED-FRUIT FOCACCIA

MAKES ONE 17-BY-12-INCH BREAD *Try this bread toasted in the morning for breakfast.*

2 cups dried cherries	½ cup granulated sugar
1 cup golden raisins	1 tablespoon instant yeast
3 cups boiling water	1 tablespoon coarse salt
1 cup extra-virgin olive oil	¼ teaspoon ground cinnamon
1 pound 10 ounces (about 5 cups) all-purpose flour, plus more for dusting	¼ cup sanding sugar

In a large bowl, combine the cherries and raisins with the boiling water; let soak for 10 to 15 minutes. Drain fruit, reserving 2 cups of the soaking liquid; set fruit aside. Add ¼ cup olive oil to the soaking liquid. In the bowl of an electric mixer fitted with the dough hook, combine the flour, granulated sugar, yeast, salt, and cinnamon; mix just to combine. With mixer on low speed, add reserved fruit and soaking liquid. Mix until the fruit is evenly distributed but the dough is still tacky, about 3 minutes.

Turn out the dough onto a lightly floured work surface, and knead for 1 minute. Pour ½ cup olive oil onto a 17-by-12-inch rimmed baking sheet, coating the bottom completely. Place the dough on top of the oil, and use your hands to spread it out as much as possible without tearing (it doesn't have to fill the pan). Cover the dough loosely with plastic wrap, and continue to pat and press the dough toward the edges. Set the pan in a warm place, and let rest, pressing out the dough every 10 minutes until it fills the pan, about 45 minutes. Let rest until doubled in bulk, about 1 hour. Meanwhile, place a baking stone on the floor of the oven. Preheat the oven to 425°F.

Drizzle dough with remaining ¼ cup olive oil, and sprinkle evenly with the sanding sugar. Set the baking sheet directly on the stone and bake, rotating sheet halfway through, until the focaccia is deep golden brown on top and bottom, 35 to 40 minutes. Immediately slide the focaccia onto a cutting board to cool. Use a pizza wheel or serrated knife to cut bread into thick strips, and serve warm. Focaccia can be kept at room temperature, wrapped in plastic, for 2 to 3 days.

ROASTED-TOMATO BREAD

MAKES ONE 17-BY-12-INCH BREAD *This bread is also delicious garnished with fresh marjoram or oregano; coarsely chop one-quarter cup herbs, then sprinkle over baked bread.*

4 pints cherry tomatoes, sliced into 1/4-inch rounds	3 1/2 cups milk
3/4 cup plus 3 tablespoons extra-virgin olive oil, plus more for pan	1 1/2 pounds (about 5 1/4 cups) all-purpose flour
4 teaspoons coarse salt, plus more for sprinkling	10 ounces (about 1 3/4 cups) semolina flour
	1 1/2 ounces fresh yeast

Preheat the oven to 300°F. Divide tomatoes evenly between two rimmed baking sheets; drizzle with 1/4 cup olive oil, and sprinkle with 2 teaspoons salt. Bake until tomatoes begin to shrivel and juice on the pan has reduced, about 45 minutes; remove from oven. Lightly brush another rimmed baking sheet with olive oil; set aside. Raise oven temperature to 425°F.

In a medium saucepan over low heat, bring milk to a simmer. In the bowl of an electric mixer fitted with the paddle attachment, combine remaining 2 teaspoons salt, the flours, 3 tablespoons olive oil, and the yeast. Mix on low speed, gradually pouring in the hot milk until combined, scraping down the sides of the bowl as needed. Once combined, mix on medium speed for 1 minute. The dough will be very sticky.

Transfer to the prepared baking sheet. Using lightly oiled hands, spread the dough evenly, making sure it fills the pan. Cover tightly with oiled plastic wrap and set in a warm place until the dough reaches just below the edge of the pan, about 30 minutes. Using your fingers, dimple the dough, in an uneven pattern, leaving 2 inches between each dimple. Evenly arrange half of the roasted tomatoes on the dough. Drizzle with 1/4 cup of olive oil, and sprinkle with salt.

Bake, rotating sheet halfway through, until golden brown, about 20 minutes. Remove from the oven, and drizzle with the remaining 1/4 cup olive oil. Transfer to a wire rack to cool. Scatter the remaining tomatoes on top, then sprinkle with salt. Cut into slices with a serrated knife or pizza wheel. The bread can be kept, wrapped tightly in plastic, at room temperature for 2 to 3 days.

CIABATTA

MAKES TWO 16-BY-6-INCH LOAVES OR SIX 8-BY-4-INCH LOAVES *The puffy, rectangular shape of Ciabatta is thought to have inspired its name, which means "slipper" in Italian.*

Focaccia dough (page 323)
All-purpose flour, for dusting

Fine cornmeal, for dusting

Prepare the Focaccia dough, following the recipe through the second 1-hour rise. Turn out dough onto a well-floured work surface, and pat it out into a 16-by-12-inch rectangle, about 1 inch thick. Divide the dough into two 16-by-6-inch rectangles (for large loaves), or six 8-by-4-inch rectangles (for small loaves). Sprinkle a large wooden peel (or the flat side of a heavy baking sheet) with cornmeal.

Working in batches if necessary, transfer the dough to the prepared peel. Lightly dust the tops of the loaves with flour, and drape with plastic wrap. Let dough rest until slightly puffed, 20 to 25 minutes. Meanwhile, place a baking stone on the floor of the oven. Preheat the oven to 450°F.

Working quickly, slide the loaves onto the stone, and bake until the bread is deep golden and sounds hollow when tapped on the bottom—35 to 40 minutes for the larger loaves and 20 to 25 minutes for the smaller ones. Transfer the loaves to a wire rack to cool completely before slicing. This bread can be wrapped in plastic and kept at room temperature for up to 3 days.

PIZZA MARGHERITA

MAKES TWO 12-INCH PIZZAS *Keep dough in an airtight container in the refrigerator for up to one day; before using, let it come to room temperature. If freezing, dough should be shaped and wrapped well in plastic first. Thaw completely in the refrigerator.*

1 cup warm water (about 110°F)
¼ teaspoon sugar
1 envelope (¼ ounce) active dry yeast
14 ounces (about 2¾ cups) unbleached all-purpose flour, for dusting
1 teaspoon table salt
1½ tablespoons olive oil, plus more for bowl and drizzling
Fine cornmeal, for dusting

Pizza Sauce (recipe follows)
1 pound fresh mozzarella, thinly sliced
½ cup loosely packed fresh basil, plus more for garnish
Coarse salt and freshly ground pepper
½ cup grated Parmesan, preferably Parmigiano-Reggiano

In a small bowl, sprinkle sugar and yeast over warm water; stir with a fork until yeast and sugar dissolve. Let stand until foamy, about 5 minutes.

In a food processor, pulse flour and table salt to combine. Add yeast mixture and oil; pulse until mixture comes together but is still slightly tacky. Dough should pull away cleanly from your fingers after it's squeezed. Turn out dough onto a lightly floured work surface; knead four or five times, until a smooth ball forms.

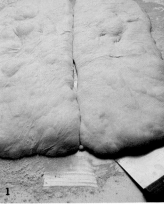

CIABATTA HOW-TO
1. After the dough is patted into a 16-by-12-inch rectangle, it is divided in half using a bench scraper or sharp knife. **2.** Dough is proofed on a peel that has been lightly dusted with cornmeal.

Place the dough in a lightly oiled bowl, smooth side up. Cover with plastic wrap; let rise in a warm place until doubled in bulk, about 40 minutes.

Punch down dough. Fold dough back onto itself four or five times, then turn smooth side up. Replace plastic wrap; let dough rise again in a warm place until doubled in bulk, 30 to 40 minutes.

Punch down dough; turn out onto a lightly floured work surface. Using a bench scraper or knife, divide dough into two equal pieces. Knead each piece four or five times, then form a smooth ball. Return one ball to oiled bowl; cover with plastic wrap. Pat remaining ball into a flattened disk; cover with plastic wrap, and let rest 5 minutes. Sprinkle a large wooden peel (or the flat side of a heavy baking sheet) with cornmeal. Using your hands or a rolling pin, stretch or press dough into desired shape, working from center outward in all directions. Transfer to the prepared peel.

Place a baking stone in the bottom of the oven. Preheat the oven to 450°F. Spread a thin layer of Pizza Sauce over the round, leaving a 1-inch border uncovered. Arrange half the mozzarella slices over the sauce, and scatter with a handful of basil leaves. Sprinkle with coarse salt, pepper, and half the grated Parmesan.

Slide pizza onto the baking stone. Bake until cheese is melted and crust is crisp and golden brown, 12 to 15 minutes. Meanwhile, repeat rolling and topping with the remaining dough and ingredients; bake when first pizza is removed from the oven. Garnish with remaining basil, and slice pizza into wedges using a pizza wheel or sharp knife, and serve immediately.

PIZZA MARGHERITA HOW-TO
The crust is formed and transferred to a wooden peel that has been dusted with cornmeal. The dough is spread with a thin layer of sauce, leaving a 1-inch border, and covered with slices of fresh mozzarella. Then it's sprinkled with basil leaves, coarse salt, freshly ground pepper, and some grated Parmesan before baking.

PIZZA SAUCE

ENOUGH FOR TWO 12-INCH PIZZAS (ABOUT 1 QUART) *This sauce can be refrigerated for up to one week or frozen for up to one month; let cool completely before storing in an airtight container. Thaw frozen sauce completely in the refrigerator.*

- ¼ cup olive oil
- 2 cans (28 ounces each) whole peeled tomatoes
- 1½ teaspoons dried oregano
- Coarse salt and freshly ground pepper

Heat oil in a large skillet set over medium heat. Using your hands, crush tomatoes into a bowl, then add to skillet along with oregano. Season with salt and pepper. Cook over medium-low heat, breaking up tomatoes with a spoon, until sauce has thickened, 40 to 50 minutes.

For a smooth sauce, pass it through a food mill, or press through a sieve with a wooden spoon, into a large bowl; discard solids. Let cool slightly before using.

PISSALADIÈRE

MAKES ONE 17-BY-12-INCH TART *Pissaladière is a specialty of the southern French town of Nice. Named for pissalat ("salted fish"), this tart always includes anchovies, either whole or puréed, which are spread over the dough before baking.*

Pissaladière Dough
(recipe follows)

¼ cup olive oil, plus more
    for pan and plastic wrap

4 medium garlic cloves,
    finely chopped

3 medium onions, thinly sliced

2 teaspoons coarse salt

1 tablespoon fresh thyme leaves

¼ cup fresh flat-leaf parsley,
    coarsely chopped

1½ pounds ripe plum tomatoes

24 anchovies

¼ cup Niçoise olives, pitted and
    thinly sliced lengthwise

Lightly oil a 17-by-12-inch rimmed baking sheet, and set aside. Roll out dough to a 17-by-12-inch rectangle, and fit into sheet, folding up the edges slightly to form a small lip. Prick dough all over with a fork. Cover with oiled plastic wrap, and let rise in a warm place until slightly puffed, about 30 minutes.

Preheat the oven to 450°F, with a rack in the center. Heat olive oil in a large skillet over medium heat. Add garlic, onions, and salt. Cook, stirring occasionally, until onions begin to brown, about 10 minutes. Add thyme and parsley; set aside to cool.

Cut tomatoes in half lengthwise, and scoop out seeds with a melon baller or small spoon. Slice tomato halves lengthwise into ¼-inch-thick strips; distribute evenly over dough. Arrange the onions on top, then add anchovies in a decorative pattern to form X shapes. Dot with olives. Bake 12 minutes. Rotate sheet, and continue baking until crust is golden, about 15 minutes more. Remove from oven; using a large spatula, transfer to a cutting board. Slice into pieces, and serve warm or at room temperature. Although Pissaladière is best eaten the day it is baked, it can be reheated the next day; place in a 200°F oven for 10 to 15 minutes or until heated through.

PISSALADIÈRE DOUGH

MAKES ENOUGH FOR ONE 17-BY-12-INCH TART

¾ cup warm water (110°F)

½ teaspoon sugar

1 teaspoon active dry yeast

1 tablespoon olive oil,
    plus more for bowl

1 teaspoon salt

9 ounces (about 1¾ cups)
    bread flour, plus more
    for dusting

In a medium bowl, sprinkle sugar and yeast over ¼ cup warm water. Stir with a fork until sugar and yeast are dissolved. Let stand until foamy, about 5 minutes. Add remaining ½ cup warm water, along with the oil, salt, and flour. Using a wooden spoon, stir until a dough forms. Transfer to a lightly floured work surface; knead until smooth, about 5 minutes. Place dough in a lightly oiled bowl, turning to coat. Cover with plastic wrap; let rise in a warm place until doubled in bulk, about 1 hour.

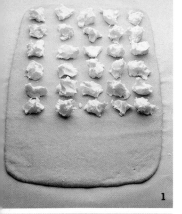

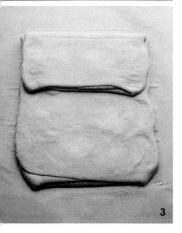

DANISH DOUGH HOW-TO
1. The dough is rolled out to a large rectangle, then dotted with butter over two-thirds of its surface. **2.** The unbuttered third is folded up over the dough, then folded once more to seal in the butter. **3.** The dough is rolled out and folded again to complete the first turn.

danish and croissants

DANISH DOUGH

MAKES ENOUGH FOR 2 DOZEN DANISH *This is a laminated dough that is created with layers of dough and butter. It's the foundation of many breakfast pastries, such as the ones on the following pages. This recipe makes enough dough for two batches.*

1 cup warm milk (110°F)	1 tablespoon coarse salt
2 envelopes (¼ ounce each) active dry yeast	½ teaspoon ground cardamom
1 pound 4 ounces (about 4½ cups) all-purpose flour, plus more for dusting	1 pound (4 sticks) unsalted butter, room temperature, cut into tablespoons
⅓ cup plus 1 tablespoon sugar	2 large whole eggs, plus 1 large egg yolk

In a small bowl, sprinkle the yeast over the warm milk; stir until dissolved. Let sit until foamy, about 5 minutes. In the bowl of an electric mixer fitted with the dough hook, combine the flour, sugar, salt, cardamom, and 4 tablespoons butter; beat on low speed until butter is incorporated and the mixture resembles coarse meal, 3 to 4 minutes. Pour in the yeast-milk mixture; mix until dough just comes together. Add the eggs and yolk; mix until just combined, 2 to 3 minutes. Do not overmix.

Turn out the dough onto a lightly floured work surface, making sure to include any loose bits left at the bottom of the bowl. Gently knead to form a smooth ball, about 30 seconds. Wrap well with plastic, and refrigerate at least 2 hours or overnight.

On a lightly floured work surface, roll out dough to an 18-by-10-inch rectangle, about ¼ inch thick, keeping the corners as square as possible. Remove any excess flour with a dry pastry brush. With a short side facing you, evenly distribute the remaining butter over two-thirds of the dough. Fold the unbuttered third over as you would a business letter, followed by the remaining third. This seals in the butter.

Roll out dough again to an 18-by-10-inch rectangle, then fold dough into thirds as described above; refrigerate for 1 hour. This is the first of three turns. Repeat rolling and folding two more times, refrigerating for at least 1 hour between turns. To help you remember how many turns have been completed, mark the dough after each one: Make one mark for the first turn, two for the second, and three for the third.

Refrigerate dough, tightly wrapped in plastic, for at least 4 hours or overnight. Dough can also be frozen, tightly wrapped in plastic, for up to 2 weeks; before using, thaw the dough in the refrigerator overnight.

PRUNE PINWHEEL HOW-TO
1. A pastry wheel is used to make diagonal cuts in the corners of every 4-inch square of dough. **2.** To form the pinwheel shapes, every other point is folded into the center. **3.** When four points meet in the center of the square, they are pressed firmly to seal, and then covered with a dollop of Prune Filling.

PRUNE PINWHEELS

MAKES 1 DOZEN *These pastries would be delicious with a cup of tea in the afternoon.*

All-purpose flour, for dusting
½ recipe Danish Dough (page 334)
Prune Filling (recipe follows)

1 large egg, lightly beaten
Granulated sugar, for sprinkling

Line two large baking sheets with parchment paper; set aside. On a lightly floured work surface, roll out the dough to a 17-by-13-inch rectangle about ¼ inch thick. Using a ruler and a pizza wheel or pastry cutter, trim the edges of the dough to form a 16-by-12-inch rectangle. Then cut the dough into twelve 4-inch squares.

To form the pinwheels, use a pastry cutter or pizza wheel to make diagonal cuts three-quarters of the way toward the center, leaving a 1-inch square. (Each piece should have eight points, two at each corner.) Fold every other point toward the center, pressing down to seal.

Spoon about 1 tablespoon of Prune Filling onto the center of each pinwheel. Place the pinwheels on the prepared baking sheets, six to a sheet. Cover with plastic wrap, and let rest in a warm place until doubled in bulk, about 45 minutes.

Preheat the oven to 375°F, with racks in the upper and lower thirds. Brush the dough lightly with beaten egg. Sprinkle with sugar. Bake, rotating sheets halfway through, until evenly browned, 20 to 25 minutes. Transfer pinwheels to a wire rack. Serve warm or at room temperature. These are best eaten the same day they are made.

PRUNE FILLING
MAKES ENOUGH FOR 1 DOZEN PINWHEELS

2 pounds pitted prunes
½ cup sugar
2 tablespoons light corn syrup

Pinch of salt
Pinch of ground cinnamon

Combine all ingredients with 1 cup water in a small saucepan. Cook over medium-high heat, stirring constantly, until most of the liquid has evaporated, about 10 minutes. Remove from heat; let cool completely.

Transfer mixture to a food processor, and process until puréed. Use immediately, or store in an airtight container in the refrigerator for up to 1 week.

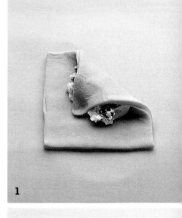

CHEESE DANISH
MAKES 1 DOZEN

All-purpose flour, for dusting

½ recipe Danish Dough (page 334)

Cheese Filling (recipe follows)

1 large egg, lightly beaten

Sugar, for sprinkling

Sliced almonds, for garnish (optional)

Line two large baking sheets with parchment paper; set aside. On a lightly floured work surface, roll out the dough to a 17-by-13-inch rectangle about ¼ inch thick. Using a ruler and a pizza wheel or pastry cutter, trim the edges of the dough to form a 16-by-12-inch rectangle. Then cut the dough into twelve 4-inch squares.

Place Cheese Filling in a pastry bag fitted with a ½-inch plain tip (such as an Ateco #806). Holding the bag above the squares, pipe 1½ to 2 tablespoons filling into the center of each square. (Alternatively, scoop the filling with a tablespoon.)

To form each danish, fold the upper right corner over the filling, about two-thirds of the way toward the opposite corner; press down firmly to seal. Bring the lower left corner up and over first fold, pressing down to adhere. (Be careful not to fold too tightly, or you may force out some of the filling.) Repeat with the remaining corners. Place the danish on the prepared baking sheets, six to a sheet. Cover with plastic wrap, and let rest in a warm place until dough is doubled in bulk, about 45 minutes.

Preheat the oven to 375°F. Brush dough with the beaten egg; sprinkle with the granulated sugar and sliced almonds, if desired. Bake, rotating sheets halfway through, until evenly browned, 20 to 25 minutes. Transfer to a wire rack to cool. Serve warm or at room temperature. These are best eaten the same day they are made.

CHEESE FILLING
MAKES ENOUGH FOR 1 DOZEN DANISH

1 pound farmer's cheese

¾ cup sugar

1 large egg

½ cup golden raisins

2 tablespoons all-purpose flour

1 teaspoon grated lemon zest

In the bowl of an electric mixer fitted with the paddle attachment, beat cheese and sugar on low speed until well combined. Add the egg, beating to combine and scraping down the sides of the bowl as needed. Add raisins, flour, and zest; mix just to combine. Filling can be refrigerated in an airtight container for up to 3 days.

CHEESE DANISH HOW-TO
1. The top right corner is folded over the cheese filling, then pressed to seal. **2.** The bottom left corner is folded over in the same manner. **3.** The remaining corners are folded in to completely encase the cheese filling.

APRICOT BOW TIE HOW-TO
1. Two apricot halves are placed on top of a dollop of Pastry Cream, along the diagonal of the dough square. **2.** The top right corner of the square is folded over the filling and pressed down to seal. **3.** The opposite corner is folded over the first to create an open-ended roll.

APRICOT BOW TIES

MAKES 1 DOZEN *Using canned apricots instead of fresh allows you to make these breakfast pastries year-round. Choose the prettiest halves and reserve the rest for another use.*

All-purpose flour, for dusting	2 cans (15 ounces each) apricot halves, drained
½ recipe Danish Dough (page 334)	
1 cup Pastry Cream (page 392)	1 large egg, lightly beaten
	Sugar, for sprinkling

Line two large baking sheets with parchment paper; set aside. On a lightly floured work surface, roll out the dough to a 17-by-13-inch rectangle about ¼ inch thick. Using a ruler and a pizza wheel or pastry cutter, trim the edges of the dough to form a 16-by-12-inch rectangle. Then cut the dough into twelve 4-inch squares.

Place Pastry Cream in a pastry bag fitted with a ½-inch plain tip (such as an Ateco #806). Pipe a dollop of cream into the center of each square. (Alternatively, scoop the filling with a tablespoon.) Arrange two apricot halves over the cream, overlapping them slightly, one in the upper left corner and the other in the lower right.

To form the bow ties, fold the upper right corner over the apricot filling, about two-thirds of the way toward the opposite corner; press down firmly to seal. Bring the lower left corner up and over first fold, pressing down to adhere. (Be careful not to fold too tightly, or you may force out some of the filling.) Repeat with the remaining squares. Place the bow ties on the prepared baking sheets, six to a sheet. Cover with plastic wrap, and let rest in a warm place until dough is approximately doubled in bulk, about 45 minutes.

Preheat the oven to 375°F, with racks in the upper and lower thirds. Lightly brush bow ties with the beaten egg, and sprinkle with sugar. Bake, rotating sheets halfway through, until pastries are evenly browned, 20 to 25 minutes. Transfer to a wire rack to cool. Serve at room temperature. Bow ties are best eaten the same day they are made.

CHOCOLATE-PISTACHIO DANISH

MAKES 1 DOZEN *Use the best-quality chocolate you can find for this recipe; some of our favorites are Valrhona, Callebaut, and Scharffen Berger.*

1 tablespoon pistachio paste
1½ cups Pastry Cream (page 392)
All-purpose flour, for dusting
½ recipe Danish Dough (page 334)

1 large egg, lightly beaten
12 ounces best-quality semisweet chocolate, coarsely chopped (2 scant cups)

Line two large baking sheets with parchment paper; set aside. In a small bowl, stir the pistachio paste into the Pastry Cream with a rubber spatula; set aside. On a lightly floured work surface, roll out dough to a 17-by-13-inch rectangle, about ¼ inch thick.

Using an offset spatula, spread the pistachio-cream mixture evenly over the dough, leaving a ½-inch border all around. Brush the border with beaten egg. Sprinkle the chocolate over the cream. With a short side facing you, roll the dough lengthwise to form a tight log. Smooth the log with your hands, and pat in at the ends. Transfer log to a parchment-lined baking sheet and refrigerate until firm, about 30 minutes. Using a sharp knife, trim the ends and then slice the log into 12 rounds. Place the slices on the prepared baking sheets, six to a sheet. Cover with plastic wrap, and let rest in a warm place until dough is approximately doubled in bulk, about 45 minutes.

Preheat the oven to 375°F. Brush the top and sides of each slice with beaten egg. Bake, rotating sheets halfway through, until pastries are evenly browned, 20 to 25 minutes. Transfer to a wire rack to cool. Serve warm or at room temperature. These are best eaten the same day they are made.

CHOCOLATE-PISTACHIO DANISH HOW-TO After the dough is rolled out to a large rectangle, it is topped with a mixture of pistachio paste and Pastry Cream, then sprinkled with chopped chocolate. The dough is rolled into a log, chilled, and then sliced into rounds.

STICKY BUNS

MAKES 1 DOZEN *Baking these buns in muffin tins ensures that each one will have a crisp, sugary edge, as well as a delicious, soft center.*

- ½ recipe Danish Dough (page 334)
  Unsalted butter, for pans
- 3⅓ cups (13 ounces) pecan halves
- 2¼ cups light corn syrup
- ¾ cup plus ⅔ cup packed dark-brown sugar
  All-purpose flour, for dusting
- ¾ cup sour cream
- 1 tablespoon ground cinnamon

Let dough stand at room temperature until slightly softened, about 15 minutes. Line a large baking sheet with parchment paper; set aside. Generously butter two 6-cup jumbo muffin pans (each cup should have a 7-ounce capacity). Chop 2 cups pecans, and break the remaining 1⅓ cups in half lengthwise, keeping the two groups separate. Pour 3 tablespoons corn syrup into each muffin cup, and sprinkle with 1 tablespoon brown sugar. Divide halved pecans evenly among the muffin cups.

On a lightly floured work surface, roll out the dough to an 18-by-14-inch rectangle, about ¼ inch thick. Using a spatula, spread the sour cream over the surface of the dough, leaving a ½-inch border. Dust the sour cream with cinnamon, and sprinkle with chopped pecans and remaining ⅔ cup brown sugar. Roll up the dough tightly lengthwise to form a log about 3 inches in diameter, and trim the ends using a serrated knife. Transfer log to the prepared baking sheet. Refrigerate until firm, about 30 minutes. Meanwhile, preheat the oven to 350°F.

Using a sharp knife and a sawing motion, slice the dough crosswise into 12 rounds, about 1½ inches thick, and place in prepared pans. Cover loosely with plastic wrap, and let rise in a warm place until ½ inch above the cups, 20 to 30 minutes. Transfer to the oven, placing a baking sheet on the rack below to catch drips. Bake, rotating pans halfway through, until buns are dark golden brown, about 40 minutes.

Immediately turn out the buns onto a parchment-lined baking sheet. Replace any pecan halves that have fallen off. Place the baking sheet on a wire rack to cool. Serve warm or at room temperature. Sticky buns are best eaten the day they are baked.

STICKY BUNS HOW-TO
1. Danish Dough is spread with sour cream, then sprinkled with cinnamon, pecans, and brown sugar. **2.** Dough is rolled into a log. **3.** The log is sliced into rounds, which are placed atop a sugary pecan mixture in jumbo muffin cups.

SUGAR BUNS

MAKES 20 *These sugar-dusted buns, which are similar to doughnuts but baked instead of fried, have a surprise cream-filled center.*

All-purpose flour, for dusting	4 tablespoons unsalted butter,
½ recipe Danish Dough (page 334)	melted and cooled
1¼ cups Pastry Cream (page 392)	Sugar, for coating
1 large egg, lightly beaten	

Line a large rimmed baking sheet with parchment paper; set aside. On a lightly floured work surface, roll out dough to a 15-by-12-inch rectangle, about ⅜ inch thick. Using a ruler and pizza wheel or pastry cutter, cut dough into twenty 3-inch squares.

Transfer the Pastry Cream to a pastry bag fitted with a ½-inch plain tip (such as an Ateco #806). Pipe 1 tablespoon into the center of each square. Brush the edges of each square with the beaten egg. Gather the edges around Pastry Cream, pinching the seams together, making sure the bun is completely sealed.

On a piece of parchment paper, gently roll each bun with floured hands, keeping it seam side down, to form a compact ball. Repeat with remaining dough. Place shaped balls, smooth side up, on the prepared sheet, about 3 inches apart. Cover with plastic wrap, and let rise in a warm spot until doubled in size, about 45 minutes. Meanwhile, preheat the oven to 400°F.

Brush gently with the beaten egg. Bake, rotating sheet halfway through, until buns are golden brown, 25 to 30 minutes. Transfer to a wire rack to cool completely.

Brush the butter over the top of the buns. Place sugar in a wide bowl; dip buttered side of buns into sugar to coat. Serve at room temperature. These buns are best eaten the day they are made.

SUGAR BUNS HOW-TO
1. A dollop of Pastry Cream is piped into the center of each dough square. The corners of the dough are pinched together to seal in the cream.
2. The filled dough balls are rolled gently back and forth to seal the seam.

CROISSANT HOW-TO
1. After the dough is rolled out, the butter package is placed over the bottom half. **2.** The uncovered half is folded over the butter package, and the open edges are pinched together to seal. **3.** The dough and butter package is rolled out, then folded into thirds.

CROISSANTS

MAKES 2 DOZEN *If using dry yeast instead of fresh, heat the milk to about 110°F, then stir in the yeast to dissolve. Let stand until foamy, about five minutes, and proceed with the recipe. The dough can be made ahead through all of the turns and frozen for up to three months; before using, defrost the dough in the refrigerator for twenty-four hours. After baking, Croissants are best eaten within six hours.*

2 cups cold milk	½ cup sugar
2 tablespoons honey	1½ ounces fresh yeast, crumbled
1½ pounds (about 4½ cups) bread flour, plus more for dusting	1 tablespoon plus 1½ teaspoons salt
4 ounces (1 scant cup) unbleached pastry flour	1¼ pounds (5 sticks) unsalted butter, cold
	1 large egg, lightly beaten

Make the dough package: Pour the milk and honey into a 1-quart liquid measuring cup, and stir to combine; set aside. In the bowl of an electric mixer fitted with the dough hook, stir together 1 pound 6 ounces (about 4¼ cups) bread flour, the pastry flour, sugar, yeast, and salt; stir to combine. Add milk mixture, and mix on low speed until the dough just comes together, 2 to 3 minutes.

Turn out dough onto a lightly floured work surface; gently knead to form a smooth ball, about 45 seconds. Wrap in plastic and refrigerate at least 1 hour or overnight.

Make the butter package: Lay the butter sticks side by side on a piece of plastic wrap, and sprinkle with the remaining 2 ounces (about ¼ cup) flour. Pound with a rolling pin until flour is incorporated, and roll into an 8-inch square. Wrap tightly and refrigerate for at least 1 hour or overnight.

Remove dough package from the refrigerator; place on a lightly floured work surface. Roll out to a 16-by-10-inch rectangle, about ½ inch thick, with a short side facing you. Remove butter package from the refrigerator; place on the bottom half of the dough; fold the top half of the dough over the butter, and pinch the edges to seal.

Roll out the dough to a 20-by-10-inch rectangle about ½ inch thick, with a short side facing you; keep the corners as square as possible. Remove any excess flour with a dry pastry brush. Starting at the far end, fold the rectangle in thirds, as you would a business letter. This completes the first of three turns. Wrap in plastic and refrigerate for 1 hour.

Repeat rolling and folding as above two more times, starting with the flap opening on the right, as if it were a book, and refrigerate at least 1 hour between turns. To help you remember how many turns have been completed, mark the dough after each: Make one mark for the first turn, two for the second, and three for the third. After the third, wrap dough in plastic, and refrigerate 6 to 8 hours, or overnight.

Turn out chilled dough onto a lightly floured work surface. Roll out the dough to a 30-by-16-inch rectangle. (If the dough becomes too elastic, cover with plastic wrap, and let rest in the refrigerator for 10 minutes.) Using a pizza wheel or pastry cutter, cut the dough in half lengthwise to form two 30-by-8-inch rectangles. Stack one piece

of dough on top of the other, lining up edges. Using the pizza wheel, cut dough into triangles, each with a 4-inch base (you will have scraps at both ends). Cut a 1-inch slit in the center of the base of each triangle. Place triangles in a single layer on a clean work surface.

To shape croissants, stretch the two lower points of each triangle to enlarge the slit slightly. Fold the inner corners formed by the slit toward the outer sides of the triangle, and press down to seal. Using your fingertips, roll the base of the triangle up and away from you, stretching the dough slightly outward as you roll; the tip should be tucked under the croissant. Pull the two ends toward you to form a crescent. Transfer the crescents to two parchment-lined baking sheets, 2 inches apart (12 on each sheet). Cover loosely with plastic wrap, and let rise in a warm place until very spongy and doubled in bulk, 45 to 60 minutes.

Preheat the oven to 400°F, with the racks in the upper and lower thirds. Lightly brush crescents with the beaten egg. Bake, rotating sheets halfway through, until the croissants are puffed and golden brown, about 20 to 25 minutes. Transfer sheets to a wire rack to cool. Serve warm or at room temperature.

WHOLE-WHEAT CROISSANTS VARIATION Follow instructions for Croissants, reducing the amount of bread flour to 1 pound 2 ounces (about 3¾ cups) and omitting the pastry flour. Reduce the butter to 1 pound (4 sticks) and the salt to 2 teaspoons. Add 10 ounces (about 2 cups) whole-wheat flour with bread flour and other ingredients.

ALMOND CROISSANTS

MAKES 1 DOZEN *This recipe is a perfect way to use day-old or store-bought croissants.*

½ recipe Simple Syrup (page 389)
12 croissants
    Almond Cream (page 392)

1 cup sliced almonds
    Confectioners' sugar, for dusting

Preheat the oven to 400°F. Line a large baking sheet with parchment paper; set aside. Pour the Simple Syrup into a wide, shallow bowl; set aside.

Using a serrated knife, slice the croissants in half horizontally. Using a small offset spatula, spread a scant tablespoon of Almond Cream on each bottom half. Sandwich with the top halves. Spread the top of each croissant with another scant tablespoon of cream, and sprinkle with sliced almonds. (Press down lightly so that the almonds are embedded in the cream.) Dip the top of each croissant into the syrup; keep it submerged for a few seconds to coat completely.

Transfer croissants to the prepared baking sheet, coated sides up. Bake until almonds are golden brown and croissants are crisp, about 10 minutes. Dust with confectioners' sugar, and serve immediately.

BABA AU RHUM

MAKES 1 DOZEN *These cakes are traditionally served with unsweetened, fresh whipped cream. You can top them with fresh berries, if you like. The recipe is easily doubled.*

- 10 ounces (about 2 cups) bread flour
- ½ cup warm milk (about 110°F)
- ½ ounce fresh yeast
- 1 stick (½ cup) unsalted butter, melted and cooled, plus more at room temperature, for molds
- 3 large whole eggs, plus 2 large egg yolks

- 2 teaspoons granulated sugar
- 2 teaspoons salt
- 3 cups assorted fresh berries (optional)
- 2 tablespoons superfine sugar (optional)
- Rum Syrup (recipe follows)
- 2 cups heavy cream

In the bowl of an electric mixer, whisk 2½ ounces (½ cup) flour, the warm milk, and yeast. Cover with plastic wrap; let rise in a warm place until doubled in bulk, 1½ to 2 hours. Butter twelve 3-ounce baba molds; place on a rimmed baking sheet.

When flour mixture has doubled, attach bowl to mixer fitted with the paddle attachment. Add whole eggs and egg yolks, one at a time, beating on low speed until incorporated after each addition. Add the remaining 7½ ounces (1½ cups) flour, the granulated sugar, and the salt; beat until smooth with no lumps, about 2 minutes. With the mixer on low speed, gradually pour melted butter down the side of the bowl in a thin stream; beat until incorporated and the dough pulls away from the sides of the bowl, about 4 minutes more.

Place dough in a pastry bag fitted with a ½-inch plain tip (such as an Ateco #806); pipe dough into prepared molds, filling each halfway. Let dough rise in a warm place until it reaches tops of molds, 30 to 40 minutes. Meanwhile, preheat the oven to 375°F. If desired, toss berries with superfine sugar in a bowl; set aside to macerate.

Bake, rotating sheet halfway through, until golden and a cake tester inserted in the center comes out clean, about 25 minutes. Immediately turn out baba onto a wire rack; let cool completely. Use a slotted spoon to gently drop two baba at a time into the hot Rum Syrup, submerging completely; let soak until there are no more bubbles. Place on a rack set over a rimmed baking sheet. Whisk heavy cream to soft peaks. To serve, split baba lengthwise, and top with whipped cream and berries, if desired.

BABA AU RHUM HOW-TO
1. The batter is piped into the molds until it reaches halfway up the sides. **2.** Baba are fully proofed when they rise slightly over the tops of the molds.

RUM SYRUP
MAKES ENOUGH FOR 1 DOZEN BABA (ABOUT 7½ CUPS)

- 4 cups sugar
- 1 cup best-quality dark rum

Combine sugar, rum, and 5 cups water in a medium saucepan. Bring to a boil over medium heat, and continue cooking until the liquid is clear, about 2 minutes. Remove from heat. Use immediately or reheat before soaking.

KOUIGN AMANS

MAKES 18 *The kouign aman (pronounced QUEEN-ah-man) is a traditional Breton pastry whose name means "butter cake" in the local dialect. Our recipe was inspired by an appearance by pastry chef Florian Bellanger on Martha's syndicated television show.*

1¾ cups warm water (110°F)

1 envelope (¼ ounce) active dry yeast

1¾ pounds (about 5 cups) all-purpose flour, plus more for dusting

1½ teaspoons salt

4 sticks (1 pound) unsalted butter, cold, plus 2 tablespoons melted

Sugar, for dusting and sprinkling (about 2 cups)

In a bowl, stir the yeast into the warm water until dissolved. Let stand until foamy, about 5 minutes. In the bowl of an electric mixer fitted with the dough hook, combine the flour, salt, and the melted butter on low speed. Add the water-yeast mixture, and continue to mix until well combined, about 2 minutes.

Cover the bowl with plastic wrap, and let rise in a warm place until doubled in bulk, about 1 hour. Punch down the dough; cover with plastic wrap, and place on a large baking sheet. Transfer to the refrigerator, and chill for 2 hours.

Meanwhile, lay the remaining 4 sticks of butter side by side on a nonstick baking mat (such as a Silpat); roll into an 8-inch square, about ½ inch thick. Wrap butter in parchment paper, and refrigerate until firm, about 30 minutes.

On a lightly floured work surface, roll out the chilled dough to an 18-inch square. Place the chilled butter square on top of the dough, with each side of the butter facing a corner of the dough, in a diamond fashion. Fold the corners of the dough over the butter to enclose, and pinch the edges to seal. Roll out the dough into a 24-by-8-inch rectangle. Fold the dough into thirds as you would a business letter, aligning the edges carefully and brushing off any excess flour. (The goal is to ensure that the butter is distributed evenly throughout so the pastry will puff evenly when baked.) Wrap the dough in plastic; chill for 20 minutes. This completes the first of three turns.

Repeat the rolling and folding process two more times; start with the flap opening on the right, as if it were a book, and refrigerate at least 1 hour between turns. To help you remember how many turns have been completed, mark the dough after each one: Make one mark for the first turn, two for the second, and three for the third. After the third turn, wrap dough in plastic, and refrigerate 6 to 8 hours, or overnight.

Preheat the oven to 425°F. Line two baking sheets with nonstick baking mats. On a well-sugared work surface, roll out dough to a 24-by-12-inch rectangle, about ¼ inch thick. Using a pizza wheel or pastry cutter, cut dough into eighteen 4-inch squares. Working with one square at a time, fold each corner toward the center, pressing down firmly to seal, resulting in a smaller square. Repeat, folding corners toward the center and firmly pressing down. Sprinkle generously with sugar (about 1 teaspoon per pastry). Place pastries on prepared baking sheets as you work. Cover loosely with plastic wrap; let rise in a warm place until slightly puffed, 30 to 40 minutes.

Bake, rotating sheets halfway through, until the pastries are golden brown, 35 to 40 minutes. Immediately transfer to a wire rack to cool completely. These are best eaten the same day they are made.

KOUIGN AMAN HOW-TO
1. Squares of dough are placed on a well-sugared surface and all corners are folded into the center. **2.** The corners are folded into the center a second time, and pressed down to seal.

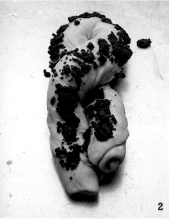

CHOCOLATE BABKAS

MAKES 3 LOAVES *A babka can be frozen in the pan for up to a month before baking. When ready to bake, remove from freezer; let stand at room temperature for about five hours. Be careful not to underbake; otherwise, the center may not set properly.*

1½ cups warm milk (110°F)	3½ sticks (1¾ cups) unsalted butter, cut into 1-inch pieces, room temperature, plus more for bowl and pans
2 envelopes (¼ ounce each) active dry yeast	
1¾ cups plus a pinch of sugar	2 pounds semisweet chocolate, very finely chopped
3 whole large eggs, plus 2 large egg yolks, room temperature	1 tablespoon plus 1 teaspoon ground cinnamon
6 cups all-purpose flour, plus more for dusting	1 tablespoon heavy cream
1 teaspoon salt	Streusel Topping (recipe follows)

In a small bowl, sprinkle yeast and a pinch of sugar over the warm milk; stir until dissolved. Let stand until foamy, about 5 minutes. In a medium bowl, whisk together ¾ cup sugar, 2 eggs, and the yolks; add yeast mixture, and whisk to combine.

In the bowl of an electric mixer fitted with the paddle attachment, combine flour and salt. Add the egg mixture, and beat on low speed until almost all the flour is incorporated, about 30 seconds. Switch to the dough hook. Add 2 sticks butter, and beat until completely incorporated and a smooth, soft dough forms, about 10 minutes. The dough should still be slightly sticky when squeezed.

Turn out dough onto a lightly floured work surface, and knead a few times until smooth. Place dough in a well-buttered bowl, and turn to coat with butter. Cover tightly with plastic wrap. Let rise in a warm place until doubled in bulk, about 1 hour.

In a bowl, stir together chocolate, remaining cup sugar, and the cinnamon. Using a pastry blender, cut in remaining 1½ sticks butter until combined; set aside filling.

Generously butter three 9-by-5-by-2¾-inch loaf pans and line with parchment paper, leaving a 1½-inch overhang along the long sides. Brush more butter over the parchment, and set aside. Punch down the dough, and transfer to a clean work surface. Let the dough rest 5 minutes.

Meanwhile, beat the remaining egg with the cream. Cut dough into three equal pieces. On a well-floured work surface, roll out one piece of dough to a 16-inch square, about ⅛ inch thick. (Keep other pieces covered with plastic wrap while you work.) Brush edges of dough with the egg wash. Crumble one-third of the chocolate filling evenly over dough, leaving about a ½-inch border on the long sides. Roll up dough lengthwise into a tight log, pinching ends together to seal. Twist dough evenly down the length of the log, a full five or six times. Brush the top of the log with egg wash. Crumble 2 tablespoons filling down the center of the log, being careful not to let mixture slide off. Fold log in half into a horseshoe shape, then cross the right half over the left. Pinch ends together to seal and form a figure eight. Twist two more times, and fit into a prepared pan. Repeat with remaining dough and filling.

Preheat the oven to 350°F, with a rack in the lower third. Brush the top of each loaf with egg wash; sprinkle with one-third of the Streusel Topping. Loosely cover each pan with plastic wrap, and let rise in a warm place until dough has expanded and feels pillowy, about 40 minutes.

Bake loaves, rotating halfway through, until golden, about 55 minutes. Reduce oven temperature to 325°F; bake until loaves are deep golden, 20 to 30 minutes more. (If the tops begin to brown too quickly, tent with aluminum foil.) Transfer pans to wire racks to cool completely. Babkas can be wrapped in plastic and kept at room temperature for up to 3 days.

STREUSEL TOPPING
MAKES ENOUGH FOR 3 LOAVES (ABOUT 3 CUPS)

1²/₃ cups confectioners' sugar	1¹/₂ sticks (³/₄ cup) unsalted butter, room temperature
1¹/₃ cups all-purpose flour	

Combine sugar and flour in a large bowl. Using a pastry blender, cut in butter until mixture resembles coarse crumbs with some larger clumps remaining.

chapter six

PASTRIES

recipes

P

Who hasn't marveled at the
array of pastries in a bakery's display case?
These exquisite baked goods can be little
works of art or architectural feats
in miniature. You may be surprised at how
easily you can create them at home.

ÂTE À CHOUX and puff pastry, two classic doughs, are the foundations for many dazzling pastries. In this chapter, you'll learn to make the doughs from scratch, and then use them to create homemade Éclairs, Napoleons, Fruit Turnovers, and more. The pastries will make a fine presentation, of course, but thanks to their wonderful freshness and flavors, they will also make especially fine eating.

Pâte à choux is an uncomplicated dough that is stirred together in minutes right on the stove. It is famously used for Cream Puffs. Balls of the egg-rich dough "inflate" in the oven, so they end up hollow—making them perfect vessels for fillings. Pipe in a vanilla custard for Cream Puffs or add ice cream and top with chocolate sauce for Profiteroles. Pâte à choux can also be used to make savory snacks: By adding cheese and herbs to the dough, you can make delectable hors d'oeuvres called Gougères.

Puff pastry, made by rolling and folding butter and dough together multiple times, requires a bit more patience. But the efforts are rewarded richly, with delicate layers of paper-thin pastry that earn their name by puffing dramatically when baked. This pastry is versatile enough to produce a Chocolate Napoleon or a scrumptious Cheese Straw.

Once you've mastered pâte à choux and puff pastry, you may want to try your hand at the more elaborate pastry doughs in this chapter, such as those used to create our crunchy Sfogliatelle or Cherry-Cheese Strudel. Whichever recipes you choose, you'll need only your kitchen counter, not a baker's display case, to marvel at the array.

To form pâte à choux puffs or gougères in advance, pipe them onto a baking sheet lined with parchment paper or a nonstick baking mat. Freeze them until solid, about 1 hour. Transfer them to resealable plastic bags, and store in the freezer until you're ready to bake, up to 3 weeks. You do not need to thaw the puffs or gougères before baking.

When piping pâte à choux onto a baking sheet, **leave about 2 inches between each shape,** as they will almost double in size while baking.

To smooth tops of cream puffs or gougères, dip your index finger in water, and dab the top of each piped puff to soften pointy edges. Rounded tops will promote even rising.

Set aside plenty of time to prepare puff pastry; chilling the dough and letting it rest is very important and should not be rushed. The gluten needs time to relax after rolling or the dough will become tough and difficult to work with. Keeping the dough cold will ensure that the butter layers are even.

When rolling out puff pastry, make sure that your **work surface is well dusted with flour.** However, before making any turns in the dough, brush off any loose flour with a dry pastry brush. Excess flour can make for tough puff pastry.

To keep puff pastry from sticking, lift the dough periodically while rolling it out. If you can see part of the butter package through the dough, flour that area heavily and continue rolling; the excess flour will act as a natural patch for the dough. Just be sure to brush off the excess before proceeding.

Keep track of how many turns you have completed in your puff pastry by marking the dough with your thumb, or the parchment paper with a pen.

If you will not be using your puff pastry dough within a day, cut it into 1-pound pieces (preferably square). **Tightly cover the dough in plastic wrap, and freeze** it for up to 3 months. Defrost frozen puff pastry in the refrigerator; this will take about 4 hours (you can allow it to defrost overnight if you wish). Don't leave puff pastry in the refrigerator for more than 1 day or it will lose its ability to puff properly in the oven.

If your oven has a convection function, use it to bake puff pastry. The pastry will rise and brown evenly. It's a good idea to start baking with the oven at 425 degrees; once the pastry has risen and begun to turn golden (after about 10 minutes), reduce the oven temperature to 350 degrees and finish baking. Watch closely; the baking time will be shorter than it is for a conventional oven.

Finished desserts that are constructed with baked puff pastry, such as napoleons, are best **cut with a serrated knife, using a sawing motion.** This will produce the least amount of crumbs, while also preventing the layers from collapsing.

When making strudel, **always make the filling first and set it aside.** Once the dough has been stretched to the right size, fill it immediately. Otherwise, the dough will become too brittle to roll.

Let strudel dough rest thoroughly, at least 1 hour, before attempting to stretch it. The gluten in the dough must relax in order for the dough to be pulled until it is paper-thin.

An extra-large work surface is essential for making strudel. If your kitchen lacks the proper space, a dining room table works well. You will also need a large, clean cloth or sheet.

PÂTE À CHOUX

MAKES 3 DOZEN *This dough is the building block for many classic French pastries.*

- 1 stick (½ cup) unsalted butter, cut into pieces
- 1 teaspoon sugar
- ½ teaspoon salt
- 1¼ cups all-purpose flour
- 4 large whole eggs, plus 1 large egg white, if needed

In a medium saucepan, combine butter, sugar, salt, and 1 cup water. Bring to a boil over medium-high heat, and immediately remove from heat. Using a wooden spoon, quickly stir in the flour until combined. Return pan to medium-high heat, and cook, stirring constantly, until mixture pulls away from the sides and a film forms on the bottom of the pan, about 3 minutes.

Transfer mixture to the bowl of an electric mixer fitted with the paddle attachment. Mix on low speed until slightly cooled, about 1 minute. Increase the speed to medium, and add the whole eggs, one at a time, beating until each is incorporated before adding the next. Test the batter by touching it with your finger and lifting to form a soft peak. If a soft peak does not form, the batter needs more egg. If you have added all the whole eggs and the batter still does not form a soft peak, lightly beat the remaining egg white, and add a little at a time. Use immediately.

PÂTE À CHOUX HOW-TO 1. The dough is best prepared in a heavy-bottom saucepan. Once the butter has melted, flour is added all at once and vigorously stirred to combine. **2.** The mixture should come together into a solid mass and pull away from the sides of the pan. It is ready for the next step when a thin film coats the bottom of the pan, after about 3 minutes. **3.** Once the mixture is removed from the heat, it is allowed to cool slightly before eggs are added, one at a time, and mixed to combine. The batter will be smooth and shiny, and should form a soft peak when touched.

PUFF PASTRY
MAKES ABOUT 3 POUNDS

3 cups (14 ounces) all-purpose flour, plus more for dusting

1 cup (5 ounces) cake flour (not self-rising)

1 tablespoon salt

1 tablespoon sugar

1 pound (4 sticks) unsalted butter, cold, plus 1 stick (½ cup), cold, cut into small pieces

1 teaspoon white wine vinegar or freshly squeezed lemon juice

In a large bowl, combine 2¾ cups all-purpose flour with the cake flour, salt, and sugar. With a pastry blender, cut in the butter pieces (1 stick) until the mixture resembles coarse meal, with a few larger clumps remaining. Make a well in the center, and pour in 1 cup cold water and the vinegar, gradually drawing the flour mixture over the water, gathering and combining until mixture comes together to form a dough. If the dough is too dry, add more cold water, 1 tablespoon at a time. Knead gently in the bowl, and form dough into a rough ball. Wrap in plastic, and refrigerate until well chilled, at least 40 minutes or up to 2 hours.

Sprinkle 2 tablespoons all-purpose flour on a sheet of parchment. Lay remaining 4 sticks of butter on top, side by side; sprinkle with remaining 2 tablespoons flour. Top with more parchment; pound butter with a rolling pin until it's about ½ inch thick. Remove top paper, fold butter in half, replace paper; pound butter until it's ½ inch thick. Repeat two or three more times until it is pliable. Using a bench scraper, shape butter into a 6-inch square; wrap in plastic, and refrigerate until chilled, about 10 minutes.

Lightly dust work surface with flour. Roll out dough to a 9-inch round; place butter package in center. Using a paring knife or bench scraper, lightly score dough to outline butter square. Remove butter; set aside. Starting from each side of marked square, gently roll out dough to form four flaps, each 4 to 5 inches long; do not touch square. Return butter to center square; fold flaps over butter. Press with your hands to seal.

With the rolling pin, gently pound the dough all over in regular intervals until it is about 1 inch thick; this will soften the dough, making it easier to roll. Working in only one direction (lengthwise), gently roll out the dough to a 20-by-9-inch rectangle, squaring corners with the side of the rolling pin or your hands as you go. Using a dry pastry brush, sweep off excess flour. With a short side facing you, fold the rectangle in thirds like a business letter. Turn the dough a quarter-turn clockwise, so the flap opening faces right, like a book. (This completes the first turn.) Roll out the dough again to a 20-by-9-inch rectangle, rolling in the same lengthwise direction; fold dough again into thirds. (This completes the second turn.) Wrap dough in plastic and refrigerate until well chilled, about 1 hour.

Repeat the rolling, turning, and chilling process for a total of six turns; always start each turn with the opening of the dough to the right. (If at any time, the dough becomes too soft to work with, return it to the refrigerator until firm.) Wrap dough in plastic; refrigerate 3 to 4 hours before using the dough.

PUFF PASTRY HOW-TO **1.** A cold stick of butter that has been cut into small pieces is added to a bowl of all-purpose and cake flours, sugar, and salt. **2.** A pastry blender is used to cut the butter pieces into the flour mixture until the mixture resembles coarse meal, with some larger clumps remaining (as shown on spoon). **3.** After a well is made in the center of the mixture, a combination of cold water and vinegar is poured into the well and gradually stirred in to combine.

4. Once a dough has formed, it is shaped into a rough ball; afterward, it is wrapped in plastic and refrigerated until well chilled. **5.** To form the butter package, 4 sticks of cold butter are placed side by side on a floured work surface, then sprinkled with more flour. **6.** A piece of parchment paper is placed over the butter, and a rolling pin is used to pound the butter until it is about $1/2$ inch thick. The paper is removed, and the butter is folded in half, and then covered and pounded once again. This process is repeated two or three more times until the butter is pliable.

7. The butter package is shaped into a 6-inch square and refrigerated until chilled. **8.** Meanwhile, the dough is rolled out to a 9-inch round (not pictured); the chilled butter is placed in the center, and its edges are lightly outlined with a knife or bench scraper. The butter is removed, and the dough is rolled out away from these marks to form four flaps, leaving the square in the center untouched. The butter package is returned to the square; the flaps are folded over to enclose the butter and pressed down to seal. **9.** With a rolling pin, the dough is pounded at regular intervals until it is about 1 inch thick.

10. The dough is gently rolled out on a piece of parchment into a 20-by-9-inch rectangle, keeping the corners square; a dry pastry brush is used to remove excess flour. The rectangle is folded into thirds like a business letter. **11.** The folded dough is turned one-quarter turn clockwise, so that the open edge faces right. The process of rolling and folding is repeated as above. After the second turn, the dough is marked with an indentation before chilling. The dough is refrigerated for at least 1 hour, before the process is repeated twice more, for a total of six turns.

CREAM PUFFS

MAKES 3 DOZEN *Once the pastry puffs are formed and frozen on the baking sheets, they can be stored in resealable freezer bags for up to three weeks. Top with rounds of Tart Dough and bake as directed; they do not need to be thawed first.*

All-purpose flour, for marking	¾ cup heavy cream
Pâte à Choux (page 358)	Pastry Cream (page 392)
1 cup granulated sugar, for sprinkling	Confectioners' sugar, for dusting
½ recipe Tart Dough (page 224)	

Line three large baking sheets with nonstick baking mats, such as Silpats, or with parchment paper. Dip a 2-inch round cookie cutter in flour, and mark circles 2 inches apart on the prepared sheets. Transfer Pâte à Choux to a pastry bag fitted with a ⅝-inch plain tip (such as an Ateco #808) and pipe puffs to fit in the flour circles. Gently smooth the pointed peaks with a moistened finger, rounding tops to ensure even rising. Freeze pastry puffs (on sheets) until firm, about 30 minutes.

Meanwhile, sprinkle a clean work surface with ½ cup granulated sugar, and place Tart Dough on top of sugar, patting out dough into a rough round. Sprinkle another ½ cup sugar on top of dough and roll to a scant ⅛-inch thickness, continually coating both sides of dough with sugar to keep dough from sticking to the rolling pin or work surface. Using a 1½-inch cookie cutter, cut out three dozen rounds, and place a round on top of each frozen puff. Return to freezer until firm, at least 15 minutes. Preheat the oven to 375°F, with racks in the upper and lower thirds.

Bake puffs, rotating sheets halfway through, until light golden brown all over, 25 to 30 minutes. Transfer sheets to a wire rack to cool completely. Once cool, the puffs can be kept overnight in an airtight container at room temperature before proceeding with the recipe.

In a medium bowl, whip cream to stiff peaks. Stir Pastry Cream to soften. Working in two batches, fold whipped cream into Pastry Cream. Transfer to a pastry bag fitted with a ½-inch plain tip (such as an Ateco #806). Insert tip into bottom of each pastry puff, and fill. Dust with confectioners' sugar. Once filled, these are best enjoyed within a few hours; store in an airtight container in the refrigerator.

CREAM PUFFS HOW-TO
1. A floured cookie cutter marks circles on a nonstick baking mat; the circles serve as guides for piping the Pâte à Choux.
2. Sugared Tart Dough cutouts are placed on top of the puffs before baking. **3.** A combination of whipped cream and Pastry Cream is piped into the bottom of each baked puff to fill.

CHOCOLATE ÉCLAIRS

MAKES 32 *The French traditionally fill their éclairs with pastry cream; the British prefer whipped cream. Our recipe borrows from both, for a filling that is at once rich and light.*

Pâte à Choux (page 358)

6 ounces semisweet chocolate, finely chopped

2¼ cups heavy cream

1 tablespoon light corn syrup

Pastry Cream (page 392)

Preheat the oven to 425°F, with racks in the upper and lower thirds. Line two large baking sheets with parchment paper or nonstick baking mats, such as Silpats. With a ruler and a pencil, mark lines about 3½ inches long on the parchment, spacing them about 1½ inches apart (you should be able to fit 16 lines on each sheet). Turn parchment over, marked sides down. Fill a pastry bag fitted with a ½-inch plain tip (such as an Ateco #806) with Pâte à Choux; pipe along the lines on the prepared baking sheets. Gently smooth tops with a moistened fingertip to ensure even rising.

Bake for 10 minutes; reduce oven temperature to 350°F. Continue to bake, rotating sheets halfway through, until pastries are golden brown, 25 to 30 minutes more. Transfer pastries and parchment to a wire rack to cool completely.

Place chocolate in a medium heatproof bowl. Heat ¾ cup cream and corn syrup in a small saucepan over medium heat until bubbles begin to appear around the edges, about 5 minutes; pour mixture over chocolate. Let stand 5 minutes, then stir until smooth. Let cool, stirring occasionally, about 5 minutes.

To fill the pastries, insert a wooden skewer into one end of each shell. (You can also use a small pastry tip, such as the one you will use for filling, to create the hole.)

In a medium bowl, stir the Pastry Cream to soften. In another bowl, whip the remaining 1½ cups heavy cream to stiff peaks. Fold the whipped cream into the Pastry Cream in two batches to lighten. Transfer to a pastry bag fitted with a ¼-inch plain tip (such as an Ateco #802). Insert the tip into the opening of each pastry, and pipe to fill with the whipped Pastry Cream.

Dip the top of each Éclair into the chocolate glaze; let excess drip off, and place, coated side up, on a wire rack set over a rimmed baking sheet. Refrigerate Éclairs in a single layer in an airtight container until glaze is set, about 10 minutes or up to 1 day.

ÉCLAIR HOW-TO

1. Pâte à Choux is piped onto marked lines on parchment-lined baking sheets.
2. Once baked, the cream filling is piped into each Éclair; the tops are then dipped in chocolate glaze.

Chocolate Éclairs

Gougères (Blue Cheese–Walnut variation)

Gougères

Profiterole

PROFITEROLES

MAKES 3 DOZEN *The pastry puffs can be baked a day in advance and kept in an airtight container at room temperature. If they soften, place them on a baking sheet and reheat in a 300-degree oven for about ten minutes to restore their crispness. Let them cool completely before filling with ice cream. Allow three profiteroles per person.*

All-purpose flour, for marking	2 tablespoons light corn syrup
Pâte à Choux (page 358)	15 ounces semisweet chocolate, finely chopped
¾ cup heavy cream	
½ cup milk	2 pints vanilla ice cream

Line two large baking sheets with nonstick baking mats, such as Silpats, or with parchment paper. Dip a 2-inch round cookie cutter in flour, and mark circles 1 inch apart on the prepared sheets. Transfer Pâte à Choux to a pastry bag fitted with a ⅝-inch plain tip (such as an Ateco #808), and pipe puffs to fit in the floured circles. Gently smooth the pointed peaks with a moistened finger, rounding tops to ensure even rising. Freeze puffs (on sheets) until firm, about 30 minutes.

Meanwhile, in a saucepan, combine cream, milk, and corn syrup; bring to a simmer over medium-high heat. Remove from heat; add chocolate, stirring with a wooden spoon until melted. Set chocolate sauce aside to cool slightly. Preheat the oven to 375°F.

Remove puffs from freezer. Bake, rotating sheets halfway through, until puffs are golden brown, 25 to 30 minutes. Transfer sheets to wire racks to cool completely. Using a serrated knife, slice off the top third of each puff; set aside. Place a scoop of ice cream on the bottom of each puff; replace tops. Drizzle with sauce. Serve immediately.

GOUGÈRES

MAKES 5 DOZEN *These savory cheese puffs are a specialty of Burgundy, France, and are the perfect accompaniment to a cocktail or glass of wine. We've flavored our version with fresh herbs, but feel free to omit them. To prepare the gougères in advance, pipe the dough, top with cheese, and freeze on a baking sheet until firm; transfer to resealable plastic bags, and freeze until ready to bake, up to three weeks.*

GOUGÈRES HOW-TO After the Pâte à Choux has finished cooking on the stove (but before the eggs are added), it is flavored with chopped fresh herbs and grated Gruyère and Parmesan cheeses.

1¼ cups all-purpose flour, plus more for marking	1½ cups grated Gruyère cheese (5 ounces)
1 stick (½ cup) unsalted butter	¼ cup grated Parmesan cheese, plus ¼ cup for sprinkling (about 1 ounce total)
2 teaspoons salt	
1 teaspoon sugar	
¼ teaspoon paprika	2 tablespoons chopped fresh dill
¼ teaspoon freshly ground black pepper	2 tablespoons chopped fresh chives
¼ teaspoon freshly grated nutmeg	4 large whole eggs, plus 1 large egg white if needed

Preheat the oven to 425°F. Line three large baking sheets with nonstick baking mats, such as Silpats, or parchment paper. Dip a 1½-inch round cookie cutter in flour, and mark circles about 1 inch apart on the prepared sheets; set aside.

In a medium saucepan, combine 1 cup water with the butter, salt, sugar, paprika, pepper, and nutmeg over medium-high heat. Bring mixture to a boil, and immediately remove from heat. Using a wooden spoon, add flour, stirring vigorously, until flour is no longer visible. Return pan to medium-high heat. Cook, stirring constantly, until mixture pulls away from the sides of the pan and forms a film on the bottom, about 4 minutes. Stir in both cheeses and the herbs, and mix just until the cheese is melted.

Transfer mixture to the bowl of an electric mixer fitted with the paddle attachment. Mix on low speed until slightly cooled, about 1 minute. Add 3 eggs, one at a time, mixing on medium speed until incorporated. Lightly beat the last egg, and add a little at a time until the batter is smooth and shiny. Test the batter by touching it with your finger and lifting—it should form a soft peak. If a soft peak does not form, the batter needs more egg. If you have added all the egg and the batter still won't form a soft peak, add the egg white, a little at a time, until it does.

Transfer dough to a pastry bag fitted with a ⅝-inch plain tip (such as an Ateco #808); pipe puffs to fit in the floured circles. Sprinkle each puff with remaining Parmesan. Bake, rotating sheets halfway through, until puffs are golden, about 20 minutes. Serve immediately, as Gougères are best eaten warm from the oven.

BLUE CHEESE-WALNUT GOUGÈRES VARIATION Follow instructions for Gougères, omitting the Gruyère and Parmesan cheeses and fresh dill and chives. Coarsely chop 1 ounce (about ⅓ cup) walnuts; set aside. Transfer dough to a pastry bag fitted with a ½-inch plain tip (such as an Ateco #806), and pipe rings of dough in the floured circles. Dividing evenly, sprinkle 5 ounces (about ¾ cup) finely crumbled blue cheese in the center of the rings, then sprinkle with chopped nuts. Proceed with the recipe.

BLUE CHEESE-WALNUT GOUGÈRES HOW-TO
Instead of being piped in rounds, the Pâte à Choux is piped in rings; the center of each ring is then sprinkled with crumbled blue cheese and chopped walnuts.

CHOCOLATE NAPOLEON

MAKES ONE 12-BY-4-INCH NAPOLEON *This famous French pastry is commonly known as mille-feuille ("a thousand leaves"). The name is believed to be derived from the term "Napolitain," alluding to the tradition of layered desserts in Naples, Italy.*

All-purpose flour, for dusting

1 pound Puff Pastry (page 359)

½ cup confectioners' sugar

1 tablespoon unsalted butter, melted and cooled

1 teaspoon light corn syrup

1 to 2 tablespoons milk

2 teaspoons Dutch-process cocoa powder

Chocolate Pastry Cream (page 392)

On a lightly floured piece of parchment paper, roll out Puff Pastry to a 12-inch square, about ⅛ inch thick. Using a pastry cutter or pizza wheel, cut square into three 12-by-4-inch strips. Transfer dough and parchment to a large baking sheet; prick all over with a fork. Cover with plastic wrap; chill in the refrigerator or freezer until firm, about 30 minutes. Meanwhile, preheat the oven to 425°F.

Transfer sheet to oven; bake, rotating sheet halfway through, until pastry is puffed and golden around the edges, about 10 minutes. Set another baking sheet directly on pastry strips and continue baking until pastry is light golden in the center, 6 to 8 minutes more. Remove top baking sheet; bake until pastry is baked through and golden brown, 6 minutes more. Transfer to a wire rack to cool completely.

In a small bowl, whisk together the sugar, butter, corn syrup, and 1 tablespoon milk. If the mixture is too thick to pour, add additional milk, 1 teaspoon at a time, until it reaches the consistency of sour cream. Transfer a quarter of the glaze to a small bowl; whisk in cocoa. Transfer chocolate glaze to a paper cornet; set aside.

Pour white glaze onto one of the pastry strips; spread evenly with an offset spatula. Cut the tip of the paper cornet, and pipe lines of chocolate glaze crosswise over the white glaze, about ½ inch apart. Drag the tip of a wooden skewer down the length of the glazed strip, in alternating directions, to create a decorative pattern.

Fit a pastry bag with a ⅝-inch plain tip (such as an Ateco #808) and fill with half of the Chocolate Pastry Cream. Pipe an even layer onto another pastry strip. Top with the remaining pastry strip, pressing gently to secure. Fill the pastry bag with remaining pastry cream, and pipe evenly onto the strip. Place the glazed pastry on top. Once assembled, the Napoleon is best eaten the same day; slice with a serrated knife.

CHOCOLATE NAPOLEON HOW-TO 1. A pastry strip is spread with an even layer of white glaze. After piping lines of chocolate glaze on top, a wooden skewer is used to create a decorative finish. **2.** The other pastry strips are layered with Chocolate Pastry Cream before being topped with the glazed strip.

LEMON-BLUEBERRY NAPOLEONS

MAKES 6 *The puff pastry can be baked a day in advance; keep in an airtight container at room temperature. The blueberry sauce can be refrigerated for up to three days.*

All-purpose flour, for dusting
1¾ pounds Puff Pastry (page 359)
2 pints (about 1¼ pounds) fresh blueberries
2 teaspoons freshly squeezed lemon juice

Pinch of salt
3 tablespoons sugar, plus ¼ cup for sprinkling
Lemon Custard (recipe follows)

Line two baking sheets with parchment paper; set aside. On a lightly floured work surface, roll out Puff Pastry dough to slightly less than ⅛ inch thick. Prick the dough all over with a fork. Using a 3-inch flower-shaped cookie cutter, cut out 18 identical pieces. Transfer cutouts to prepared baking sheets. Cover with plastic wrap; refrigerate for 1 hour, or freeze for up to 1 week (no need to thaw before baking).

Preheat the oven to 425°F. Remove plastic wrap and place another piece of parchment directly on top of pastry; top with another baking sheet. Bake, rotating sheets halfway through, until pastry is golden brown around the edges and crisp, about 15 minutes. Remove top baking sheet and parchment paper; continue baking until pastry is golden in the center, 5 to 7 minutes more. Transfer to a wire rack to cool completely.

In a medium saucepan, combine 1 pint blueberries with the lemon juice, salt, and 3 tablespoons sugar. Cook over medium heat, stirring occasionally, until berries have burst and their juice has thickened enough to coat the back of a wooden spoon, about 5 minutes. Set aside to cool completely. Once cool, stir in remaining pint blueberries.

Whisk the Lemon Custard to soften, and spoon or pipe about 2 tablespoons onto six of the pastry flowers; top each with 2 tablespoons blueberry sauce, letting some drizzle down the sides. Layer each with another pastry flower and 2 tablespoons each custard and blueberry sauce. Then sprinkle each of the six remaining pastry flowers with 2 teaspoons of sugar, and brown the tops with a small kitchen torch. (Alternatively, place the sugared pastry flowers briefly under the broiler.) Place these pieces on top of the assembled layers, and serve immediately.

LEMON-BLUEBERRY NAPOLEON HOW-TO
1. Chilled Puff Pastry cutouts are placed on a baking sheet, then topped with parchment and another sheet.
2. The weight of the sheet helps flatten the layers of Puff Pastry as it bakes, resulting in a flaky texture.

LEMON CUSTARD

MAKES ENOUGH FOR 6 LEMON-BLUEBERRY NAPOLEONS *If you want to quickly cool the hot custard, pour it into a large bowl set in a larger bowl filled with ice and cold water. Stirring the custard frequently will help to cool it even faster.*

1 large whole egg, plus
  1 large egg yolk
2 tablespoons freshly squeezed
  lemon juice
¼ cup plus 2 tablespoons sugar
  Finely grated zest of 1 lemon

1 cup milk
3 tablespoons cornstarch
⅛ teaspoon salt
1 tablespoon unsalted butter,
  cut into small pieces

In a medium bowl, whisk together the whole egg, egg yolk, lemon juice, and ¼ cup sugar. In a medium saucepan, combine the lemon zest, milk, remaining 2 tablespoons sugar, cornstarch, and salt. Bring to a boil over medium-high heat, whisking constantly. Remove from heat; slowly pour about a third of the hot milk mixture into the egg mixture, whisking constantly until combined. Pour mixture back into remaining milk, whisking constantly.

Return saucepan to medium-high heat. Whisking constantly, cook until mixture is bubbling in the center and thick enough to hold a deep trail when stirred with a wooden spoon, about 2 minutes.

Strain mixture through a fine sieve into a medium bowl; whisk in butter. Press a sheet of plastic wrap directly on the surface of the custard to prevent a skin from forming. Let cool completely. Cover and refrigerate until ready to use, up to 1 day.

PITHIVIERS

MAKES ONE 9-INCH TART *This classic tart has a filling of frangipane (an almond-flavored cream) and caramelized pears enclosed between two layers of puff pastry. The tart is named for the French town in which it was created. It is best eaten the day it is baked.*

½ cup plus 2 tablespoons sliced
  blanched almonds
2 tablespoons all-purpose flour,
  plus more for dusting
½ cup plus 1 tablespoon sugar
¼ teaspoon salt
3 tablespoons unsalted butter,
  cold, cut into ½-inch pieces

2 large eggs
1 pound Puff Pastry (page 359)
1 ripe but firm D'Anjou pear,
  peeled, cored, and cut into
  ¼-inch-thick wedges
2 tablespoons freshly squeezed
  lemon juice
1 tablespoon heavy cream

Preheat the oven to 375°F. Spread the almonds in a single layer on a rimmed baking sheet. Toast until fragrant and light golden brown, 7 to 9 minutes. Remove from oven and transfer to a plate to cool completely. In a food processor, pulse toasted almonds, flour, ½ cup sugar, and salt until fine crumbs form. With the machine running, add the butter and 1 egg, processing until mixture is smooth. Refrigerate frangipane until chilled, about 30 minutes.

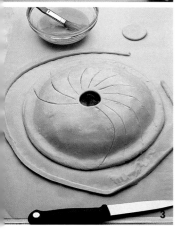

Meanwhile, on a lightly floured work surface, roll out Puff Pastry dough to an 18-by-11-inch rectangle, about ⅛ inch thick. Wrap in plastic, and freeze until chilled, about 10 minutes. In a medium skillet, combine the pear, remaining tablespoon sugar, and the lemon juice; cook over medium heat until pear slices are caramelized on both sides, about 4 minutes. Transfer pears to a plate with a slotted spoon, and refrigerate until chilled, about 10 minutes. In a small bowl, whisk together the remaining egg with the heavy cream; set egg wash aside.

Transfer the dough to a lightly floured piece of parchment paper. Using a 9-inch round cake pan as a guide, cut out two 9-inch rounds with a sharp knife; do not remove from the dough. With a floured 1-inch cookie cutter, cut a hole out of the center of one of the rounds, and discard. Using a floured 2-inch cookie cutter, cut a circle from the excess dough; set aside. (This will later be used to decorate the finished Pithiviers.) Reserve remaining dough for another use.

Place the uncut round and the cutout circle on a parchment-lined baking sheet. Using a pastry bag fitted with a ½-inch plain tip (such as an Ateco #806), pipe the chilled frangipane evenly over the center of the round, leaving a 1½-inch border. Evenly distribute the pear mixture over the frangipane. Working quickly, lightly brush egg wash over the dough surrounding the frangipane, leaving a ½-inch border around the edge. Cover with the other round of dough, lining up the edges. Gently lift to allow air to escape, then smooth any remaining air bubbles with your hands. Press the edges together firmly to seal, and trim with a sharp paring knife. With the knife, score the top of the pastry, making curved lines from the hole in the center out toward the edges, to resemble a pinwheel. Place the filled tart in the freezer until firm, about 20 minutes.

Brush the top of the tart and the cutout circle with egg wash, being careful not to let any drip over cut edges, as it will prevent even puffing. Bake for 30 minutes (remove cutout after 15 minutes). Reduce oven temperature to 350°F; cover edge of pastry with foil to prevent it from burning. Bake until center is well browned, about 30 minutes more. Remove from oven, and slide onto a wire rack to cool. Serve at room temperature, placing the cutout circle in the center if desired.

PITHIVIERS HOW-TO
1. A cake pan is used to cut two 9-inch rounds from a large rectangle of dough. A small piece is cut from one of the rounds, and a larger piece is cut from the excess dough. **2.** The frangipane is piped over one round, then topped with the pear filling. **3.** The tart is trimmed, scored, and brushed with egg wash before baking.

FRUIT TURNOVERS

MAKES 8 *Turnovers are always a favorite; their light Puff Pastry shells burst with fresh fruit. Our three fillings provide this classic dessert with a fresh twist: five-spice powder lends its subtle aroma to pear, peach chunks blend with homemade raspberry jam, and sage plays off the sweetness of summer blueberries. All the fillings can be used interchangeably—simply prepare and fill the dough as instructed.*

All-purpose flour, for dusting	1 large egg yolk
1 pound Puff Pastry (page 359)	1 tablespoon heavy cream
Fruit Fillings (recipes follow)	Sugar, for sprinkling

Line a baking sheet with parchment paper; set aside. On a lightly floured work surface, roll out Puff Pastry dough to a 17½-by-9½-inch rectangle, about ⅛ inch thick. Using a dry pastry brush, sweep off excess flour. Using a pastry cutter or pizza wheel, trim to a 16-by-8-inch rectangle. Cut out eight 4-inch squares. Place squares on the prepared baking sheet; cover with plastic wrap and chill until firm, at least 1 hour or up to 8 hours. Meanwhile, prepare desired Fruit Filling, and set aside.

In a small bowl, whisk together egg yolk and cream; set egg wash aside. Divide the filling equally among the pastry squares, placing it in the center. Brush edges with egg wash. Fold dough diagonally over filling to form a triangle, and press to seal. If desired, crimp the edges using the floured tines of a fork. Place filled turnovers on a baking sheet, cover with plastic wrap, and freeze until firm, 20 to 30 minutes. The filled turnovers can be frozen for up to 3 weeks; no need to thaw before proceeding.

Preheat the oven to 375°F. Brush tops of turnovers with egg wash, being careful not to let it drip over the edges, as this will prevent even puffing. Sprinkle generously with sugar, and bake, rotating sheet halfway through, until turnovers are puffed and deep golden, 30 to 35 minutes. Using a thin metal spatula, immediately transfer turnovers to a wire rack to cool. They are best eaten the same day they are baked.

FRUIT FILLINGS
MAKES ENOUGH FOR 8 FRUIT TURNOVERS

PEAR FILLING Peel, core, and cut 2 medium pears into ½-inch dice. In a medium bowl, combine the pears with 2 tablespoons cornstarch, 2 teaspoons freshly squeezed lemon juice, ½ teaspoon five-spice powder, a pinch of salt, and 2 teaspoons sugar.

RASPBERRY-PEACH FILLING In a small bowl, stir together 3 tablespoons freshly squeezed lemon juice with 1 tablespoon cornstarch; set aside. In a small saucepan, combine ¾ cup fresh raspberries, 1¼ cups sugar, and a pinch of salt. Cook, stirring, over medium heat until mixture begins to simmer. Stirring constantly, add the cornstarch mixture, and simmer, stirring occasionally, until mixture has thickened, 8 to 10 minutes. Transfer to a bowl, and refrigerate until chilled. Meanwhile, cut 1 medium peach into ½-inch dice, and place in a medium bowl. Strain raspberry mixture into the saucepan, then add ¾ cup raspberries. Cook until bubbling and thickened. Let cool, then stir into the peaches.

Fruit Turnovers

BLUEBERRY FILLING Slice 10 fresh sage leaves into fine julienne; set aside. In a small saucepan, combine 1 cup fresh blueberries, 3 tablespoons freshly squeezed lemon juice, and a pinch of salt. Cook over medium heat until blueberries begin to burst. Stir in ¾ cup sugar, and simmer until mixture thickens enough to coat the back of a spoon, 6 to 8 minutes. Transfer mixture to a medium bowl, and refrigerate until well chilled. Stir ½ cup blueberries into chilled blueberry sauce. Follow instructions for filling turnovers, sprinkling the blueberry filling with 1 teaspoon sage.

POPPY SEED–PARMESAN CHEESE STRAWS

MAKES 56 *To help these hors d'oeuvres retain their twisted shapes, thoroughly chill them before baking. You can freeze the formed straws for up to three weeks (no need to thaw), but once they're baked, it's best to serve them as soon as possible.*

All-purpose flour, for dusting
1 pound Puff Pastry (page 359)
1 large egg, lightly beaten
2 tablespoons poppy seeds

½ cup finely grated Parmesan cheese (2 ounces)
1 tablespoon paprika
Coarse salt

CHEESE STRAW HOW-TO
After being rolled out and coated with poppy seeds and grated cheese, the Puff Pastry is cut into strips. The strips are then twisted and chilled before baking.

On a lightly floured work surface, roll out Puff Pastry dough to a 17-by-14-inch rectangle, about ⅛ inch thick. Transfer dough to a large baking sheet; lightly brush with some of the beaten egg, then sprinkle evenly with poppy seeds. Gently press poppy seeds into dough with a rolling pin, taking care not to stretch the rectangle further. Refrigerate dough until firm, 10 to 15 minutes. In a small bowl, combine cheese, paprika, and a large pinch of salt; set aside.

Invert the dough onto the work surface, then brush uncoated side with remaining beaten egg. Sprinkle evenly with the cheese mixture; use a rolling pin to gently press cheese mixture into the dough. Return dough to baking sheet, cheese side up; chill until firm, 10 to 15 minutes.

With a pizza wheel or pastry cutter, divide dough in half crosswise to make two rectangles, each 14 by 8½ inches. Cut each half crosswise into 28 strips (each ½ inch wide), for a total of 56. Twist each strip, then transfer to two large unlined baking sheets, pressing the ends onto the sheet to hold their shape. Refrigerate strips until firm, at least 30 minutes or overnight.

Preheat the oven to 375°F. Bake, rotating sheets halfway through, until straws are light golden, 20 to 24 minutes. Transfer to a wire rack to cool. Cheese straws are best eaten the day they are made, but they can be kept in an airtight container at room temperature for up to 2 days. If desired, reheat in a 200°F oven for about 20 minutes.

SFOGLIATELLE

MAKES ABOUT 20 *These pastries are a specialty of Naples, Italy. The key to making them is using the freshest ricotta you can find. Do not substitute packaged ricotta, which can't compare with artisanal varieties in terms of flavor or consistency.*

3 cups all-purpose flour, plus more for dusting	⅔ cup semolina flour
1½ teaspoons salt	2 large whole eggs, plus 2 large egg yolks
3 tablespoons extra-virgin olive oil	½ teaspoon ground cinnamon
1½ sticks (¾ cup) unsalted butter, room temperature	¼ teaspoon freshly grated nutmeg
1 cup vegetable shortening	1 teaspoon pure vanilla extract
2½ cups fresh ricotta cheese	1 teaspoon finely grated orange zest
1 cup granulated sugar	Confectioners' sugar, for dusting

In a large bowl, combine all-purpose flour with 1¼ teaspoons salt, the olive oil, and ¾ cup water; stir together until a dough forms (it will be slightly dry). If the dough is too dry to absorb all of the flour, add more water, 1 tablespoon at a time. Transfer the dough to a lightly floured work surface, and knead until soft and elastic, about 5 minutes. Wrap dough in plastic and refrigerate for 1 hour.

In the bowl of an electric mixer fitted with the paddle attachment, beat butter and shortening on medium speed until light and fluffy, about 1 minute. Transfer mixture to a small bowl, and set aside. In a food processor, blend ricotta cheese until smooth and creamy, about 30 seconds; set aside.

In a medium saucepan, combine 1 cup water with the granulated sugar, and bring to a boil over medium heat. Add semolina flour, and stir until there are no visible lumps and mixture is slightly thickened, about 1 minute. Whisk in ricotta cheese, and cook over medium heat until mixture is smooth and thickened, 1 minute. Remove from heat, and whisk in whole eggs and yolks, one at a time. Return pan to heat and continue to cook until mixture is slightly thickened, about 1 minute more. Stir in the cinnamon, nutmeg, vanilla, orange zest, and remaining ¼ teaspoon salt. Transfer to a medium bowl. Press a sheet of plastic wrap directly on the surface of the custard to prevent a skin from forming, and refrigerate until well chilled, about 1 hour.

Remove dough from the refrigerator, and cut into four equal pieces. Lightly dust each one with flour. Using a rolling pin, roll out each piece to a thickness that will easily fit through the widest setting on a manual pasta machine (it should be about 5½ inches). Pass each piece of dough, one after the other, through every other setting, ending with the thinnest setting.

Place one of the strips of dough on a lightly floured work surface, and trim both the rounded ends. Using an offset spatula, evenly spread one quarter of reserved butter mixture on the dough. With a short side facing you, begin rolling the dough into a tight log; gently stretch the ends as you roll to make them thinner (the log should

SFOGLIATELLE HOW-TO
1. The dough is first passed through a pasta machine. **2.** Once the dough is thin enough, it is spread with a mixture of butter and shortening, and then rolled into a log. **3.** The log is cut into slices, the centers of which are slowly pushed out to form a clamshell shape and then filled with a ricotta mixture.

be about 8 inches long). Repeat with remaining three pieces of dough. Refrigerate until firm, about 1 hour.

Preheat the oven to 425°F. Stack two baking sheets, and line the top one with parchment paper; set aside. Transfer chilled custard to a pastry bag fitted with a ½-inch plain tip (such as an Ateco #806). Slice each log of dough crosswise into ½-inch pieces (dip your knife in flour to prevent sticking). With your thumbs, slowly push out the center of each roll to form a clamshell shape. Fill the opening with custard; pinch openings to seal. Transfer filled pastries to prepared baking sheet, about 1 inch apart.

Bake, periodically basting pastries with the accumulated melted butter, until golden brown, 25 to 30 minutes. Transfer to a wire rack to cool completely. Before serving, dust with confectioners' sugar.

Cherry-Cheese Strudel

CHERRY-CHEESE STRUDEL

MAKES ONE 24-INCH STRUDEL *Fresh sour cherries usually appear in farmers' markets in early July, but the season is short—about three weeks. If you can't find fresh sour cherries, substitute two pounds of frozen ones; defrost before using. To make the strudel, you'll need a large, clean cloth and a work surface that you can easily walk around, such as an island or your kitchen table.*

5 tablespoons unsalted butter, melted and cooled, plus more for pan	12 ounces cream cheese, room temperature
3 pounds fresh sour cherries, stemmed and pitted, juices reserved	1 large egg yolk
	All-purpose flour, for dusting
	Strudel Dough (recipe follows)
1¼ cups granulated sugar	1 teaspoon vegetable oil, for brushing
½ teaspoon salt	
2 whole cinnamon sticks or ¼ teaspoon ground cinnamon	Sanding sugar, for sprinkling
	Whipped cream or ice cream, for serving (optional)
1¾ teaspoons cornstarch	

Brush a large rimmed baking sheet with melted butter; set aside. Combine the cherries and their juice, ¾ cup granulated sugar, ¼ teaspoon salt, and cinnamon sticks in a medium high-sided skillet. Place over medium-high heat, and bring to a boil. Cook until juice is reduced to ¼ cup, about 10 minutes. Transfer 2 tablespoons of juice to a small bowl; add the cornstarch, and whisk until combined. Return mixture to skillet and cook, stirring until thickened, about 2 minutes. Set aside to cool completely.

In the bowl of an electric mixer fitted with the paddle attachment, beat cream cheese, remaining ½ cup granulated sugar, and ¼ teaspoon salt on medium-high speed until very smooth, 2 to 3 minutes. Add the egg yolk, and beat to combine.

Lay a large, clean cloth or sheet (at least 3 feet long and wide) on a work surface, and sprinkle well with flour. Place dough in center of cloth, and roll out to a 12-inch square. Cover with plastic wrap, and let stand for 15 minutes.

Preheat the oven to 400°F. Roll out dough again to about a 20-inch square, and lightly brush entire surface with oil. Slide both hands, with slightly curved palms facing down, under dough toward the center. Holding this position, lift the dough off the cloth with your knuckles, and begin stretching from the center out to the edges until it is too large to stretch easily with your hands. Carefully set dough back on cloth, spreading it to smooth out any wrinkles or folds. Starting in the center again, continue to stretch out the dough in all directions, maintaining a rectangular shape, until the dough is almost translucent everywhere except the edges, which should be thicker. Don't worry if the dough tears while stretching: Once you're done, you will be able to patch any holes with some of the excess stretched dough.

Using a pizza wheel or kitchen scissors, trim all the thick edges until the dough is about 30 by 28 inches. Drizzle 4 tablespoons melted butter evenly over the dough. With a short side facing you, and starting about 6 inches from the top edge, spread the cream cheese mixture in a 6-inch-wide layer, horizontally, leaving a 3-inch border

STRUDEL HOW-TO
1. A square of strudel dough is placed on a well-floured sheet on top of a large work surface. 2. The dough is rolled and brushed with oil, then stretched into a very large, nearly translucent rectangle. 3. If the dough tears, it can be easily patched with extra dough.

on each end. Arrange the cherry mixture evenly on top of the cream cheese. Using the cloth, lift up and flip the 6-inch top edge of the dough over the filling. Repeat lifting and folding once, leaving sides open. Then fold in sides of dough to enclose the filling. Continue lifting and folding until the dough is completely rolled into a flat log. If the ends are very thick, trim them as you work.

Place the prepared baking sheet lengthwise next to the log. To transfer, gently flip one end of the log onto the baking sheet, seam side down, then flip the other end, curving to form a crescent shape. Brush the surface evenly with the remaining tablespoon butter, and generously sprinkle with sanding sugar. Using a wooden skewer, prick the surface of the dough to allow steam to escape.

Bake until strudel is deep golden, about 1 hour. Transfer sheet to a wire rack to cool, 10 minutes. Using two large offset spatulas, release strudel from the sheet and slide it onto the rack. Serve with whipped cream or ice cream, as desired.

STRUDEL DOUGH
MAKES ENOUGH FOR ONE 24-INCH STRUDEL

2 cups plus 2 tablespoons all-purpose flour, plus more for dusting

¼ teaspoon salt

3 tablespoons vegetable oil

¾ cup warm water

In the bowl of an electric mixer fitted with the paddle attachment, combine flour and salt. Add oil and warm water; mix on medium-low speed until dough just comes together, about 1 minute. Switch to the dough hook; mix until dough is smooth and shiny and doesn't stick to your fingers, about 5 minutes.

Turn out dough onto a lightly floured work surface. Knead the dough, dusting with flour as you go and periodically slamming it against the work surface, until it is soft, smooth, and elastic. Leave dough on work surface; cover with an overturned bowl. Let rest at room temperature at least 1 hour or up to 4 hours.

STRUDEL HOW-TO **4.** Sweetened cream cheese is spread in a layer across the top of the dough, then covered with sour cherry filling. **5.** The cloth helps support the dough as it is folded around the filling. **6.** The flat log is transferred to a rimmed baking sheet, the ends curved to form a crescent. A skewer is used to prick holes in the surface.

BASIC RECIPES

frostings and glazes

Swiss Meringue Buttercream

Brown Sugar Buttercream

Strawberry Meringue Buttercream

Seven-Minute Frosting

Chocolate Ganache

Mint-Chocolate Ganache

Dark Chocolate Frosting

Royal Icing

Mocha Glaze

fillings, custards, and creams

Basic Caramel

Simple Syrup

Lemon Curd

Lime Curd

Passion Fruit Curd

Grapefruit Curd

Vanilla Whipped Cream

Caramel Whipped Cream

Almond Cream

Pastry Cream

Mocha Mousse

Raspberry Jam

toppings and dough

Slab Pie Pâte Brisée

Crumb Topping

Streusel

Candied Walnuts

White Chocolate Cutouts

Chocolate Curls

Fresh Coconut Curls

STORAGE TIP If you'll be using our Dark Chocolate Frosting or buttercreams within several hours, they should be covered with plastic wrap and kept at room temperature. They can also be refrigerated in an airtight container for up to 3 days, or frozen for up to 1 month. Before using, bring to room temperature, and beat with an electric mixer on the lowest speed until smooth.

SWISS MERINGUE BUTTERCREAM

MAKES 4 CUPS *This is an excellent all-purpose frosting that can be used to top any cake—from cupcakes to a multitiered wedding cake. Its flavor is adaptable, too; two of our favorite variations are lemon (which we paired with our Lemon Curd Cake, page 153) and chocolate (which adorns the Dobos Torte, page 203).*

    4 large egg whites
 1¼ cups sugar
    3 sticks (1½ cups) unsalted butter,
        room temperature, cut into tablespoons
    1 teaspoon pure vanilla extract

In the heatproof bowl of an electric mixer set over a saucepan of simmering water, combine the egg whites and sugar. Cook, whisking constantly, until the sugar has dissolved and the mixture is warm to the touch (about 160°F).

Attach the bowl to the mixer fitted with the whisk attachment. Beat the egg-white mixture on high speed until it holds stiff (but not dry) peaks. Continue beating until the mixture is fluffy and cooled, about 6 minutes.

Switch to the paddle attachment. With the mixer on medium-low speed, add the butter several tablespoons at a time, beating well after each addition. (If the frosting appears to separate after all the butter has been added, beat on medium-high speed until smooth again, 3 to 5 minutes more.) Beat in vanilla. Beat on lowest speed to eliminate any air bubbles, about 2 minutes. Stir with a rubber spatula until frosting is smooth.

LEMON SWISS MERINGUE BUTTERCREAM VARIATION Follow instructions for Swiss Meringue Buttercream, omitting the vanilla extract and stirring in ¾ cup Lemon Curd (page 390) with a rubber spatula at the end.

CHOCOLATE SWISS MERINGUE BUTTERCREAM VARIATION Follow instructions for Swiss Meringue Buttercream, omitting the vanilla extract, decreasing the sugar to 1 cup, and adding 8 ounces melted best-quality bittersweet chocolate after the butter has been incorporated (let chocolate cool slightly before mixing in).

BROWN SUGAR BUTTERCREAM
MAKES ABOUT 2 CUPS

    2 large egg whites
 ½ cup packed light-brown sugar
 1½ sticks (¾ cup) unsalted butter, cold,
        cut into tablespoons

In the heatproof bowl of an electric mixer set over a saucepan of simmering water, combine the egg whites and sugar. Cook, whisking constantly, until the sugar has dissolved and the mixture is warm to the touch (about 160°F).

Attach the bowl to the mixer fitted with the whisk attachment. Beat the egg-white mixture on high speed until it holds stiff (but not dry) peaks. Continue beating until the mixture is fluffy and cooled, about 6 minutes.

Switch to the paddle attachment. With the mixer on medium-low speed, add the butter several tablespoons at a time, beating well after each addition. (If the frosting appears to separate after all the butter has been added, beat on medium-high speed until smooth again, 3 to 5 minutes more.) Beat on lowest speed to eliminate any air bubbles, about 2 minutes. Stir with a rubber spatula until frosting is smooth.

STRAWBERRY MERINGUE BUTTERCREAM
MAKES 5 CUPS

4 large egg whites

1¼ cups sugar

3 sticks (1½ cups) unsalted butter,
room temperature, cut into tablespoons

1 teaspoon pure vanilla extract

1½ cups (12 ounces) strawberry jam,
puréed in a food processor

In the heatproof bowl of an electric mixer set over a saucepan of simmering water, combine the egg whites and sugar. Cook, whisking constantly, until the sugar has dissolved and the mixture is warm to the touch (about 160°F).

Attach the bowl to the mixer fitted with the whisk attachment. Beat the egg-white mixture on high speed until it holds stiff (but not dry) peaks. Continue beating until the mixture is fluffy and cooled, about 6 minutes.

Switch to the paddle attachment. With the mixer on medium-low speed, add the butter several tablespoons at a time, beating well after each addition. (If the frosting appears to separate after all the butter has been added, beat on medium-high speed until smooth again, 3 to 5 minutes more.) Beat in vanilla. Beat on lowest speed to eliminate any air bubbles, about 2 minutes. Stir in strawberry jam with a rubber spatula until frosting is smooth.

SEVEN-MINUTE FROSTING
MAKES ABOUT 8 CUPS

1½ cups sugar

2 tablespoons light corn syrup

6 large egg whites

1 teaspoon pure vanilla extract

In the heatproof bowl of an electric mixer set over a saucepan of simmering water, combine sugar, corn syrup, ¼ cup water, and the egg whites. Cook over medium heat, stirring frequently, until the mixture registers 160°F on an instant-read thermometer, about 2 minutes.

Attach the bowl to the mixer fitted with the whisk attachment. Beat the mixture on high speed until glossy and voluminous, about 5 minutes. Beat in the vanilla. Use immediately.

CHOCOLATE GANACHE

MAKES ABOUT 3 CUPS *Ganache will thicken as it sits. To cover a cake, it should be pourable but still thick enough to coat. If not, place the bowl of ganache over a pan of simmering water and stir until it reaches the right consistency.*

2 cups heavy cream

1 pound best-quality semisweet chocolate,
finely chopped

In a small saucepan over medium-high heat bring cream to a full boil; turn off heat. Add the chocolate, and swirl pan to completely cover it with cream. Let stand about 5 minutes. Slowly whisk mixture until smooth. Transfer to a clean bowl. Let cool, stirring frequently.

MINT-CHOCOLATE GANACHE

MAKES ABOUT 7 CUPS *Ganache can be kept, tightly covered, in the refrigerator for up to three days. Before using, warm ganache by setting it over a saucepan of simmering water, then let cool, stirring frequently.*

    4 cups heavy cream
    2 pounds best-quality semisweet
       chocolate, finely chopped
    ¼ cup light corn syrup
    ¼ teaspoon salt
    1½ teaspoons pure peppermint extract

In a small saucepan over medium-high heat, bring the cream to a full boil; turn off the heat. Add the chocolate, and swirl pan to completely cover with cream. Slowly whisk mixture until smooth. Add the corn syrup, salt, and peppermint extract, and stir until combined. Transfer to a clean bowl.

DARK CHOCOLATE FROSTING

MAKES ABOUT 5 CUPS *If you want to give this frosting extra flavor, add a teaspoon of mint, orange, or coffee extract after the chocolate has been incorporated. To frost a four-layer cake you will need to increase the ingredients accordingly: use 24 ounces chocolate, 4½ sticks butter, ¾ cup sugar, and ½ cup plus 1 tablespoon each cocoa and boiling water. Alternatively, halving this recipe makes just enough for a standard sheet cake or a dozen cupcakes.*

    1 pound best-quality semisweet
       chocolate, finely chopped
    6 tablespoons Dutch-process cocoa powder
    6 tablespoons boiling water
    3 sticks (1½ cups) unsalted butter,
       room temperature
    ½ cup confectioners' sugar
       Pinch of salt

Place chocolate in a heatproof bowl set over (but not touching) simmering water. Turn off the heat; stir occasionally until chocolate has melted completely, about 15 minutes. Set bowl on countertop, and let chocolate cool to room temperature, 25 to 30 minutes. Meanwhile, combine cocoa powder and boiling water in a small bowl; stir until cocoa is dissolved.

In the bowl of an electric mixer fitted with the paddle attachment, beat butter, confectioners' sugar, and salt on medium-high speed until light and fluffy, 3 to 4 minutes. Add melted chocolate; beat on low speed until combined, 1 to 2 minutes, scraping down the sides of the bowl as needed. Beat in the cocoa mixture.

ROYAL ICING

MAKES ABOUT 2½ CUPS *If not using immediately, transfer to an airtight container (icing hardens quickly when exposed to air), and store at room temperature for up to one week. Beat with a rubber spatula before using.*

- 1 pound confectioners' sugar
- 5 tablespoons meringue powder
- Liquid or gel-paste food coloring (optional)

In the bowl of an electric mixer fitted with the paddle attachment, combine sugar, meringue powder, and a scant ½ cup water on low speed. Beat until mixture is fluffy yet dense, 7 to 8 minutes.

To thin the icing for flooding (filling in areas with a thin layer of icing), stir in additional water, 1 teaspoon at a time. Test the consistency by lifting a spoonful of icing and letting it drip back into the bowl; a ribbon should remain on the surface for 5 to 7 seconds.

To tint icing, dip a toothpick or wooden skewer into food coloring, and gradually mix it in until the desired shade is reached.

MOCHA GLAZE
MAKES ENOUGH FOR ONE 10-INCH CAKE

- 2 cups confectioners' sugar
- 1 tablespoon Dutch-process cocoa powder
- 1 tablespoon instant espresso powder
- ¼ cup plus 2 tablespoons boiling water

Sift together sugar and cocoa powder into a medium bowl. In a small bowl, stir the espresso powder in the boiling water to dissolve. Pour the espresso mixture into the dry ingredients, and stir with a wooden spoon until smooth. Use immediately.

BASIC CARAMEL

MAKES 1½ CUPS *This recipe produces a caramel that, once cooled, is quite stiff—the ideal consistency for making bar cookies. If you plan to pour it over cake or ice cream, simply double the amount of heavy cream. This caramel can be refrigerated, tightly covered, for up to three days.*

- 2 cups sugar
- ¼ teaspoon cream of tartar
- ¾ cup heavy cream

In a medium heavy-bottom saucepan, combine the sugar and cream of tartar with ½ cup water. Cook over high heat without stirring until sugar begins to melt and turn golden at the edges. Continue cooking, swirling the pan to cover evenly, until the sugar turns golden amber. Carefully pour the heavy cream down the side of the pan in a slow, steady stream (it will spatter), stirring constantly with a wooden spoon until combined. Transfer to a medium bowl, and let cool.

SIMPLE SYRUP
MAKES 4 CUPS

- 3 cups sugar
- 3 cups water

Prepare an ice bath, and set aside. In a medium saucepan, bring the sugar and water to a boil over medium-high heat. Cook, stirring occasionally, until sugar has completely dissolved. Transfer to a medium bowl set in the ice bath; let stand until chilled, stirring occasionally, before using or storing. Simple Syrup can be kept in an airtight container in the refrigerator for up to 1 month.

LEMON CURD

MAKES 2 CUPS

    8 large egg yolks
       Finely grated zest of 2 lemons
  1/2 cup plus 2 tablespoons freshly
       squeezed lemon juice (about 3 lemons)
    1 cup sugar
  1/8 teaspoon salt
 1 1/4 sticks (10 tablespoons) unsalted
       butter, cold, cut into pieces

Combine yolks, lemon zest, lemon juice, and sugar in a heavy-bottom saucepan; whisk to combine. Cook over medium-high heat, stirring constantly with a wooden spoon (be sure to scrape the sides of the pan), until the mixture is thick enough to coat the back of the spoon, 8 to 10 minutes, and registers 160°F on an instant-read thermometer.

Remove saucepan from heat. Add salt and butter, one piece at a time, stirring until smooth. Strain through a fine sieve into a medium bowl. Cover with plastic wrap, pressing it directly onto the surface of the curd to prevent a skin from forming. Refrigerate until chilled and set, at least 1 hour or up to 1 day.

LIME CURD

MAKES 2 CUPS

    8 large egg yolks
  1/4 cup plus 2 tablespoons freshly
       squeezed lime juice (3 to 4 limes)
  1/4 cup plus 2 tablespoons freshly
       squeezed lemon juice (about 2 lemons)
       Finely grated zest of 2 limes
    1 cup sugar
  1/8 teaspoon salt
 1 1/4 sticks (10 tablespoons) unsalted
       butter, cold, cut into pieces

Combine yolks, lime juice, lemon juice, half of the zest, and the sugar in a heavy-bottom saucepan; whisk to combine. Cook over medium-high heat, stirring constantly with a wooden spoon (be sure to scrape the sides of the pan), until the mixture is thick enough to coat the back of the spoon, 8 to 10 minutes, and registers 160°F on an instant-read thermometer.

Remove saucepan from heat. Add salt and butter, one piece at a time, stirring until smooth. Strain through a fine sieve into a medium bowl. Stir in the remaining zest. Cover with plastic wrap, pressing it directly onto the surface of the curd to prevent a skin from forming. Refrigerate until chilled and set, at least 1 hour or up to 1 day.

PASSION FRUIT CURD

MAKES 1 3/4 CUPS

    8 large egg yolks
  1/2 cup passion fruit juice
    1 cup sugar
  1/8 teaspoon salt
 1 1/4 sticks (10 tablespoons) unsalted
       butter, cold, cut into pieces

Combine yolks, passion fruit juice, and sugar in a heavy-bottom saucepan; whisk to combine. Cook over medium-high heat, stirring constantly with a wooden spoon (be sure to scrape the sides of the pan), until the mixture is thick enough to coat the back of the spoon, 8 to 10 minutes, and registers 160°F on an instant-read thermometer.

Remove saucepan from heat. Add salt and butter, one piece at a time, stirring until smooth. Strain through a fine sieve into a medium bowl. Cover with plastic wrap, pressing it directly onto the surface of the curd to prevent a skin from forming. Refrigerate until chilled and set, at least 1 hour or up to 1 day.

GRAPEFRUIT CURD
MAKES 2 CUPS

      8 large egg yolks
    1/4 cup freshly squeezed ruby red
         grapefruit juice (about 1/2 grapefruit)
    1/4 cup plus 2 tablespoons freshly
         squeezed lemon juice
         Finely grated zest of 1 ruby red grapefruit
      1 cup sugar
    1/8 teaspoon salt
  1 1/4 sticks (10 tablespoons) unsalted butter,
         cold, cut into pieces

Combine yolks, grapefruit juice, lemon juice, half of the zest, and the sugar in a heavy-bottom saucepan; whisk to combine. Cook over medium-high heat, stirring constantly with a wooden spoon (be sure to scrape the sides of the pan), until the mixture is thick enough to coat the back of the spoon, 8 to 10 minutes, and registers 160°F on an instant-read thermometer.

Remove saucepan from heat. Add salt and butter, one piece at a time, stirring until smooth. Strain through a fine sieve into a medium bowl. Stir in the remaining zest. Cover with plastic wrap, pressing it directly onto the surface of the curd to prevent a skin from forming. Refrigerate until chilled and set, at least 1 hour or up to 1 day.

VANILLA WHIPPED CREAM

MAKES ABOUT 3 CUPS *When making whipped cream, it's always a good idea to chill the bowl (preferably metal) as well as the cream in the freezer for about ten minutes before you begin.*

      2 cups heavy cream
      2 tablespoons pure vanilla extract
      2 tablespoons confectioners' sugar

In a medium bowl, whisk the cream, vanilla, and sugar until soft peaks form. (Alternatively, whip the cream in the bowl of an electric mixer fitted with the whisk attachment.) The cream can be covered and refrigerated for up to 2 hours at this point. Just before serving, finish whipping the cream to stiff peaks.

CARAMEL WHIPPED CREAM
MAKES ABOUT 2 CUPS

    1/4 cup sugar
  1 3/4 cups heavy cream

Prepare an ice bath; set aside. Pour sugar into a small saucepan; cover and cook over medium-high heat, without stirring, until sugar is completely melted. Remove lid, and cook, swirling pan to cover evenly, until sugar turns golden amber. Carefully pour 3/4 cup heavy cream down the side of the pan in a slow, steady stream (it will spatter), stirring constantly with a wooden spoon until combined. Transfer caramel to a bowl set in ice bath; let sit until cool, stirring occasionally.

Meanwhile, whip the remaining cup cream until medium-stiff peaks form. Fold in the caramel until combined. Use immediately.

ALMOND CREAM
MAKES ENOUGH FOR 1 DOZEN CROISSANTS

4 tablespoons butter, room temperature

¼ cup sugar

1 large egg

½ cup whole blanched almonds,
  finely ground in the food processor

¼ cup all-purpose flour

¼ teaspoon pure almond extract

  Pinch of salt

In the bowl of an electric mixer fitted with the paddle attachment, beat the butter and sugar on medium-high speed until light and fluffy, about 2 minutes. Beat in the egg. Add the ground almonds and flour, and beat until combined. Stir in the almond extract and salt. Continue beating until the mixture is light and fluffy, about 2 minutes, scraping down the sides of the bowl as needed. The almond cream can be refrigerated in an airtight container for up to 1 week.

NOTE Raw eggs should not be used in food prepared for pregnant women, babies, young children, the elderly, or anyone whose health is compromised.

PASTRY CREAM
MAKES ABOUT 2½ CUPS

2 cups whole milk

½ cup sugar

½ vanilla bean, split lengthwise, seeds scraped
  Pinch of salt

4 large egg yolks

¼ cup cornstarch

2 tablespoons unsalted butter, cut into small pieces

In a medium saucepan, combine the milk, ¼ cup sugar, vanilla bean and seeds, and salt. Cook over medium heat until mixture comes to a simmer.

In a medium bowl, whisk together the egg yolks, cornstarch, and remaining ¼ cup sugar. Whisking constantly, slowly pour about ½ cup of the hot-milk mixture into the egg-yolk mixture. Continue adding milk mixture, ½ cup at a time, until it has been incorporated. Pour mixture back into saucepan, and cook over medium-high heat, whisking constantly, until it thickens and registers 160°F on an instant-read thermometer, about 2 minutes. Remove and discard vanilla bean.

Transfer to the bowl of an electric mixer fitted with the paddle attachment. Add the butter, and beat on medium speed until the butter melts and the mixture cools, about 5 minutes.

Cover with plastic wrap, pressing it directly onto the surface of the pastry cream to prevent a skin from forming. Refrigerate until chilled, at least 2 hours or up to 2 days. Just before using, beat on low speed until smooth (you can also whisk by hand).

CHOCOLATE PASTRY CREAM VARIATION Follow instructions for Pastry Cream, adding 8 ounces finely chopped best-quality semisweet chocolate along with the butter. Beat until both butter and chocolate have melted and the mixture has cooled, about 5 minutes. Strain Pastry Cream into a medium bowl; chill and store as directed above.

MOCHA MOUSSE

MAKES ENOUGH FOR ONE 18-INCH ROULADE *Prepare the mousse at least four hours or up to two days in advance. Refrigerate, covered with plastic wrap.*

- 1½ cups heavy cream
- 6 ounces best-quality bittersweet chocolate, finely chopped
- 2 tablespoons instant espresso powder
- 2 tablespoons boiling water
- ¼ cup sugar
- 2 tablespoons light corn syrup
- 4 large egg yolks

In the bowl of an electric mixer fitted with the whisk attachment, whip the cream to soft peaks; cover with plastic wrap and refrigerate. In a heatproof bowl set over (but not touching) simmering water, melt the chocolate. Remove from heat. In a small bowl, stir the espresso powder into the hot water until dissolved.

In a small saucepan, bring the sugar, corn syrup, and 1 tablespoon water to a boil over medium heat, and cook until mixture registers 238°F on a candy thermometer, about 3 minutes; remove from heat.

In the bowl of an electric mixer fitted with the whisk attachment, beat the yolks on medium speed until lightened, about 3 minutes, scraping down the sides of the bowl as needed. With the mixer on medium speed, gradually pour the sugar syrup down the side of the bowl in a slow, steady stream. With the mixer on high speed, beat until the mixture holds a ribbon-like trail on the surface for 2 seconds when the whisk is raised, about 2 minutes more. Beat in the melted chocolate and the espresso mixture to combine. Using a rubber spatula, gently fold in the chilled whipped cream until there are no streaks and the mixture is well combined.

RASPBERRY JAM
MAKES 1¼ CUPS

- 3½ cups fresh raspberries
- 1½ tablespoons freshly squeezed lemon juice
- ¾ cup sugar
- 1 tablespoon cornstarch
- ¼ teaspoon salt

In a medium saucepan, stir to combine 2 cups raspberries, lemon juice, sugar, cornstarch, and salt. Simmer over medium-low heat until berries have begun to break down and become juicy, about 5 minutes.

Strain raspberry mixture through a fine sieve into a clean medium saucepan; discard solids. Add remaining 1½ cups raspberries to saucepan, and return to a simmer over medium heat. Cook until raspberries have broken down and jam has thickened enough to coat the back of a wooden spoon, about 10 minutes.

Transfer jam to a small bowl. Cover with plastic wrap, pressing it directly onto the surface to prevent a skin from forming; refrigerate for up to 2 weeks.

SLAB PIE PÂTE BRISÉE
MAKES ENOUGH FOR ONE 15-BY-10-INCH PIE

- 3¾ cups all-purpose flour
- 2½ teaspoons coarse salt
- 1½ teaspoons sugar
- 3 sticks (1½ cups) unsalted butter, cold, cut into small pieces
- ½ cup ice water, plus more if needed

Place the flour, salt, and sugar in the bowl of a food processor, and pulse for a few seconds to combine. Add the butter, and pulse until the mixture resembles coarse crumbs, about 10 seconds.

With machine running, pour the ice water through the feed tube in a slow, steady stream, until the dough just holds together when squeezed. If needed, add more ice water 1 tablespoon at a time. Do not process for more than 30 seconds.

Turn out the dough onto a clean work surface. Divide into two pieces, one slightly larger than the other. Form into flattened rectangles. Wrap each in plastic, and refrigerate at least 1 hour or overnight.

CRUMB TOPPING
MAKES ENOUGH FOR ONE 13-BY-9-INCH CAKE

- 3 cups all-purpose flour
- 1 cup packed light-brown sugar
- 1 tablespoon ground cinnamon
- 1½ teaspoons coarse salt
- 3½ sticks (1¾ cups) unsalted butter, room temperature

In a medium bowl, whisk to combine the flour, sugar, cinnamon, and salt; cut in the butter using a pastry blender, until large, moist clumps form. (Alternatively, mix together in a food processor.) Topping can be refrigerated in an airtight container for up to 2 weeks.

STREUSEL
MAKES 4 CUPS

- 2¼ cups all-purpose flour
- ¾ cup packed light-brown sugar (or ¾ cup confectioners' sugar)
- 2¼ teaspoons ground cinnamon
- 1 teaspoon coarse salt
- 1½ sticks (¾ cup) unsalted butter, room temperature

In a medium bowl, combine the flour, sugar, cinnamon, and salt; cut in the butter using a pastry blender, until large, moist clumps form. Streusel can be refrigerated in an airtight container for up to 2 weeks.

CANDIED WALNUTS

MAKES 24 *You can also use other whole nuts, such as almonds, macadamia nuts, pecans, or cashews. It is best to make these on a day with low humidity.*

- ¾ cup sugar
- ⅛ teaspoon freshly squeezed lemon juice
- 24 walnut halves

Line a baking sheet with parchment paper; set aside. In a medium saucepan over high heat, combine sugar, lemon juice, and ¼ cup water. Cook without stirring, until mixture turns golden amber, 3 to 4 minutes; remove from heat. (Be careful not to let caramel turn too dark, as it will continue to cook.)

Add the walnuts, and stir with a wooden spoon to coat. Using a fork, transfer nuts one at a time to the prepared baking sheet, letting excess caramel drip off the nuts before setting them on the parchment. Once the caramel has hardened, about 5 minutes, gently remove nuts from parchment.

Caramelized nuts are best used immediately, but can be kept in an airtight container at room temperature for up to 1 day.

WHITE CHOCOLATE CUTOUTS

MAKES 3 DOZEN *These shapes are used to top the Petits Fours (page 192). Use the same set of cutters for the cakes and the cutouts.*

2¼ pounds best-quality white chocolate, finely chopped

Liquid or gel-paste food coloring

Line three rimmed baking sheets with parchment; set aside. In a heatproof bowl set over (but not touching) simmering water, melt white chocolate, stirring constantly. Divide melted chocolate evenly among three small bowls; tint each with food coloring to desired shade. Pour a colored chocolate onto the prepared baking sheet, spreading it with an offset spatula into a layer about ⅛ inch thick. Transfer to the refrigerator; chill until chocolate is firm, 10 to 15 minutes. Repeat with the remaining colored chocolates.

Working with one color at a time, cut out shapes; leave shapes in place on the sheet. (If chocolate is still soft in any area, return to the refrigerator to harden, 1 to 2 minutes.) Refrigerate until completely firm. Separate the shapes from borders with a small offset spatula. (Scraps can be discarded, or remelted and used again.) Cutouts can be refrigerated, between sheets of parchment paper, in an airtight container for up to 1 week.

CHOCOLATE CURLS

MAKES ENOUGH FOR 2 DOZEN CUPCAKES *These chocolate curls add a playful touch to the tops of cakes, pies, and tarts. Working with a block of chocolate (instead of a bar) makes it easier to form the curls. It also helps if the chocolate is slightly warm; if necessary, microwave it for about ten seconds, being careful not to let it melt.*

Best-quality semisweet chocolate

Line a rimmed baking sheet with parchment paper, and set aside.

Using a sharp knife or bench scraper, scrape the chocolate at a 45-degree angle to form chocolate curls. (Alternatively, use a vegetable peeler.)

With a wide spatula, transfer chocolate curls to the prepared baking sheet. Refrigerate, covered with plastic wrap, up to 4 days.

FRESH COCONUT CURLS

MAKES ENOUGH FOR ONE 9-INCH LAYER CAKE *Look for a coconut that is heavy for its size; when you shake it, you should be able to hear the liquid sloshing inside. The husk should be dark brown without any cracks (which could allow moisture to escape), and the eyes should be dry and free of mold.*

1 medium fresh coconut

Preheat the oven to 350°F. Test each of the three eyes at the stem end of the coconut to see which is the softest. Then use an ice pick (or a screwdriver) and a hammer to pierce two of the eyes. Strain milk through a fine sieve into a bowl; reserve for another use or discard.

Place the coconut on a rimmed baking sheet, and bake for 30 minutes, or until coconut shell begins to crack. Set aside until cool enough to handle.

Wrap coconut in a clean kitchen towel; holding the coconut with one hand, hit it with the hammer in the same place several times to crack the outer shell and split the coconut into several large pieces.

Separate coconut flesh from the shell, and use a vegetable peeler to remove dark outer skin. Rinse the coconut in cold water, then use the vegetable peeler to take off long, thick strips from the outer (cut) edges. Use immediately, or store, layered between damp paper towels in an airtight container, in the refrigerator for up to 6 hours.

SOURCES

equipment

BABA AU RHUM MOLDS
Bridge Kitchenware

BAKING SHEETS, HEAVY-DUTY ALUMINUM
Broadway Panhandler

BAKING STONE
Sur La Table

BAMBOO SKEWERS
Kalustyan's

BENCH SCRAPER
Sur La Table

BRIOCHE MOLD
Sur La Table

CAKE BOARDS (SQUARES AND RECTANGLES, 8" AND 9")
Pastry Chef Central

CAKE PAN (10")
Sur La Table

CAKE TURNTABLE
Pastry Chef Central

CANDY THERMOMETER
Pastry Chef Central

CANNELÉ MOLDS
Pastry Chef Central

CARDBOARD ROUNDS
Pastry Chef Central

CERAMIC BAKING DISHES (ASSORTED SIZES)
Sur La Table

CHEESECLOTH
Bridge Kitchenware

CHERRY PITTER
Bridge Kitchenware

CITRUS REAMER
Bridge Kitchenware

COFFEE GRINDER
Williams-Sonoma

COOKIE CUTTER SETS
Pastry Chef Central

COOLING RACKS
Sur La Table

ENGLISH-MUFFIN RING MOLDS (2.75")
J. B. Prince

ENTREMETS RINGS, 9" AND 4"
J. B. Prince

FINANCIER MOLDS
J. B. Prince

FINE-MESH SIEVE
Sur La Table

FLAN RINGS (VARIOUS SIZES)
Sur La Table

KITCHEN SHEARS
Bridge Kitchenware

KITCHEN TORCH
Sur La Table

KNIVES, SERRATED
Sur La Table

LOAF PANS
PULLMAN (PAIN DE MIE)
Pastry Chef Central
9" x 5"
Bridge Kitchenware
8.5" x 4.5"
Williams-Sonoma
6" x 3" x 2"
Sur La Table

MADELEINE MOLDS
Williams-Sonoma

MANDOLINE
Bridge Kitchenware

MELON BALLER (SMALL AND LARGE)
Bridge Kitchenware

METAL SPATULAS (VARIOUS SIZES)
Williams-Sonoma

MUFFIN PANS (JUMBO, STANDARD, AND MINI)
J. B. Prince

NUTMEG GRATER
Sur La Table

PANETTONE MOLD
Sur La Table

PARCHMENT ROUNDS (9" AND 10")
Kitchen Krafts

PASTA MACHINE, HAND-CRANKED
Williams-Sonoma

PASTRY BAGS, ASSORTED TIPS AND COUPLERS
Sweet Celebrations

PASTRY BLENDER
Williams-Sonoma

PASTRY BRUSHES
Pastry Chef Central

PASTRY CUTTERS
J. B. Prince

**PIE PANS, GLASS
AND METAL**
Sur La Table

PIZZA PEEL
The Baker's Catalogue
at King Arthur Flour

POPOVER TIN
The Baker's Catalogue
at King Arthur Flour

**RASPS AND
TRADITIONAL ZESTERS**
The Baker's Catalogue
at King Arthur Flour

**RIMMED BAKING
SHEETS**
Sur La Table

ROLLING PIN
The Baker's Catalogue
at King Arthur Flour

**ROUND CAKE PANS
(8" AND 9")**
Williams-Sonoma

RULER, METAL
Dick Blick

SCALES, DIGITAL
Williams-Sonoma

**SILPAT NONSTICK
BAKING MATS**
Sur La Table

**SPATULAS, HEAT-PROOF
SILICONE**
Sur La Table

SPRINGFORM PANS
Williams-Sonoma

**SQUARE BAKING PANS
(ASSORTED SIZES)**
Sur La Table

**TART PANS
(VARIOUS SHAPES AND
SIZES, INCLUDING
BOTTOMLESS FLUTED
AND FLAN RINGS)**
Bridge Kitchenware

**TART PANS, FLUTED
(9.5")**
Pastry Chef Central

**THERMOMETER,
FOLDING OVEN**
Bridge Kitchenware

**THERMOMETER,
INSTANT READ**
Sur La Table

TIMERS, DIGITAL
Pastry Chef Central

**TONGS
(VARIOUS SIZES)**
Sur La Table

TUBE PANS
Bridge Kitchenware

WHISKS
Sur La Table

SOURCES

ingredients

ALMOND PASTE
Kalustyan's

ALMONDS, BLANCHED
Kalustyan's

ANISE SEEDS
Kalustyan's

APRICOTS, DRIED
Economy Candy

BARLEY MALT SYRUP
The Baker's Catalogue
at King Arthur Flour

BREAD FLOUR
The Baker's Catalogue
at King Arthur Flour

CHARENTAIS MELON
Whole Foods

**CHERRIES, FRESH
(IN SEASON)**
Whole Foods

**CHERRIES, SOUR
(FROZEN AND DRIED)**
Friske Orchards

**CHESTNUTS, FRESH
(IN SEASON)**
Diamond Organics

CHOCOLATE, VALRHONA
Chocolatesource.com

CRANBERRIES, DRIED
Friske Orchards

CRÈME FRAÎCHE
Whole Foods

**CURRANTS (FRESH,
RED AND BLACK)**
Whole Foods

DATES (FRESH)
Whole Foods

DURUM WHEAT
The Baker's Catalogue
at King Arthur Flour

FENNEL SEEDS
Kalustyan's

FLAXSEEDS
The Baker's Catalogue
at King Arthur Flour

**FONTINA CHEESE,
ITALIAN**
Murray's Cheese

**GEL-PASTE
FOOD COLORING**
Sweet Celebrations

GIANDUJA CHOCOLATE
Chocolatesource.com

GINGER, CRYTALLIZED
Sur La Table

GOOSEBERRIES
Whole Foods

GRAHAM FLOUR
The Baker's Catalogue
at King Arthur Flour

GRUYÈRE CHEESE
Murray's Cheese

HAZELNUTS, BLANCHED
Kalustyan's

**HERBS, FRESH
(THYME, MARJORAM,
OREGANO, BASIL, SAGE)**
Whole Foods

KEY LIMES (IN SEASON)
Whole Foods

**LAVENDER
(DRIED AND FRESH)**
Eatwell Farm

MANCHEGO CHEESE
Murray's Cheese

MAPLE SYRUP, GRADE B
New Hampshire Gold

MASCARPONE CHEESE
Whole Foods

**NUT FLOURS (ALMOND
AND HAZELNUT)**
The Baker's Catalogue
at King Arthur Flour

OLIVES, NIÇOISE
Kalustyan's

ORANGE OIL
Kalustyan's

PASSION FRUIT JUICE
Kalustyan's

PASTRY FLOUR
The Baker's Catalogue
at King Arthur Flour

PEACHES, DRIED
Economy Candy

PEAR, D'ANJOU
Whole Foods

**PIMENTON DE LA VERA
(SPANISH SMOKED
PAPRIKA)**
igourmet.com

PISTACHIO EXTRACT
Amoretti

PISTACHIO PASTE
Amoretti

**PISTACHIOS, NATURAL
SHELLED**
Kalustyan's

POPPY SEEDS
The Baker's Catalogue
at King Arthur Flour

**RASPBERRIES,
GOLDEN (IN SEASON)**
Whole Foods

RHUBARB (IN SEASON)
Whole Foods

**RICOTTA CHEESE,
FRESH**
Murray's Cheese

RYE FLOUR
The Baker's Catalogue
at King Arthur Flour

SANDING SUGAR
Sur La Table

SEA SALT
The Baker's Catalogue
at King Arthur Flour

SEMOLINA FLOUR
The Baker's Catalogue
at King Arthur Flour

**SESAME SEEDS,
UNHULLED**
Kalustyan's

TALEGGIO CHEESE
Murray's Cheese

VANILLA BEANS
The Baker's Catalogue
at King Arthur Flour

YEAST, FRESH
Whole Foods

SOURCES

directory

AMORETTI
800-266-7388
www.amoretti.com

THE BAKER'S CATALOGUE
AT KING ARTHUR FLOUR
135 Route 5 South
P.O. Box 1010
Norwich, VT 05055
800-827-6836
www.kingarthurflour.com

BRIDGE KITCHENWARE
711 Third Avenue
New York, NY 10017
800-274-3445
212-688-4220
www.bridgekitchenware.com

BROADWAY PANHANDLER
477 Broome Street
New York, NY 10013
212-966-3434
www.broadwaypanhandler.com

CHOCOLATESOURCE.COM
9 Crest Road
Wellesley, MA 02482
800-214-4926
www.chocolatesource.com

DIAMOND ORGANICS
1272 Highway 1
Moss Landing, CA 95039
888-674-2642
www.diamondorganics.com

DICK BLICK ART MATERIALS
P.O. Box 1267
Galesburg, IL 61402
800-828-4548
www.dickblick.com

EATWELL FARM
2657 Portage Bay East #3
Davis, CA 95616
800-648-9894
www.lavenderfarm.com

ECONOMY CANDY
108 Rivington Street
New York, NY 10002
800-352-4544
www.economycandy.com

FRISKE ORCHARDS
10743 North U.S. 31
Ellsworth, MI 49729
888-968-3554
www.friske.com

IGOURMET.COM
877-446-8763
www.igourmet.com

J.B. PRINCE
36 East 31st Street
New York, NY 10016
800-473-0577
www.jbprince.com

KALUSTYAN'S
123 Lexington Avenue
New York, NY 10016
212-685-3451
www.kalustyans.com

KITCHEN KRAFTS
P.O. Box 442
Waukon, IA 52172
800-776-0575
www.kitchenkrafts.com

MURRAY'S CHEESE
254 Bleecker Street
New York, NY 10014
888-692-4339
www.murrayscheese.com

NEW HAMPSHIRE GOLD
P.O. Box 291
Huckleberry Road
New Hampton, NH 03256
888-819-4255
www.nhgold.com

PASTRY CHEF CENTRAL
1355 West Palmetto Park Road, suite 302
Boca Raton, FL 33486
888-750-2433
www.pastrychef.com

SUR LA TABLE
800-243-0852
www.surlatable.com

SWEET CELEBRATIONS
P.O. Box 39426
Edina, MN 55439
800-328-6722
www.sweetc.com

WHOLE FOODS
212-924-5969
www.wholefoods.com

WILLIAMS-SONOMA
800-541-2233
www.williams-sonoma.com

Herb Biscuits, 30
Honey Whole-Wheat
  Bread, 294, *295*

I

Ice cream scoops, 70
Icing(s)
  Black and White, 78, *79*
  Royal, 389
  royal, piping onto
    cookies, 82
Instant-read thermometer,
  288
Irish Soda Bread, 52, *53*

J

Jam. *See* Raspberry Jam

K

Key Lime Slices, Candied,
  260, 261
Key Lime Tart, *260,* 261
Kitchen scale, 12
Kitchen shears, 14
Kitchen timer, 16
Knife, serrated, 14, 144
Kouign Amans, *350,* 350–51

L

Lame, 288
Lavender Syrup, Summer
  Fruit Tart with, 252, *253*

Lemon(s)
  -Blueberry Napoleons,
    370, *371*
  Citrus Bars, *120,* 121–22
  Curd, 390
  Curd Cake, *152,* 153
  Custard, 372
  -Ginger Scones, 42
  Madeleines, *197,* 199
  Pound Cake, Glazed,
    61–64, *62*
  Sugar Snaps, 93–95, *94*
  Swiss Meringue
    Buttercream, 386
Lime(s)
  Citrus Bars, *120,* 121–22
  -Coconut Lace Tuiles,
    133–34, *135*
  Curd, 390
  Glaze, *102,* 103
  -Glazed Cookies, *102,*
    102–3
  Key, Slices, Candied,
    260, 261
  Key, Tart, *260,* 261
Linzer Hearts, *116,* 117
Linzertorte, *170,* 171
Loaf pans, 26

M

Macadamia Nut–Coconut
  Cookies, 103–4, *104*
Macaroons
  Chocolate, *136,* 137
  French Almond, *136,* 137
  Strawberry, *136,* 137
Madeleine pan, 142

Madeleines, Lemon, *197,* 199
Mango-Pineapple Upside-
  Down Cake, *182,* 183
Maple Buttercream, 164
Maple-Walnut Cupcakes,
  164, *165*
Marble Cake with White-
  Chocolate Glaze, *63,* 65
Martha's Birthday Cake,
  204–5, *206–7*
Marzipan Carrots,
  Mini, 167
Mascarpone cheese
  Frosting, 158
  Savory Caraway Cheese
    Crisps, 90, *91*
Mat, nonstick baking, 16
Measuring cups
  choosing, 18
  dry, 12
  liquid, 12
Measuring spoons, 12
Meringue, Swiss. *See* Swiss
  Meringue
Meringues
  Pavlovas with Mixed
    Berries, 194, *195*
Metal pie tins, 220
Mexican Wedding Cookies,
  96–99, *97*
Milk Glaze, 55
Mint Leaves, Chocolate, 160
Mixing bowl, 12

Mocha
  Buttercream, 213
  Glaze, 389
  Mousse, 393
  Pastry Cream, 214
  -Pistachio Wedding Cake,
    209–13, *210–11, 215*
  Roulade, *186,* 187
Molds, specialty
  baba, 288
  barquette, 222
  brioche, 288
  cannelé, 142
  panettone, 288
Mousse, Mocha, 393
Mozzarella cheese
  Easter Pie, *275,* 276
  Pizza Margherita,
    329–30, *331*
Muffin pans
  preparing, 29
  scooping batter into, 29
  sizes, 26
Muffins
  baking equipment, 26
  Blueberry, 37, *38*
  cooling, 29
  Cranberry-Zucchini,
    37–39, *38*
  Date-Bran, *38,* 40
  filling muffin cups, 29
  Plum Coffee-Cake, *38,* 39
  preparing, general tips
    for, 25
Mushrooms
  Corn and Shiitake Tart,
    273, *274*